The Literary Essay: Writing About Fiction

Lucy Calkins, Kathleen Tolan, and Alexandra Marron

Photography by Peter Cunningham

HEINEMANN ◆ PORTSMOUTH, NH

This book is dedicated to Lauren Fontana, Barbara Rosenblum, and all the teachers and students at PS 6.

DEDICATED TO TEACHERS™

*first*hand
An imprint of Heinemann
361 Hanover Street
Portsmouth, NH 03801–3912
www.heinemann.com

Offices and agents throughout the world

The authors and publisher wish to thank those who have generously given permission to reprint borrowed material:

Excerpts from *Fox* written by Margaret Wild, illustrated by Ron Brooks. Copyright © text Margaret Wild 2000. Copyright © illustrations, Ron Brooks 2000. Reproduced by permission of the publisher, Kane Miller, A Division of EDC Publishing and with permission from Allen and Unwin Publishers Sydney, Australia.

Excerpts from "The Marble Champ" from *Baseball in April and Other Stories,* by Gary Soto. Copyright © 1990 by Gary Soto. Published by Houghton Mifflin Harcourt. Reprinted by permission of the publisher.

Excerpts from "Eleven" from *Woman Hollering Creek.* Copyright © 1991 by Sandra Cisneros. Published by Vintage Books, a division of Random House Inc., and originally in hardcover by Random House Inc. By permission of Susan Bergholz Literary Services, New York, NY and Lamy, NM and by permission of Bloomsbury Publishing Plc. All rights reserved.

Cataloging-in-Publication data is on file with the Library of Congress.

ISBN-13: 978-0-325-04739-3
ISBN-10: 0-325-04739-1

Production: Elizabeth Valway, David Stirling, and Abigail Heim
Cover and interior designs: Jenny Jensen Greenleaf
Series includes photographs by Peter Cunningham, Nadine Baldasare, and Elizabeth Dunford
Composition: Publishers' Design and Production Services, Inc.
Manufacturing: Steve Bernier

Printed in the United States of America on acid-free paper
17 16 15 14 13 VP 1 2 3 4 5

Acknowledgments

A UNIT OF STUDY in writing literary essays straddles many fields of knowledge, making this an especially rich, provocative, and challenging enterprise, and that, in turn, makes our list of thank-yous long. We are especially grateful to Kate Montgomery, who has been a thought companion to the three of us from start to finish. We love mulling over ideas in her company and being able to go to her for clear thinking when our minds are muddled. We are grateful for her close reading of this text and her many principled suggestions.

Our thinking about reading is enriched not only by the colleagues who are right on hand, at the Teachers College Reading and Writing Project, but also by more distant thought companions. We're grateful to Steph Harvey, Dick Allington, Peter Johnston, Tim Rasinski, Kylene Beers, Ellin Keene, and Smokey Daniels for their books, their companionship, and their ideas.

This book is one in a progression of books on opinion/argument writing, and we are thankful to all those who have helped us develop a curriculum that enables youngsters to grow up learning to state bold opinions, to back them with evidence, and to write persuasively. Mary Ehrenworth, Shana Frazin, Kate Roberts, Kelly Boland Hohne, and Cory Gillette have been especially helpful with that work. We are also grateful to a think tank on learning progressions in argument writing that was sponsored by the Council of Chief School State Officers and conducted with ETS.

The book represents a composite of classrooms. Student work from the original classroom in which the first version of this book was piloted is still here—and we thank Kathy Doyle for that. The imprints of Kathy and her students' work are still a force in this new book. Nekia Wise from PS 59 and Molly Feeney from PS 199 have also contributed to this book and to many related projects, for which we are grateful.

Thanks to Kara Fischer, a brilliant writer and staunch advocate for all children, who helped us write sessions in the book's early stages and who later helped us develop some of the homework. Thanks also to Lisa Cazzola, who compiled the CD-ROM with a smile and an ever-present "can-do" attitude, and to Mary Ann Mustac, who does so much to make our lives possible.

The stunning photography in this book is the work of Peter Cunningham, an extraordinary artist and great friend to the Project, who has an incredible ability to capture the beauty in New York City classrooms. We thank Adele Schroeter and the teachers and children at PS 59 in Manhattan for welcoming Peter and his camera into their writing workshops. We are grateful also to Abby Heim, production mastermind at Heinemann, who has cobbled together a beautiful text, bringing photos, icons, white space, and text into a coherent manuscript. Your sky-high standards and attention to detail are an inspiration to us.

And finally, special thanks to Julia and Hannah. We've watched you go to the ends of the earth to help out, doing anything and everything to make these books the best they can be. Thanks for your hard work.

The class described in this unit is a composite class, with children and partnerships of children gleaned from classrooms in very different contexts, then put together here. We wrote the units this way to bring you both a wide array of wonderful, quirky, various children and also to illustrate for you the predictable (and unpredictable) situations and responses this unit has created in classrooms across the nation and world.

Contents

BEND I   Writing about Reading: Literary Essays

1. Close Reading to Generate Ideas about a Text • 2

In this session, you'll teach students that reading with an attentiveness to detail can spark ideas and that writing can be a vehicle for developing those ideas.

2. Gathering Writing by Studying Characters • 14

In this session, you'll teach students that experts know that certain aspects of their subjects merit special attention. Literary essayists know it pays off, for example, to study characters.

3. Elaborating on Written Ideas Using Prompts • 25

In this session, you'll teach students one way writers elaborate on their ideas— using simple prompts.

4. Finding and Testing a Thesis • 36

In this session, you'll teach students that writers select ideas to craft into theses. You'll show writers ways to question and revise their theses, making sure these are supported by the whole text.

5. Using Stories as Evidence • 48

In this session, you'll teach students ways that essayists select mini-stories as evidence to support their ideas.

6. Citing Textual Evidence • 60

In this session, you'll teach students that writers use direct quotes to support their claims about a text. You'll teach them ways writers are discerning, choosing only the quotes that best support their ideas.

7. Using Lists as Evidence • 69

In this session, you'll teach students that writers not only use stories and quotes as evidence, they also use lists to support their claims.

8. Putting It All Together: Constructing Literary Essays • 77

In this session, you'll teach students some of the ways that writers create drafts out of collections of evidence. You'll also teach children ways to study published literary essays to find structures for their own literary essays.

BEND II   Raising the Quality of Literary Essays

9. Writing to Discover What a Story Is *Really* About • 88

In this session, you'll teach students that writers seek out patterns in their books or short stories, using those patterns to develop ideas about the story's theme or message.

BEND III Writing Compare-and-Contrast Essays

Welcome to the Unit

JUST AS WRITING allows us to pause in the hurry of our lives to really notice, experience, and reflect, so too, writing can give us a tool to pause in our hurried reading to really pay attention to characters and ideas in books. This unit aims to make reading a more intense, analytical experience for young people, equipping them with tools they need to write expository essays that advance an idea about a piece of literature. This unit relies upon your students' prior experience writing personal and persuasive essays. You'll essentially suggest that in this unit, they'll do work that is similar to that earlier work with essays—and different. While students will have learned to write with evidence, they did not learn about citing texts. That's one of the new challenges of this unit. The Common Core State Standards (CCSS) are clear that students must be able to write opinion pieces not only on topics, but also on texts (W.4.1).

The unit is designed so that students will receive repeated practice writing arguments about texts. Their work with this progresses from rather simple to much more complex, beginning with the fourth-grade CCSS standards and addressing many fifth-grade standards by the end of the unit. For instance, at the start of the unit, the students' essays defend basic ideas about texts, and your instruction focuses to a large extent on the structure of an effective literary essay. Students will be reminded to carry forward all they have learned to do in opinion writing so far: to state a clear opinion, to craft a solid organizational structure, to support their claim with both reasons and evidence, to use transitional phrases for clarity and cohesiveness, and to provide a conclusion that relates to the stated claim (W.4.1).

Eventually your students progress to writing about more complex, interpretative ideas and learn to write in ways that address not only the theme of a story (RL.5.2), but that ask them to interpret and analyze the ways words,

phrases, and ideas are used in a text (R.5.4). After developing a complex, interpretative thesis, writers are asked not only to support that claim, but to do so in a way that logically groups ideas to support their purpose (W.5.1). Finally, in the third bend of the unit, students learn to write comparative essays, comparing and contrasting interpretations across multiple texts (R.4.9, R.5.9).

The practice that your students will gain in writing literary essays during this unit will open the door to many crucial pathways for them. It will offer them a bridge between reading and writing. It will help them learn not only that writing can be a way to hold onto one's thinking about a particular subject or, more specifically, about a particular text, but that writing can also help them clarify and elaborate on their thinking. Through this unit, you will help your students become more skilled in what the Common Core State Standards refer to as "opinion writing"—that is, the logical idea-based writing that was introduced through the personal and persuasive essay unit earlier in the year. Meanwhile, you'll move your students along in their journey toward the text-based, analytic work that is foundational in high school and college classrooms. In fact, the skill of responding to a text with a reasoned, well-crafted piece of writing is emphasized across several of the CCSS: it is touched on not only in the standards for opinion writing, but also in the standards for speaking and listening, in the research standards, and even, to some extent, in the information writing standards. In short, this task, writing about reading, could be seen as the gold standard of the CCSS.

When teaching *Boxes and Bullets: Personal and Persuasive Essays,* you will have taught your fourth-graders to create organizational structures in which they group related ideas, to chunk evidence—facts and details—and to elaborate on and explain their ideas with specific examples. Furthermore, you will have taught them to craft introductory and concluding sections related to their opinions and to provide closure in the essay. This unit will help you show children how to transfer and apply that learning to the new challenge of writing about literature, and then it will help you extend the learning they've already done about essay writing in general. You will now teach them more nuanced ways to develop theses and organize their essays, to cite evidence, and to elaborate. In this way, *The Literary Essay* will help you set them well on their way toward meeting the ambitious fifth-grade standards called for by the CCSS.

While this unit is first and foremost a writing unit, we'd be remiss if we didn't acknowledge the purposeful and large-scale ways it enriches students' reading skills as well. That is to say, the unit begins by helping children to read closely and carefully, mining a text for ideas about characters' traits, motivations, troubles, changes, and relationships. They will learn to use close reading as a way to generate provocative ideas. Later, children will move to thinking more interpretatively about texts, analyzing characters and plotlines for character's complexities, lessons learned, and overarching themes that are advanced within a text. Students will not only infer and interpret, but will learn to sustain and support the theories they develop. In this way, children's theories (and accompanying evidence) will build in complexity and in richness as the unit progresses, and they will devote themselves to developing accountable ideas. In the final portion of the unit, students will compare and contrast their analyses across two books, raising the level of their thinking and allowing them to play closer attention to the nuances of the texts (RL.4.6, 4.9). The Common Core State Standards spotlight the importance of textual comparisons, and this unit will teach children to, as the fourth-grade standard for textual analysis and comparison states, "compare and contrast the treatment of similar themes and topics . . . and patterns and events" (RL.4.9).

Last but not least, this unit will offer you a chance to teach into and shore up the areas in argument writing about which your students are unsure. You will want to have all of your data at hand from across the year to ensure that you are helping students to move along a trajectory of work and make progress in large, visible ways.

OVERVIEW OF THE UNIT

To write well about reading, students not only need to learn more about *writing*; they also need to learn more about *reading*. Throughout the unit,

students are taught the value of close reading of complex texts. From Day One, students will learn to read literature closely—and to write about the literature they are reading. They'll first learn to notice the details in a text, to appreciate that authors choose the setting, objects, word choices, metaphor, and characters they put into their texts for reasons, and therefore, readers are wise to read, asking, "Why might this author have made this decision?" This work, so central to the Common Core, is especially powerful work for students who are analyzing texts for ideas and interpretations. Students will learn that there are certain aspects of a story that are especially central to the story, and they'll learn to read texts with attentiveness, noticing what the author has done and fashioning evidence-based theories about the text.

From the get-go, students will learn to write structured, compelling essays in which they make and support claims and analyze, unpack, and incorporate evidence. In Bend I, you'll remind students of the work they did on essays prior to this unit, in which they were taught strategies for doing much of this challenging work. Students will focus on arguing for ideas about characters while carrying forward what they have been taught about planning and drafting a boxes-and-bullets essay, writing introductions and conclusions, and marshalling evidence in support of reasons. This allows the main focus of teaching to be devoted to the special challenges of writing essays about texts.

After drafting and revising essays about a familiar short text in Bend I, students will be given feedback on their first cycle of essay writing, and then you'll ask them to repeat that cycle in the second bend, this time applying all they have learned and also working to write more interpretively and analytically. On the first day of this new bend, you will launch a small sequence of work that aims to teach youngsters the power of higher-level interpretive reading. Writing about favorite texts—novels, read-alouds, short stories—students will learn to resist closure on an issue, to value complexity, and to commit themselves to examining all sides of an issue with the most open mind possible. In doing so, they will also learn new and more complex ways of structuring an essay and more nuanced ways to mine a text for the evidence they need.

Finally, the unit ends with the third bend, in which students will learn to write compare-and-contrast essays, noting the different texts' approaches to the same theme or issue. Children will learn to compare and contrast themes and topics in literature, writing to analyze the similarities and differences in the approaches two texts take. Students will learn to write in ways that take into account not only the subject of a text, but also the author's treatment of that subject. In this way, students will be taught to write more about point of view, emphasis, and interpretation and to be aware of the craft moves that authors use. Students will also learn ways to structure a compare-and-contrast essay and to cite evidence from two texts in a seamless, purposeful way.

ASSESSMENT

You and your school will need to decide whether your assessments of your students as opinion writers will have commenced at the start of the year. Many teachers devote the first few days of the writing workshop to assessments in narrative, opinion, and information writing, and if you did that, you'll be able to track the extent to which the progress students make in other kinds of writing affects their information writing.

Before you start this unit, we recommend you take just a bit of time to establish a baseline understanding of your students' skills as opinion writers. This assessment is crucial. We've provided you with instruments—learning progressions, rubrics, checklists, and leveled exemplar texts—that will help you to see where, in the trajectory of writing development, each of your students lie. These tools will help you see clearly what some steps are to improvement. Then, too, this assessment is necessary for you to track each individual's progress—and to help your students see themselves improving.

For this assessment to provide accurate data on your writers' opinion skills at this point in the year, be careful *not* to scaffold your students' work during this assessment. You'll want to simply remind students of the basic qualities you'd expect in a piece of opinion writing, then step back and leave them to their own devices. Rather than creating an "evaluatory" feel, we suggest you make this assessment an opportunity for children to "show off" what they know about opinion writing. You might say that you can't wait to see how strong they've become since your last essay unit. We suggest you begin with the following prompt, repeating it on the day of the assessment:

> "Think of a topic or issue that you know and care about, an issue around which you have strong feelings. Tomorrow, you will have forty-five minutes to write an opinion or argument text in which you will write your opinion or claim and tell reasons why you feel that way. When you do this, draw on everything you know about essays, persuasive letters and reviews. If you want to find and use information from a book or another outside source,

you may bring that with you tomorrow. Please keep in mind that you'll have forty-five minutes to complete this, so you will need to plan, draft, revise, and edit in one sitting. In your writing, make sure you:

- "Write an introduction
- State your opinion or claim
- Give reasons and evidence
- Organize your writing
- Acknowledge counterclaims
- Use transition words
- Write a conclusion"

You will want to assess where each writer falls in the Opinion/Argument Writing Learning Progression and compare this to where they were at the end of the opinion writing unit earlier this year, *Boxes and Bullets*. Note where the bulk of your class falls, letting that information inform your plans within this unit. To do this, we suggest you read each student's draft, comparing it to the exemplar texts, not worrying too much about whether the text matches every one of the descriptors of a level. No text will do so in its entirety, and the descriptors become more useful when you want to help writers know specific steps they can take to make their writing better. That is, if a writer's essay is mostly level 5, you and that writer can look at the descriptors of, say, elaboration for level 5 and note whether the writing adheres to those. If so, tell that child—or your whole class, if this is broadly applicable—"You used to elaborate by . . . ," and read the descriptors from the prior level, "but now you . . . ," and read the level 5 descriptor. "Can I give you a pointer about a way to make your writing even better? Try . . . ," and read from the level 6 descriptor. You can even say, "Let me show you an example," and to do so, you can cite a section of the level 6 exemplar text.

When this unit ends, you'll repeat this assessment exactly, and when you collect the student writing and look between the first on-demand and the second, the progress that you see will allow for an assessment not only of your students but also of your teaching, and of this curriculum, too. We have found that when you teach knowing that judgment day will not revolve around the published texts that writers produced with your input (and ours) but will, instead, revolve around what writers do without any input in an on-demand situation, this serves as a reminder that the goal of any writing instruction is not to produce strong *writing*. It is to produce strong *writers*. If we teach in ways that lift the level of today's piece of writing, but that teaching does not leave writers able to do better work another day, on another piece, then that teaching is for naught. The good news is that will not be the case! You'll look back on the baseline data you collect at the start of this unit and at the work students eventually produce, and you'll say, "Look at this progress!"

GETTING READY

Because this unit has a reading component, you will need to spend some time beforehand planning for the texts students will write about. Throughout the sessions, we suggest several texts you might give children to read and analyze, noting the importance of having a range of texts so that students can read those that are at a just-right level for them. We use *Fox* by Margaret Wild and Ron Brooks as our demonstration text throughout the unit. Using the same book will certainly make the planning for your own lessons worlds easier, though we encourage you to use any text that is replete with opportunities for character study, interpretation work, and analysis of author's craft. In Bend II and Bend III, students write using their own texts and the short stories from Bend I, so materials can come from your classroom library or students' own collections of favorite books.

It will be incredibly important for students to have the opportunity to transfer all of their learning from *Boxes and Bullets* to this unit. Therefore, you will want to make sure to bring out charts, paper choices, and any other resources children relied on for that unit, and make them accessible for this one as well. So as not to overwhelm the room, you might consider making small, folder-size versions of a few key charts, and let children know that other resources are available in a designated area of the classroom should they need them.

Examples of particularly helpful kinds of sources you'll find on the CD-ROM are:

- Samples of student work from various stages of the writing process
- Classroom charts, lists of prompts, and other teaching tools
- The opinion writing checklist
- A list of literary terms
- An editing checklist
- Homework assignments for use throughout the unit

Close Reading to Generate Ideas about a Text

IN THIS SESSION, you'll teach students that reading with an attentiveness to detail can spark ideas and that writing can be a vehicle for developing those ideas.

GETTING READY

✔ Before starting the unit, each child will need to have read at least one of the short texts that you'll invite youngsters to study across this unit. We recommend *Fox* by Margaret Wild and Ron Brooks, "Marble Champ" by Gary Soto, "Eleven" by Sandra Cisneros, *Fireflies* by Julia Brinkloe, *The Other Side* by Jacqueline Woodson, "Gloria Who Might Be My Best Friend" and other stories from *The Stories Julian Tells* by Ann Cameron. Alternatively, you may decide to choose one of your own favorites.

✔ The touchstone text you've selected for this minilesson, one for each child

✔ The first few paragraphs of the mentor text, *Fox*, by Margaret Wild and Ron Brooks, to be displayed to the whole class

✔ "Ways to Push Our Thinking" list of prompts from Session 4 of Unit 2, *Boxes and Bullets: Personal and Persuasive Essays* (see Teaching)

✔ "How to Write a Literary Essay" chart (see Link and Share)

✔ The short texts students will study across the unit (see Link)

✔ "Questions Writers Ask of Earlier Entries" chart from Session 5 of Unit 2, *Boxes and Bullets: Personal and Persuasive Essays*, to use as a model to create a new chart for this unit, "Questions Writers Ask of Texts" (see Share)

✔ Chart paper, Post-its, and markers

COMMON CORE STATE STANDARDS: W.4.1, W.4.4, W.4.7, W.4.8, W.4.9.a, RL.4.1, RL.4.4, RL.4.10, RFS.4.4, RL.5.1, SL.4.1, SL.4.4, L.4.1, L.4.2, L.4.3.a, L.4.4.a, L.4.5.a,b

BECAUSE YOU HAVE ALREADY TAUGHT MANY UNITS OF STUDY, you enter this unit with an expectation for how a unit of study will probably go. You can count on the fact that Session 1 will invite writers into the big work of the unit while also equipping them with a particular strategy for generating the new kind of writing. You can also count on the fact that the first few minilessons will give students a repertoire of strategies for generating this new kind of writing, and then the next few will help them lift the level of the writing, and you can count on the fact that students will then select a seed idea and develop it into a piece of writing.

Because this is your students' second unit this year on opinion/argument writing, you can also count on the fact that your students will be returning to many of the skills and strategies they learned earlier, for example, writing a thesis statement with supporting reasons and evidence, this time applying those skills to a new kind of opinion writing.

But this unit is a bit different from all the others. To write well about reading, students not only need to learn more about *writing*; they also need to learn more about *reading*. These sessions, then, must support reading well in addition to writing well. Specifically, this first session is intended to help children read literature closely—and to write about the literature they are reading.

More specifically, this session invites young people to use writing as a tool for developing their ideas about stories. In the personal and persuasive essay unit, you taught your writers that essayists observe the world, then push themselves to have thoughts about what they see. This session builds upon that strategy. This time, you teach youngsters that just as they earlier observed the *world* and pushed themselves to have thoughts about it, they can now observe the *texts* they are reading and push themselves to have thoughts about those texts. Just as you have repeatedly taught writers that the tiny details of their lives are worth noticing, you'll now teach them that the tiniest details of texts are worth noticing.

Part of your attention in this session and in this unit, then, will be directed toward supporting reading within the writing workshop. You won't want reading to overwhelm writing time, so during the first two bends in the unit, we recommend channeling students to return to familiar short texts (and later, to familiar novels). As always, choice matters, so we recommend that you encourage children to select from a small folder full of optional short texts. When we taught this unit, the folder included "Spaghetti," "Slower Than the Rest," and "Boar Out There" from Cynthia Rylant's anthology, *Every Living Thing*; "Gloria Who Might Be My Best Friend" from *The Stories Julian Tells* by Ann Cameron; "The Marble Champ," a much more complex story by Gary Soto; "Eleven" by Sandra Cisneros; *Fireflies* by Julia Brinkloe; and *The Other Side* by Jacqueline Woodson. You'll make your own choices.

"Just as you have repeatedly taught writers that the tiny details of their lives are worth noticing, you'll now teach them that the tiniest details of texts are worth noticing."

You'll probably find that young writers do not enter this unit already accustomed to using an attention to the details of a text to spark big ideas. This sort of marriage of close reading and interpretation requires students to straddle two ways of thinking: it asks them to be both concretely grounded and tentatively abstract. It requires them to point to, to note, and to cite—and it requires them to question, surmise, and theorize. The power that you are looking for comes from the combination.

At the start of this unit, it is more typical for your young students to be accustomed to either close *or* interpretive reading, but not to a combination of the two, which is the trademark of truly interpretative work. That is, they are apt to either point at parts of a text, citing and collecting examples, or to be at the opposite extreme, accustomed to abstract theorizing that is unanchored to the text. If you notice that your students' writing about texts amounts either to mere retelling or to empty generalities, then, don't be surprised. This will change, and those changes will start in this session as you teach children that when people read (or live) with a wide-awake attention to detail, they can use language—and writing, in particular—to generate big, compelling ideas that are supported by evidence.

With this session, I am trying to reclaim writing about reading as a beautiful, glorious thing. I'm trying to make writing about reading feel personal—even intimate—and intense. For many children, writing about reading is a dreaded enterprise. Often children are asked to do this simply as a way to prove they read the text. Often no one reads the writing children do about reading, and nothing happens to that writing. It's not read, shared, revised, discussed—and, consequently, it feels wooden and lifeless.

Close Reading to Generate Ideas about a Text

CONNECTION

Remind children that writers first live intensely and only then write about their experiences.

"Do you remember when I told you that the great writer Annie Dillard has a photograph above her writing desk of a little boy standing in a waterfall, only his head above water? Annie posts that picture beside her writing desk because, she says, 'That little boy is completely alive. He's letting the mystery of existence beat on him. He's having his childhood and he knows it'" (*The Writing Life* 1989, 47). "Annie uses that picture to remind herself that writers need to live intensely wide-awake lives and then write about those lives."

When today's teaching calls upon previous teaching, this adds layers to today's work, bringing in far more depth and resonance. I love the lead to this unit, and I love it because of all the ways in which something as everyday and ordinary as writing about reading is made extraordinary. To me, that is the gift that writing gives—it allows us to see significance in what others might walk past.

Tell children that, in the same way, writers first read intensely and only then write about that experience.

"In this unit of study, you will be writing about your reading. Reading is one way to wake up to the intensity and meaning and truth of our own lives. The famous essayist and poet Donald Hall has said, 'Great literature, if we read it well, opens us up to the world and makes us more sensitive to it, as if we acquired eyes that could see through things and ears that could hear smaller sounds.' Before you can write a literary essay, you first need to climb inside a story, just as that little boy climbed inside the white water. You need to let the details of the story pound down on you—paying attention to what you see and hear and notice on the page. Only then can you decide what you want to say about the story."

❖ **Name the teaching point.**

"Today I hope you'll learn that to write well about reading, you need to be wide-awake readers. Some people say they read themselves to sleep, but because you are writers, you need to read yourselves *awake*! To become especially wide-awake readers, you read closely, paying attention to little details that others might pass by, and then you write to grow ideas about those details."

Notice that this teaching point is written to be memorable. The parallel construction of this helps.

TEACHING

Demonstrate by rereading a snippet of the touchstone text. Highlight the fact that you pause to attend closely to what's in the text, saying or writing what you notice.

"Readers who want to grow ideas from reading a text find it helps to not just read but to also reread a text, so let's reread the book *Fox*. I know you have already heard me read this book aloud, and we've already talked about the kinds of questions readers usually ask first. We already talked a bit about the plot and characters. This time, as we reread, let's turn our minds on high, looking for moments or details that strike us as important to the whole text, and when we find them, let's stop and talk. Put your thumb up when you find a moment or a detail in the story that seems worth growing ideas about, that may be related to the big ideas in this story."

> *Through the charred forest, over hot ash, runs Dog, with a bird clamped in his big, gentle mouth. He takes her to his cave above the river and there he tries to tend her burnt wing . . .*

Noticing that the children were listening but that none had yet put a thumb up to signal that some of the details might be worth thinking about, I said, "I don't see many thumbs up yet. I'm the same as you; sometimes I just want to let the text flow over me. But to grow big ideas about a text, especially a short text, it helps to pause early and often and to force ourselves to notice what the text is actually saying instead of zooming along."

I reread the text, as if to myself, letting the children take it in again. I did this hoping that ideas would dawn in their minds.

Then I began. "I'm noticing that Dog's mouth is described as *gentle*." I underlined the word on the large copy of the text. "That seems like a really unusual word to use for a dog's mouth. When I try to grow ideas about characters, I usually notice unusual words that the author uses to describe the character. Let me jot a quick annotation on the page to note what I'm noticing." Beside the underlined word, I wrote, "Why this word?"

The reason I suggest students look closely at the text to grow new insights is that I'm convinced writers are more apt to develop fresh ideas when they begin by attending to detail, rather than generalizing and then supplying details to illustrate those generalizations.

By stopping so early on in a text and zooming in on a detail students will otherwise be apt to have passed over, we recalibrate students' thinking. This is meant as a wake-up call and as a way to help children see the path they will need to take to get from where they are to where we want them to be.

If you do this right, your children will start to say, "Ohhh, ohhh," and climb up on their knees. You want their minds to be doing the same work you will demonstrate, because they'll learn more from your demonstration if they have been doing the exact same work and can compare their version with yours. So don't call on them just because they signal that they have something to add. This is your time to demonstrate, to teach, and to make your point.

Shifting out of the role of reader into the role of teacher, I said, "You already know how to shift between *recording* what you see in the text to *thinking* about what you see. And you know that it is important to do this even when you're not sure that you do have a thought! Something magical often happens when you use thought prompts to launch yourself into new ideas. Brand-new thoughts spill out. So let's use some thought prompts to help us take what we've noticed in our close reading and push our brains to have more thoughts about it." I pointed to the "Ways to Push Our Thinking" list of prompts from the *Boxes and Bullets: Personal and Persuasive Essays* unit, which I had brought to the front of the meeting area. Then I picked up a pen and began to jot quickly in my notebook, saying aloud what I was writing as I wrote.

> I see that Dog's mouth is called gentle, even though dogs have sharp teeth and use their
> mouths to eat other animals. <u>The thought I have about this is</u> . . .

"Hmm, what should we write?" I paused for a moment, visibly thinking this over before beginning to write. "I'm not sure what I'm thinking, but here goes."

> <u>The thought I have about this is</u> that . . .
>
> . . . even though most dogs' mouths are made to bite other animals, this dog uses his mouth in
> a different way.
>
> <u>To add on</u>, Dog is carrying a bird in that mouth. He is saving her life instead of eating her. He is
> a caring kind of a dog!

Debrief. Remind writers that when using this strategy to generate writing about texts, you note details in the text, then write your thoughts about those details.

"Writers, do you see that after I read a bit, I looked back at the story, noticing details? Because I own the book, I underlined the details. Otherwise, I would have left a sticky note to mark what I noticed. Then I picked up my pen and pushed myself to write. I used thought prompts like 'I see . . .' and 'The thought I have about this is . . .' and 'To add on . . .' to lead myself down a path of thought toward new ideas about the text. When I was writing, I wasn't quite sure what I would end up thinking, but I find that when I get my pen moving, ideas come to me."

I have come to believe that the sequence of our instruction in writing is incredibly important, because once skills have become automatic, learners can use those skills effortlessly to tackle new and more complex mental operations. This session assumes children have already learned to write entries in which they observe, then shift into reflecting on what they observe. The session also assumes that children already know how to work with conversational prompts, using these to extend their first thoughts.

The most important word that I've said might be hmm. It's crucial for us to show children that ideas don't come to any of us right away. We wait for them to nibble, like a fisherman waits for the fish to bite. So often, children expect ideas to be right there, fully articulated, in their minds, and they don't understand the experience of fishing for, waiting for, an idea to nibble.

This attentiveness to the dog's mouth shows up a bit later in this unit when we present a draft of our writing and then again when we develop a thesis. You absolutely can notice different things, but when you alter the teacher text, watch the domino effect those changes need to have.

I underline the lines from the story that ground what I say and think, because I want this physical way to remind children that our ideas are grounded in a close reading of the story. Often children glance at a text and then spin out ideas that are only tangentially related to the text. If you can find a way to give your students a copy of the entire text so they can annotate as well, that's helpful.

ACTIVE ENGAGEMENT

Channel children toward reading, scrutinizing, and annotating the next few lines of the touchstone text.

"If I hadn't been writing about *Fox*, I would have zoomed right past the detail that Dog's mouth is described as gentle. Writers see more, notice more; they live more wide-awake lives. So let's try this. I have a short excerpt from *Fox* to display for you, and you have your own copies of *Fox*. You'll read the next few lines from where we stopped, pausing when you see a detail that's worth growing ideas about. Then pay attention to that detail and see what ideas you can grow."

> He takes her to his cave above the river, and there he tries to tend her burnt wing: but Magpie does not want his help.
>
> "I will never again be able to fly," she whispers.
>
> "I know," says Dog.
>
> He is silent for a moment, then he says, "I am blind in one eye, but life is still good."
>
> "An eye is nothing!" says Magpie. "How would you feel if you couldn't run?"
>
> Dog does not answer. Magpie drags her body into the shadow of the rocks, until she feels herself melting into blackness.

Coach into children's work in ways that lift the level of it.

As children worked, I coached, "I love that you are using thought prompts to say more, like 'The thought I have about this is . . . ,' 'To add on . . . ,' and 'This shows . . . '

"Your hands are flying! It's great that you are writing fast and furiously! You can move on to your next thought prompt if you want," I said, urging them to dive right into this work and do their thinking with their pens moving. "Richard is going back to the text, grabbing another detail, and writing some more. Are you?"

Debrief by celebrating one student's work, explaining that the student successfully noticed an important detail and then composed ideas.

After another minute, I asked for attention. "Writers, can we talk?" Once I had everyone's attention, I said, "I want to share with you what Tony wrote. He read this bit of the story":

> "I will never again be able to fly," she whispers.

"Then Tony underlined the word *whispers*. Tony wrote, 'I notice Magpie could have shouted or screamed that, but instead she whispered it.'

You'll want students to read the excerpt from their own copies of the text. Another option would be to ask students to read from an enlarged copy of the passage, written on chart paper or displayed for the class. They would not be able to underline and annotate, but the logistics might be easier.

The excerpt needs to be short for many reasons. Keeping the minilesson brief is one. You also want to highlight the power of close reading, and providing a short excerpt does this. Leave plenty of white space around the part so children can annotate the text with their thinking.

When voicing over to cajole students to write more quickly, to work with more intensity, use your voice to communicate your content. Talk with urgency, using the same voice you used earlier during essay boot camp.

Notice that you will return to using "voiceovers" that you used earlier during the boot camp lesson from the Boxes and Bullets: Personal and Persuasive Essays *unit. Here you will be using these voiceovers to celebrate that your writers are reading and writing quickly—and to make it likely that more are doing this.*

"Tony could have stopped there, but he wanted to keep growing his idea, so he wrote more. He wrote, 'The thought I have about this is that Magpie is really sad. She's the kind of sad that's so big it makes you quiet instead of loud.' Then he pushed himself one last time with another thought prompt: 'To add on, she's so sad that I bet she almost wishes she'd died in the fire instead of living when she can't fly.'"

LINK

Reveal a chart showing the strategy you've taught for close reading and growing ideas about texts. Invite children to draw on this strategy, today and always.

"Today, writers, you learned a strategy for reading yourselves awake. You learned that to get big ideas about texts—and eventually grow those ideas into a literary essay—you read closely and write in response to reading." I revealed a chart showing the beginning of the process for writing about reading, with the first strategy to help that process listed.

How to Write a Literary Essay

- Grow ideas about a text.
  - Use thought prompts.

"In today's writing workshop, you'll have a chance to read as well as write. I have made available a few texts that you know. You'll see 'Eleven' by Sandra Cisneros, 'Marble Champ' by Gary Soto, *Fireflies* by Julia Brinkloe, *The Other Side* by Jacqueline Woodson, 'Boar Out There' by Cynthia Rylant, and 'Gloria Who Might Be My Best Friend' by Ann Cameron, and a few others. Because you'll be writing about these texts, use the wide margins so you can jot your thoughts. For today, would you and your partner read the same story?"

You'll report not on Tony's thinking, of course, but about what a child in your own class says. As you listen to partners talk, find or help a child to say an idea about Magpie (or the character in whatever text you read) that you believe is worth revisiting. Record the child's exact words on chart paper. You'll see that I return to what Tony has said in tomorrow's small-group work, when I teach children that as we read further in a story, we revise our first-draft ideas of it.

Supporting Close Reading

A T THE START OF ANY NEW UNIT, you'll hustle among your students, helping them begin the new work you've laid out. Today what you will be expecting children to do is to look through the folder of familiar short texts and settle on one to read and write about. It is important that most of the texts are familiar to most of the class because this way, if a reader is reading one text—say, in our instance, that Sophie is reading "Eleven"—you can still bring that student—Sophie—into a small group that is working with a different text (say, "Spaghetti"). It is also important that the texts represent a range of text difficulty, because you'll want to provision each reader with a text that he or she can read. We find that the anthology *Every Living Thing* is a wonderful source of short stories, as is *Birthday Surprises* by Johanna Hurwitz, *Baseball in April* by Gary Soto, *Hey World, Here I Am!* by Jean Little, *Going, Going, Gone!* by Judy Blume, and *The Stories Julian Tells* by Ann Cameron.

Don't be surprised if your children need quite a bit of help getting started with the work of the new unit. You have asked youngsters to engage in something that requires a different orientation than their usual writing workshop work. During writing time, they have been asked to read much more intensely than usual, inching through a text with frequent shifts between reading and writing.

So at the start of today's workshop, we suggest you survey the room and notice first whether children seem to be choosing to work with texts you think they can handle—that are not too hard for them to read. Notice next the children who are flying through the text that you hoped they'd be scrutinizing. Notice also those who are writing at a distance from the text, rarely looking from their writing to the text. These last two groups will each need a quick intervention to bring them on course.

If the entire class is working at one extreme or the other, you will want to rely on a mid-workshop teaching to right the balance; otherwise, you'll find that table conferences are especially helpful. At each table, you can watch for a minute, thinking about how best to help. Then you can intervene. One way to do so involves noticing and supporting when students are doing work you wish others were doing. The important

---

MID-WORKSHOP TEACHING   **Developing the Eyes to See and the Language to Discuss What Others Overlook**

Standing in the middle of the room, I called for children's attention. "I want to tell you about Raffi. When I came to him, he looked up from his reading and shrugged, like this, and said, 'There's not that much to see in here.'

"But then we started talking, and Raffi remembered the time he had dipped his cup into the pond, looked at the water and said, 'I didn't get any bugs or anything.' He almost threw the water back! But instead, he studied the water through a magnifying lens, and this time he found his water was swarming with creatures!" I looked out at the class and said, "So Raffi decided to look again at the story he is reading, just as he had looked again at that pond water, and you won't be surprised to hear that this time, he saw a whole lot and wrote all this." I held up his notebook to illustrate that he'd filled more than a page with observations.

"Writers, would you and your partner put the story you've both been reading between you and try, like Raffi did, to *really see* what's there? Underline intriguing things you notice. Talk about what you see and *think*."

After a few moments, I intervened. "Writers, can I stop you? When you talk about your ideas, I'm having a hard time understanding some of what you say. I want to give you two tips on how to be clear when you talk about ideas."

- "When you speak of a character, use his or her name. If you say, 'This kid, he . . . ' and then say, 'Then he . . . ,' people listening are often unclear which person your pronoun references."

- "Try to avoid talk that sounds like this: 'Well, you know, he likes all that stuff, you know.' Assume your listeners *don't* know what you are getting at. Say outright what you mean!"

---

thing is to be authentic and persuasive. "William, I *love* how you are going back and forth between the text and your own writing, underlining a part as you read and then growing ideas about it right in the margin of your paper!" I glanced around the rest of the table. "Oh my gosh, look at Raffi. He has a ton of thoughts written already too. Can the rest of you guys notice the thinking Raffi and William have gotten onto their pages, and try doing the same?"

At another table, I saw that Sophie had written an entire page and a half about a few lines from the text. I asked all the writers at the table to pause. "Look at what Sophie is doing here! She's developed such fabulous skills at writing long and strong, it's almost as if she could go on examining this one part forever!" Then I told the class, "I hope you are noticing the way that Sophie read a little bit, then wrote, and then read a little bit more, and then wrote. That way, she was able to grow ideas off of a lot of details in the story, and even started to see how some of the details worked together to support big ideas." Addressing the whole table, I said, "Take a moment to look at your own paper now. Are you finding lots of details to write about? A pattern in the details?"

To another table full of writers, who had just read a good portion of their texts but only paused once or twice to jot, I made a suggestion. "Can I teach you a totally cool trick? You all are reading *forward* in your texts, but if you go *back* to *re*read the text, you'll find that you see a lot more the second time." With this tip, I helped them slow down their reading enough to be able to notice the little details they were looking for, which others would probably pass by.

You can predict that a surprisingly large number of children will have difficulties coming up with thoughts about books. Some children, for example, will have written about personal connections rather than actually writing about the text. You can notice these writers because you will see lines like "I remember one time when I . . ." or "This reminds me of the time when I . . ." or "I found a bird once and I . . ." In these cases, you'll want to channel these writers towards the text by telling them that they are not expected to write about times from their lives but rather about the character, and their idea about the character. You may want these writers to reread the excerpts from the text that had sparked their initial entry, and coach them to this time start by restating what that passage actually said, then to reflect on it.

Other children will restate facts rather than invent their own new thoughts. So they'll write, "I think Gabriel wants company" or "I think Gabriel goes looking for what is making that sound." Neither of those is a new idea—both are stated outright in the text. To help children understand the difference, I sometimes tell them that their ideas won't be *right there* on the page of the story. If I can point to the section of the text

that comes right out and says what the child has stated, then the child is retelling the story, not growing an idea. I also sometimes tell children that ideas are often debatable.

If children are recording facts about the story rather than writing ideas, I find it helps to teach them that ideas hide inside facts. For example, it's a fact that Gabriel thought about a *butter* sandwich. To grow a thought, I need to linger with that for a fraction of a minute, asking myself, "And what do I think about that?" Sometimes a child's first instinct is to think by asking a question, "A *butter* sandwich, not peanut butter and jelly?" Nudge the child to speculate on an answer. "Maybe Gabriel remembers his butter sandwich because he is poor and it's basically just bread."

Remember that now is not the time to nitpick. Instead, it's time to do the things that will make the biggest transformational difference.

Probably one of the biggest things you can do now is to tap into the repertoire of skills the students already know. You might, therefore, be ready to remind students that whenever they're starting a new task, they will want to think, "What have I already learned that sets me up for this new task?"

Because I knew that during the share, I would want to remind students to draw on all they already know, I looked for and found a student who was stuck on what to write, and I asked her, "Is there anything you've studied before that can help you?" Of course, I had hung the "Questions Writers Ask of Earlier Entries" chart in the meeting area in preparation for today, so it wasn't long before a table full of students discovered it and decided to expand today's work with some of the strategies from the chart, such as "What surprises me about this is . . ." and "What this teaches me about life is . . ." Of course, I gave students the credit for the idea that a chart from their previous unit might be brought into this unit.

> I think that Jenny is lonely. Maybe she goes out to find the boar to either befriend him or to show everyone she is brave. Which she is. She is brave to go find the boar. The boar is also brave because he stays there with Jenny without attacking. But he is not all brave because he gets scared when he sees or knows that someone is after him. Also Jenny knows that there is more inside the boar than most people think. Even a wild boar can have a true kind heart inside. People prejudge him, but Jenny knows not to.

FIG. 1–1   Max's notebook entry after thinking about the story "Boar Out There"

Using Charts from Previous Units

Tell writers about a child who was stuck, then spotted a chart from the essay unit that supported interpretive thinking, finding ways to use strategies from the chart that relate to writing about reading.

"Writers, can I stop you for a moment? I just saw Chloe doing something that I think we'd all benefit from. As you've noticed, I've prominently displayed many of our essay charts for this unit. Just a minute ago, Chloe was looking a bit stuck and unsure of what to write next. She was looking between her text and her writer's notebook, but it was clear that no ideas were coming to her. Then, suddenly, Chloe looked up and spotted the chart 'Questions Writers Ask of Earlier Entries'—the one we used to mine our entries for ideas at the beginning of our *Boxes and Bullets: Personal and Persuasive Essays* unit. Chloe stared at this chart a moment and then quickly began writing fast and furiously." I directed children's attention to the chart.

Questions Writers Ask of Earlier Entries

- What is the important thing about this entry?
- What does this teach about me? About life?
- Why do I remember this one time? How does it connect to who I am or to important issues?
- What other entries have I written that connect to this one?
- What does this make me realize?
- What do I want readers to know about this?
- What surprises me about this?

Name the larger point—that learning from earlier units can be adapted to help with new work—then recruit the class to make a new version of the "Questions Writers Ask of Earlier Entries" chart called "Questions Writers Ask of Texts."

"What Chloe realized, and what you should all know, is that *old charts* and old learning can help you do new work. The charts from our personal and persuasive essay unit may not fit literary essay writing *perfectly*, but we can *make* them

Questions Writers Ask of Earlier Entries

- What is the important about this entry?
- What does this teach about me? About life?
- Why do I remember this one time? How does it connect to who I am or to important issues?
- What other entries have I written that connect to this one?
- What does this make me realize?
- What do I want readers to know about this?
- What surprises me about this?

into useful tools. For instance, Chloe looked at the questions chart and realized that instead of 'Questions Writers Ask of Earlier Entries,' this could be 'Questions Writers Ask of *Texts*'! She took this second bullet on the questions chart, 'What does this teach about me? About life?' and added, 'What does this teach me about the character in this text? About life?' Do you see how powerful that is? Instead of asking questions to explore *herself*, she is asking questions to explore the *character* in her text."

"Will you see if you can revise a few other bullets from the original chart? Work with your partners, or pull two partnerships together."

As students worked, I coached in, reminding them that the new goal was to develop ideas about the text, not their lives. "Remember, you want this to be a question you can ask about a song, a picture book, a novel—about any text." And later, "Chloe only needed to change the word *me* to *character*. Many of these questions only need a teeny, tiny switch."

Marie began. "My group was thinking about the bullet 'What do *I* want readers to know about this?' We thought that maybe, since it isn't about us anymore, it could be about what does *the author* want readers to know." I added to the chart.

Judah began excitedly, "We realized that some of the questions can stay exactly the same. Like the one 'What does this make me realize?' or 'What surprises me about this?'"

After a few moments, I pulled the class back together and charted out their new questions.

Questions Writers Ask of Texts

- What does this teach about the character in this text? About life?
- What does the author want readers to know about this?
- What does this make me realize?
- What surprises me about this?
- Does this text connect to others I've read?
- What issues or life topics does this connect to?
- What is the important thing about this text?

Questions Writers Ask of Texts

★ What does this teach about the character in this text? About life?

★ What does the author want readers to know about this?

★ What does this make me realize?

★ What surprises me about this?

★ Does this text connect to others I've read?

★ What issues or life topics does this connect to?

★ What is the important thing about this text?

I put down the marker. "The tools you've used all year long as writers can help you even now. When you are stuck or looking to have smarter ideas for your writing, you can think back on what you've learned and use all the charts in our room to help you." I waved my arm across the room. "As we continue on in this unit, be asking yourselves, 'What do I already know that can help me do stronger, smarter work in this literary essay unit?'"

READING WITH PASSIONATE ATTENTIVENESS

Tonight, read one of the stories we've chosen to study. Read it as carefully as you can. Read it like you'd read a treasure map or read it like you know there's more to it, if only you can figure it out. Read it as hard as you can. And write about whatever you notice, whatever it makes you think and feel and wonder and remember. I have made each of you a copy of the chart "Questions Writers Ask of Texts" so you can draw upon that tonight as you write a long entry.

Gathering Writing by Studying Characters

IN THIS SESSION, you'll teach students that experts know that certain aspects of their subjects merit special attention. Literary essayists know it pays off, for example, to study characters.

GETTING READY

✔ "How to Write a Literary Essay" chart from Session 1

✔ The next few paragraphs of the touchstone text, *Fox*, to display to the whole class (see Teaching and Active Engagement)

✔ Chart paper and markers

✔ The texts students worked with in the previous session (see Conferring and Small-Group Work)

COMMON CORE STATE STANDARDS: W.4.1, W.4.7, W.4.8, W.4.9.a, RL.4.1, RL.4.3, SL.4.1, L.4.1, L.4.2, L.4.3.a, L.4.6

I T WAS PREDICTABLE that in the first session of this unit, you'd help students know the ways that writers write about literature and you'd invite them to get started collecting notes and entries from which they'll eventually choose a seed idea. It is predictable that today you'll return to this work and extend the list of options that students have for ways to generate writing. Meanwhile, you'll channel children to choose the one text they'll study for the remainder of the bend and eventually write an essay about.

You are also still launching the unit, and as part of that, you are still helping your students recognize that this is big and important work. Buddha said, "Your job is to discover your work and to give your heart to it." We believe this matters—for kids and for us, as teachers, too. Gallup polls show that less than half of workers in today's society say that they know the goals of their workplace and feel they are a part of those goals. That is a devastating statistic—and not one that we want to characterize our classrooms as well as our workplaces. So it is important that in your teaching today, you are mindful that your job is not only to instruct, but also to rally your students to care about the work of this unit. One of the best ways to get youngsters to care about writing literary essays is by helping them care about characters.

My son began his college application essay like this:

> When I enter the class of 2009, I will bring my experiences of trekking through the mountains of Viet Nam and my memories of a 227-day stint in a lifeboat, accompanied by a Bengal tiger. When I attend freshman classes, my role will bear the imprint of my tortuous hours standing above the town square, a scarlet letter emblazoned on my chest. Reading has given me the water I swim in, the heroes I emulate, and the imagination to believe that I can make the world a better place.

I often say that as an educator, I want to give all children what I want for my own sons. I can think of few gifts that have mattered more to my sons than the gift of Nathaniel Hawthorne's Hester Prynne, Katherine Patterson's Gilly Hopkins, A. A. Milne's Eeyore,

Brian Jacques's mouse, Martin, and all the other characters who have enriched their lives. Our children can find heroes in the books they read, and better still, they can become these characters, standing for a time in their shoes.

> *"Our children can find heroes in the books they read, and better still, they can become these characters, standing for a time in their shoes."*

I want all children to empathize with characters—just as I want them to think deeply about them.

This session continues where the last one left off—teaching children another way to find and develop interesting, original, true ideas about texts. Specifically, the session encourages readers to think about characters' traits, motivations, struggles, changes, and relationships. These terms are easy to list, but they are potent. They hold unbelievable potential for revealing insight. Those who analyze and write about texts know to pay close attention to characters.

Gathering Writing by Studying Characters

CONNECTION

Remind children that they live their lives observing and need only bring this work to their study of texts.

"Writers, will you come to the carpet, and as you come, will you look around you with eagle eyes, noticing little details that you sometimes just walk right past?"

The children gathered. "Tell your partner what you just noticed with your eagle eyes," I said. As children talked, I listened in.

"Help! No more talking about what you noticed! So many of you are noticing things we need to clean up! Stop, stop," I said, covering my ears in jest. "No, seriously. You all are great observers. I started to realize that last week when I came back after you had that new substitute teacher for a day. I could have painted a portrait and written an essay about him just from the details you guys told me! It seemed like when you came into the classroom and saw him standing there at my desk, you started looking for signs that would tell you what sort of sub he'd be. You were practically spying on him! You took anything he did and used it as a clue to help you figure out the sort of sub he'd be, the sort of person he is. Am I right?"

Many children nodded, laughing. Becoming more somber, I said, "Writers, here is my point. *That's exactly what it is like for thoughtful readers when they meet new characters in a story.*"

❖ Name the teaching point.

"Today I want to teach you that skilled readers of fiction pay special attention to the characters in a story. And they especially pay attention to the main character's traits, motivations, struggles, changes, and life lessons."

I revealed our chart from yesterday, with yesterday's and today's teaching points added on.

When writing minilessons for kindergarten and first-grade children, we often use physical activity to drive home a point. As I shift between writing units for young children and doing so for older students, I can't help but think, "Will physical activity be any less engaging for nine-year-olds?" Setting kids up to notice little details as they proceed to the meeting area doesn't extend the length of the minilesson, so it's hard to see the downside to using this as a way to bring home the point.

Reading and writing well are abstract skills, so you will often go away from reading and writing to bring home what a skill means. In this instance, you help children understand what it means to grow theories about characters by talking about the way they "read" people all the time.

Notice that the list of things to follow matches story structure—and is sequenced in ways that match the progression of a story.

How to Write a Literary Essay

- Grow ideas about a text.
  - Use thought prompts.
  - Ask questions of texts.
  - Pay attention to the characters in a story, especially noting their traits, motivations, struggles, changes, and relationships.

~ How to Write a Literary Essay ~

- Grow Ideas about a text.
  - Use thought prompts.
  - Ask questions of texts.
  - Pay attention to the characters in a story, especially noting their traits, motivations, struggles, changes, and relationships.
- Find a big idea that is really important to you, then write a thesis.
- Test out your thesis by asking questions.
  - Does this opinion relate to more than one part of the text?
  - Is there enough evidence to support it?
- Collect Evidence.
  - micro-stories
  - quotes
  - lists
  - examples
- Unpack the evidence by telling the reader what it shows, using prompts like:
  - This shows that...
  - This is evidence that...
- Add transitions to glue the evidence together.

TEACHING

Point out that experts on any subject know the features of that subject that merit attention. Illustrate by talking about expertise in subjects you know well.

"I've been reading a best-selling book, *Blink*. Malcolm Gladwell, the author, suggests that an expert on a topic can listen and observe something related to that topic and figure out in a flash a whole lot about that topic.

"When I watch the Westminster Kennel Club dog show on television. I love to put myself in the judge's place, eyeing the Welsh corgis, cairn terriers, and wirehaired dachshunds. But it always happens that I am still checking out the dog's coat, ears, and shape, when suddenly the judge signals, 'Take him around.' Then, before I can take in all that new information, the judge moves on to the next dog! The secret is that the person who makes those observations is an expert, and experts know which aspects of a dog are worth noticing.

"The author Malcolm Gladwell says that the secret to being an expert who can understand things in a blink lies in the fact that experts know which features of a subject merit attention. This is true for expert readers too. When reading fiction, it pays to think about characters in general, and specifically, it pays to think about a character's traits, motivations, struggles, changes, and relationships."

One reason this unit begins by asking students to spend several days writing about reading is to teach children that writing is a vehicle not only for communicating, but also for growing ideas. I encourage children to write about ideas that are not yet fully formed in their minds, to let ideas come out of the tips of their pencils, fresh and surprising.

If you have expertise in a sport that kids care about or in currently popular television shows, by all means draw on that expertise when making your points! If you are like me, obsessed with dogs, the kids will forgive you for turning to that arena for half your examples! Bring your loves into your teaching, and the passion you feel for your subject will come into your teaching as well!

Tell students that expert readers know it pays off to attend to specific aspects of a story. Discuss these and demonstrate how you read, attending to these aspects—in this case, character.

"It's easier to *say* this than to *do* it, because authors don't come right out and say, 'Dog's character traits are . . . Dog's motivations (or hopes) are . . . ' Instead, readers need to pay close attention to details that reveal a character's traits, motivations, struggles, changes, and relationships.

"Let's look back at *Fox* again and see if this time when we read closely, we can grow ideas about Dog's traits, motivations, struggles, changes, and relationships—because after all, experts at reading literature know those are important features to notice about a story's characters. Remember that yesterday, we noticed that Margaret Wild describes Dog's mouth as 'gentle,' which made us start to think that perhaps Dog wants to care for Magpie. Let's read on with this idea in mind, paying close attention to the character, Dog." I motioned again to this strategy listed on the "How to Write a Literary Essay" chart and the features that I'd especially notice: traits, motivations, struggles, changes, and relationships.

> *Days, perhaps a week later, she wakes with a rush of grief. Dog is waiting. He persuades her to go with him to the riverbank.*
>
> *"Hop on my back," he says. "Look into the water and tell me what you see."*
>
> *Sighing, Magpie does as he asks. Reflected in the water are clouds and sky and trees—and something else.*
>
> *"I see a strange new creature!" she says.*
>
> *"That is us," says Dog.*

"Hmm," I thought aloud. "Are you noticing some new things about Dog?" I looked at the text. I left a bit of silence, knowing the children would fill it with their thoughts.

Then I continued. "I notice that when Magpie wakes, days or weeks later, Dog is waiting for her. It is such a simple sentence—'Dog is waiting'—but it shows caring, don't you think? Even patience. This fits with our earlier idea that Dog is taking care of the bird." I looked out at the children as they nodded their heads in agreement.

"We should push ourselves to see if there is more here. Let's look for more. Hmm." I returned my eyes to the text, rereading to myself, leaving space for children to have more thoughts about Dog.

Sophie piped in, "Why does he say, 'That is us'? It is sort of weird."

"Great that you are asking questions," I said and added, to the class, "The best is if you can try to also answer your questions. Will you take Sophie's question, 'Why does Dog look in the water and say, 'That is us'? and this time, say, 'Could it be that . . . ?' and try to speculate an answer. I'll throw the question out again, and you speculate about it." I repeated, "'Why does Dog look in the water and say, 'That is us'?"

When I reference Dog, I am referring to one of the main characters in Fox, *by Margaret Wild and Ron Brooks, a mentor text for this unit. This is the book we began reading in the previous session.*

This list of what stories reveal about character is a weighty one, so I say each term slowly, giving time for each term to sink in.

The story reveals more about Magpie than it does about Dog, and it would be easier to talk about her character than Dog's. It will always be the case that you choose to demonstrate with the work that is harder, leaving the more straightforward work for the children.

Watch how I extract particular pointers from my demonstration. It's not enough to simply say, "Watch me," and then hope the children will be enthralled by simply watching me read and think aloud.

Teachers, if none of your students pipe in, you could run your fingers under a few lines and reread them aloud, then ask a question such as Sophie's, doing this as if you are questioning yourself. Then you can point out the importance of asking and also answering questions.

From throughout the room, I heard one partner say to another, "Could it be that . . . ?" and soon the room was filled with conjectures.

After a minute, I brought their attention back to me by saying over the hubbub, "I heard Charlie say, 'Maybe, the dog was lonely and now he is glad to have a friend.'"

Debrief in ways that spotlight the work that you have done that can be transferred to another text, another day. Do this in ways that return to the teaching point.

"Do you see that the story often gives concrete details—it tells what the characters say and do? Readers pay attention to those like they are clues—clues to the mystery of what the characters are like and what the story is really about. You can solve some mysteries by reading closely and asking questions and thinking, 'Could it be that . . . ?'"

ACTIVE ENGAGEMENT

Set children up to try the work you've demonstrated. In this instance, ask children to look for a character's motivations, traits, and so on.

"Now it's your turn. I am going to read on. This time, will you read closely, thinking about what the details of the text show about *Magpie*?" Pointing to the chart, I said, "Notice especially her traits, motivations, struggles, changes, and relationships." I read on just a bit, giving the children a little more text to work with.

> "I see a strange new creature!" she says.
>
> "That is us," says Dog. "Now hold on tight!"
>
> With Magpie clinging to his back, he races through the scrub, past the stringy barks, past the clumps of yellow box trees, and into blueness. He runs so swiftly, it is almost as if he were flying.
>
> Magpie feels the wind streaming through her feathers, and she rejoices. "FLY, DOG, FLY! I will be your missing eye and you will be my wings."

I paused and let there be a bit of silence and thinking, aware of the growing anticipation to talk. "Partner 1," I said after a moment, "start the conversation with your partner. What big ideas are you beginning to have about Magpie's traits or motivations, her struggles, changes, or relationships?"

Immediately, Amelia turned to her partner, Charlie. "Magpie is finally happy! This is a big change from before."

"I agree," added Charlie. "I think that Magpie might need a friend, too. She thought that she had nothing because her wing was broken and she couldn't fly anymore, but having a friend will help her."

Notice that I don't suggest children pull out copies of one of the stories they've been reading during the workshop and think about the character in that story. Had my children needed lots of support, I would have chosen that option. Instead, I imagine they'll do this during the workshop itself. I don't usually want the work of the workshop to be launched (and I certainly don't want it to be compressed) during the active engagement section of a mini-lesson, leaving students little new to try once I say, "Off you go." However, when working with high-need groups of children, I often do want to launch the day's work during the mini-lessons, and therefore I'd adjust my teaching accordingly.

"And maybe," added Amelia, "Magpie is starting to think that Dog can give her what she wants—like, to fly. Like when she says, 'FLY, DOG, FLY! . . . you will be my wings.' They are good for each other."

LINK

Remind children that expert readers know which features of a story are worth studying and that it pays off to study a character's traits, motivations, struggles, changes, and relationships.

"So, readers, today and whenever you want to grow ideas about stories, it helps to remember that expert readers know the features of stories that are worth their attention. Among other things, expert readers pay attention to the main character's traits, motivations, struggles, changes, and life lessons. Today you'll be doing that, and I'm going to ask you to focus on *one* text you've been reading. I'll give you a moment to look through your texts and look back over the notes you jotted yesterday to choose a text that feels important to you. Pick carefully, because this text will be the focus of your first literary essay!" I gave the children a moment to pick a text.

I pulled the children back together. "Today you can write marginal notes some of the time, but I also hope you write long and strong in your notebook, growing your ideas about characters' traits, motivations, struggles, changes, and relationships. You can write several entries. Remember, you can draw on any strategy, from this unit or others, to help you think deeply about your text."

As you move about the carpet area, use this opportunity to steer children toward texts that you know will be best suited to their needs. Encourage them to choose texts they can read fluently. If one of your struggling readers reaches for "The Marble Champ" because he saw his best friend do the same, you might intervene. "Max," you can say. "You wrote so much about 'Spaghetti' yesterday. It seems a shame to drop all that brilliant thinking and start anew with a different text. What do you think about choosing 'Spaghetti' for your essay?" Then too, you'll want to emphasize the smart choices children make, voicing over commentary about the children who look for texts that are just right or those they've already spent some time with.

Teachers, if you feel the list laid out here of what readers could pay attention to is too long, then you can certainly shorten it. If you do so, then you might want to alter your mid-workshop teaching or share to give these other options to your students. However, if you have already taught some of these during a character study, then many of them will be familiar to your readers and they will benefit from having them revisited and laid out as options to grow ideas about their characters now.

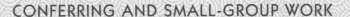

Revising Initial Theories

Y OU WILL WANT TO USE YOUR CONFERRING AND SMALL-GROUP WORK today to be sure your children are reading, rereading, and responding with a new level of investment, drawing on all they know about reading closely and about writing-to-learn.

You may notice that some students seem to read with total detachment, not seeming to care about the characters. Engagement matters in all that students do, so you will probably want to address this. You could, for example, convene a small group of these children and ask if they'd try out some work that you'd like to later share with the whole class. Then you could teach this small group that readers of fiction don't simply read like professors, growing theories about the texts. Readers of fiction also read like many of us watch great movies. It is almost as if we become the character. The character is in trouble, and our hearts beat wildly, hoping, hoping, things work out. There is a creepy sound behind the character, and we jump in our seats. Reading in this sort of empathetic way leads a reader to grow more urgent and intense theories about a character. "I can see why she'd . . . " this reader might say. "I worry that she'll . . . " This allows the reader to have a felt sense for the character's experience and to want to reach for the exact right words that capture that experience. In the share for today's workshop, you could then tell the rest of the class that empathetic reading leads a reader to hear more, see more, feel more, care more, and yes, to think more. You can source from this small group in your share session to emphasize the value of this.

When planning your small-group work, you will also want to be alert to students who seem to be prematurely settling on one hard-and-fast idea, rather than using their growing repertoire of strategies to explore multiple theories. You may decide to convene a small group of children to give them supported practice drafting and revising their ideas as they read. With one group, I said, "Once you form an idea about a character, it is important to read on, expecting you'll probably revise that idea." I had them all pull out their copy of "Spaghetti."

"Yesterday Tony had this idea." I gestured to the pad of chart paper, where I'd written an enlarged version of what Tony had told me the preceding day. He'd been using

MID-WORKSHOP TEACHING
Revising Theories about Characters

"Writers, can I have your eyes and your attention?" I waited. "I want to remind you that the ideas you develop about characters are rough drafts. Once you have drafted an idea, say to yourself, 'I'm going to continue to read and see if upcoming sections of the text can help me *add on to* or *revise* this idea.' Often when you read more, you learn that your first idea was only partly true and needs to be changed.

"Let me show you what I mean. You already know that after I read that Dog carried Magpie gently, I put in my writer's notebook that he is caring. After we talked about the part where he and Magpie look at their reflection in the water and he tells her, 'It's us,' I added that he seems to want a friend. Then I read on, knowing new information in the text would either confirm or challenge the idea that he was lonely. Listen to what I read next.

> And so Dog runs, with Magpie on his back, every day, through Summer, through Winter.

"They stay together for half a year because they are both so happy running together! To me, that goes with my idea that Dog wanted a friend, and I'm going to add that he is a loyal friend. Staying together for all those seasons tells me he is loyal."

Then, debriefing to pull out the transferable lesson I hoped they were learning, I said, "Do you see the way I continue reading, expecting to learn more, to develop and to change my theories? Will you make sure that your theory is not something you make and leave behind? Carry it with you, and expect it to change (or be confirmed) as you read on."

thought prompts, and now I underlined those in his entry to remind children of their presence.

> I notice Magpie could have shouted or screamed that she would never be able to fly again, but instead she whispered it. The thought I have about this is that Magpie is really sad. She's the kind of sad that's so big it makes you quiet instead of loud. To add on, she's so sad that I bet she almost wishes she'd died in the fire instead of living when she can't fly.

Teachers, you won't be surprised that I chose this one child's theory as worth tracking for a reason. I knew that if children followed Tony's thought and tracked Magpie's sadness, this would pay off. In the story, Magpie becomes less sad by the end. In most stories, the protagonist undergoes a change, so I wanted children to be accustomed to not just "proving" their idea about a character, but testing that idea—tracking it.

I invited the students to read on in the story with me, keeping Tony's idea that Magpie is sad in mind. "Remember," I told them, "try to let your ideas become complex. Ask, 'Could the story be saying something more complicated?'"

Near the end of the story, we learned Magpie gets to—in a sense—fly again.

> *Magpie feels the wind streaming through her feathers, and she rejoices.*
> *"FLY, DOG, FLY! I will be your missing eye and you will be my wings."*

"What are you thinking *now* about Magpie's sadness?" I asked. I again gave children time to underline relevant sections of the text, and then they talked, this time as a group. They agreed that this part showed Magpie being not so sad, and that actually she is happy to be "flying" with Dog.

Gesturing to Tony's entry, I said, "When Tony suggested at the start of the story that Magpie was sad, that she almost *wished* she'd died in the fire, do you think that the evidence *wasn't* really there to support that claim? Or what do you think is going on? Could Magpie be changing? Right now, each of you, reread the story and try to figure out your position on this. Was Magpie never sad? Does Tony need to revise his initial thought?" As children worked, I voiced over, saying, "I'm glad to see so many of you finding and underlining sections of the text that help you." After a minute, I said, "Tell your partner what you're thinking."

Tony spoke. "I still say Magpie *was* sad because she couldn't fly anymore and because she wanted to be left alone, curled up in the shadows of the cave. But I think this part at the end shows that Dog helped her to be less sad. Dog changed her."

Wanting to extrapolate the lessons that pertain to other days and other texts, I said, "This is the work that readers who write do all the time. Readers notice things in texts, grow tentative ideas, and then they read on, knowing those first ideas will be revised. Will you make sure that you are expecting to change your first ideas about whatever text you are reading? Do as we just did and think, 'Is all of the story supporting my initial idea?' Almost always, as you continue reading, you will find that stories take turns that lead you to revise your first ideas."

You might find that some of your children are not ready to revise their ideas because they are struggling to generate ideas in the first place. You may want to pull these children together to have a conversation. To do this, it will be important for them to read a shared text—even a very short one. Then you can point out that thinking about a text often begins with selecting an important part of the text and musing over why that part is important. Alternatively, you could point out that most important sections of a text can be treated as windows to the character. What does this part show about the character? After a few minutes of small-group discussion about whichever question you lead them to discuss, stop the conversation and ask the group to list ideas they now have about the story. Then you can ask the children to write about one of those ideas. As they write, coach them to go back to the text for evidence that supports their thinking.

Small groups such as the ones we describe in this write-up will be important throughout this unit.

> I think the change in Rachel in Eleven is this: she learns not to make so many Predictions and expect things Because she learned that if you always expect the best, a lot of the time you'll be disappointed or let down. Like when she expected to feel eleven and to know what to do, only to be forced to wear someone else's revolting sweater, and not knowing how to handle it. And she expected to feel eleven right away, only to find out she had to be eleven before she knows what eleven feels like.

FIG. 2–1   Max writes about the change in the character Rachel that he sees in "Eleven."

Writing to Know Characters

Tell children that when we read fiction, we can empathize with a character in ways that let us see the world through that character's eyes. Empathy is a way to grow ideas.

"A friend of mine, Ralph Fletcher, once said, 'If you want to get to know a person, don't go out to dinner with that person—instead have a flat tire together, get caught in a rainstorm together.' When we read, we're caught in rainstorms—or in whatever happens in the story—with the characters we meet on the pages. By living through the storms of life together, we form relationships with those characters—and we learn not only *about* them, but also *from* them.

"So, readers, remember that to develop ideas about characters, it helps to first live with that character through the storms of life. If you want to grow ideas about Rachel in 'Eleven,' then it helps to first imagine that *your* teacher told you, 'Put that sweater on,' and *you* look at that sweater, hanging over the front corner of your desk, knowing it's not yours. When you experience the story within the skin of a character, when you read with that kind of empathy, you should find that the character's reactions make sense to you. Empathy helps you come to smart new insights, and *that's* your goal."

When I was at college, I had a poster on my wall that said, "Love does not come from gazing into each other's eyes, but from gazing together in the same direction." When we read, we and the character gaze together in the same direction. We encounter storms, predicaments, heartaches together—and because we live through life side by side, we bond with characters.

Highlight the work you did with a few children in a small group today.

On the overhead projector, I displayed an entry Ali wrote explaining its context. "Ali tried to put herself in the main character's shoes as she read 'The Marble Champ.' In the story, after the main character, Lupe, realizes her marble-shooting thumb is weaker than the neck of a newborn chick, the text says, 'She looked out the window. The rain was letting up but the ground was too muddy to play.' Ali pictured her doing that. In fact, she imagined herself doing that, as Lupe, and pretty soon she was writing a part of the story that Gary Soto left out, imagining the details of what Lupe may have done next. You'll see she first copied a bit from the text, and then wrote 'off from' the text" (see Figure 2–2).

> She looked out the window. The rain was letting up. She gripped the brown silk bag of marbles in one hand and a piece of chalk in the other hand. She got up and walked to the door to the outside. She took a deep breath and walked back to the marbles on the bed.

> She looked out the window. The rain was letting up. She gripped the brown silk bag of marbles in one hand and a piece of chalk in the other hand. She got up and walked to the door to the outside. She took a deep breath and walked back to the marbles on the bed.
>
> ———
>
> Lupe got into the push up position. 1,2,3,4,5. She fell down. But decided to push herself 10,15,20. "Yes!" she screamed.

FIG. 2–2   Ali envisions herself as the character Lupe and writes off from "The Marble Champ."

Ali did this same kind of writing—pretending to be the character—based on other sections of the text too. After reading the part about strengthening her shooting by doing push-ups, five at a time, Ali wrote in her notebook:

> Lupe got into the push up position. 1, 2, 3, 4, and 5. She fell down. But decided to push herself
> 10, 15, 20. "Yes!" she screamed.

"All this writing and imagining made Ali realize how hard it was to practice all the time. She could feel how much each little push-up hurt!"

Ask children to try this work with a partner, using their own stories.

"I expect most of you have not yet tried writing in the shoes of a character. Let me show you how to do this. Find an intense and important part of the text, where something is happening to the main character." I left a pool of silence. "Now reread and find a line that shows the character doing or saying something. Copy that onto the top of a blank page of your notebook. Now, reread that, imagining you are the character. Look ahead to know what happens next, but first there's going to be a bit of life that you imagine. Picture where you are, what you are doing. Make a movie in your mind. And start writing, fast and furious."

After a few minutes, I asked writers to stop. "We need to end workshop time," I said. "But always remember that another way to grow ideas about a text is to live and write inside the shoes of the main character."

If your students are ready for further study of character, you may want to teach them that there is a saying, "When you go over the bumps, what's inside spills out," telling them that this is true for characters in books as well. When a character struggles, what's inside spills out, and for this reason, experienced readers pay special attention to what a character does in the face of difficulties. Often when characters struggle, they end up finding strengths inside themselves that they never knew existed, and this is one force that accounts for the way a character changes.

SESSION 2 HOMEWORK

STUDYING HOW A MENTOR AUTHOR PORTRAYS A CHARACTER

In a few days, you will reread your notebook to select a seed idea that you can develop into a literary essay. You want to make sure that you have a lot of ideas to choose from by that time. So tonight, reread the story you've selected and use a strategy or two that you haven't yet used to grow ideas. You may want to reread paying close attention to details that seem significant and important. You may want to pay close attention to the main character's traits, motivations, struggles, and changes; or then use thought prompts to write about the ideas you have:

- The thought I have about this is . . .
- To add on . . .
- This shows . . .

Before you get started, decide and record a plan for tonight's work.

Elaborating on Written Ideas Using Prompts

WHEN WE WRITE A NARRATIVE, the sequence of events can be determined by chronology. We can record events in the order in which they happen, making it very easy for us to say more. We recall the first thing that happened, then the next, then the next thing, and as long as we are taking small steps through the sequence of events, we don't quickly run out of things to say.

When we write expository texts, however, and especially when the expository text conveys our ideas, it is no easy matter to say more. To say more, to elaborate, the writer needs not only to recall what happened, but also to think more. This requires that the writer have not only stuff to say but also a plan, a structure, that determines the sequence of what he or she will say. Many students have enormous trouble with elaboration when writing expository texts, and as a result, their writing ends up with "a muddle in the middle." Your students worked through this challenge throughout the sequence of units in opinion writing and especially in the recent *Boxes and Bullets: Personal and Persuasive Essays* unit, and of course, they will work through this again in the current unit.

Your job today will be to lure your students into continuing to practice elaborating on their first thoughts—in this lesson, their first ideas about character. You'll help children to do this in writing by first encouraging them to elaborate in conversation. If children can talk well about a text they have read, making and defending and elaborating on their ideas, then it is not difficult to teach them to write well about the text. But the first goal is not a small one!

In this unit, you need to value talking well in addition to writing well about texts. The Common Core State Standards emphasize the importance of talk by having an entire category devoted to speaking and listening, asking us to make sure students can "engage effectively in a range of collaborative discussions (SL.4.1)." Yet schools often treat talk as if it's to be avoided. If a principal says to a teacher, "I passed your classroom and your children were talking," the teacher doesn't generally regard this as positive feedback. If we describe a child as "a real talker," we don't usually intend this as a compliment. But in our own adult lives, we recognize, as the Standards do, that talking is a way to grow. If we

IN THIS SESSION, you'll teach students one way writers elaborate on their ideas—using simple prompts.

GETTING READY

✔ A copy of a transcript of book club conversation you and your colleagues have had, illustrating text citations and conversational prompts (see Teaching)

✔ Mentor text, *Fox*, to be displayed to the whole class. Alternatively, you might give several copies of the book to groups of children in the meeting area.

✔ "Ways to Push Our Thinking" list of prompts, updated from the *Boxes and Bullets: Personal and Persuasive Essays* unit, one copy for each child, which can later be pasted in a notebook or placed in a folder ●

COMMON CORE STATE STANDARDS: W.4.3, W.4.4, W.4.5, W.4.9.a, RL.4.1, RL.4.3, SL.4.1, SL.4.3, L.4.1, L.4.2, L.4.3.a

need help working through an issue, we meet with someone to "talk things through." If we want to imagine possible ways to teach, we're apt to "talk over our options" or "talk out a plan."

Today you'll encourage children to tap the power of talk as a tool for thinking. Moreover, you'll help children realize that the features of a probing, generative discussion are also the features of probing, generative writing.

"Your job today will be to lure your students into continuing to practice elaborating on their first thoughts— in this lesson, their first ideas about character."

Elaborating on Written Ideas Using Prompts

CONNECTION

Remind children that when writing personal and persuasive essays, they used conversational prompts—or thought prompts—to help them extend their first ideas.

"You'll remember that when you wrote personal and persuasive essays, you found that at first you wrote only very briefly about your ideas. You'd write your idea—say, 'soccer teaches sportsmanship'—and then you weren't sure what else to say, so your entries were often short. But you came to realize that you could rely on the conversational prompts that you use in book talks to help you talk back to your own ideas as they emerge on the page. Remember?

"I won't forget, for example, when Ellie wrote this entry during the personal essay unit; she used the thought prompts—or conversational prompts—to help her get more good ideas."

> I hate it when I am doing something important and then I get interrupted.
>
> <u>For example</u>, when I'm reading a book and my mom calls, "Ellie, it's time to go to sleep" but I really want to finish the book because that's what I am into. <u>I realize that</u> this happens a lot to me, like when I'm watching TV or having fun with my friends. <u>What surprises me</u> is I always have a lot of time and no one interrupts me when I am doing things I don't like, like homework or practicing my oboe or other things.

❖ **Name the teaching point.**

"Today I want to teach you that when writers want to elaborate on their ideas—in this case ideas about a character— they can use the same prompts and phrases that people use in conversations to elaborate. These kinds of prompts help writers to elaborate, to say more, think more, and write more."

Although the connection in one day's minilesson will often refer back to the previous day's, it's also not unusual for the connection to link back to portions of a previous unit of study that relate to that day's specific point. Although in this connection you refer to instruction the children received just a month or two earlier, the truth is that for years, children have been learning to elaborate. It shouldn't surprise you that learning takes time and repeated practice. After all, you don't watch a pro tennis player serve the ball, and then presto, your serves resemble that of the pro! Learning a skill takes time and repeated practice.

TEACHING

Dramatize a discussion between you and a few colleagues about a familiar text. Set children up to notice that you incorporate thought prompts and textual evidence.

"Yesterday at lunch the other teachers and I decided to read and talk about *Fox* ourselves. We copied down a bit of our book talk so I can show you how the talk went and, specifically, so I can show you the ways that we used prompts to help us grow ideas. You're already familiar with some of these prompts from our previous essay unit. But there are some new prompts on the chart that the other teachers and I used, and that other people use a lot too when elaborating." I handed out copies of the list.

You don't need to distribute a transcript of the book talk to the kids, but it will help if they have a paper containing the list of thought prompts. If you can't duplicate and distribute, then copy this onto chart paper, and when a thought prompt is used, underline it while the kids watch on.

For each prompt we've included on this list, there are many others we could have included as well. We were selective in our choices both here and in the Boxes and Bullets: Personal and Persuasive Essays *unit because we knew that providing students with a shorter list would make it likely that they mastered a few thought prompts and that over time we could add to their repertoire. Here, students have some new additions to the list that they didn't have in the* Boxes and Bullets: Personal and Persuasive Essays *unit. And in the sessions that follow, you might ask children to add onto the list, jotting down new prompts as their work becomes more sophisticated. For the full list of prompts, see the CD-ROM.*

Ways to Push Our Thinking

In other words . . .

That is . . .

The important thing about this is . . .

As I say this, I'm realizing . . .

This is giving me the idea that . . .

An example of this is . . .

This shows . . .

Another example of this is . . .

This connects to . . .

I see . . .

The thought I have about this is . . .

To add on . . .

The reason for this is . . . Another reason is . . .

This is important because . . .

On the other hand . . .

This is similar to . . . This is different from . . .

"Instead of just reading you the transcript of our book talk, I'm going to ask the three of you," and I gestured to three volunteers, "to come up and reenact how that book talk went." I gave each child a copy of the transcript and the role of a teacher, giving away my role in the book talk as well. "As we reenact a little bit of this book talk, Partner 1, will you notice and underline *the thought prompts* (from the list) that you hear used? And Partner 2, will you keep track of the number of times *we go back to the text*, reading exact bits of the text to illustrate our points? After you listen to a bit of the book talk, I am going to give you and your partner a chance to talk about what you notice, and then all of you will take your places and continue the conversation."

Ms. Johnson: I think that Dog is caring, but also lonely. <u>For example</u>, it says that he runs through the "charred forest" and takes her to his cave below the river. There aren't any other animals around.

Mr. Cook: I agree. <u>Another example</u> of Dog being caring is that he takes care of Magpie when she's hurt, not leaving her side.

Ms. Deloy: Where do you see evidence of that? Can you go back to the text and find a specific place that shows it?

Mr. Cook: Oh, yeah. Well, Magpie finally wakes up and the text says "Dog is waiting." He didn't go anywhere for a week. He just sat and waited for Magpie. It's like she is all he has.

Ms. Deloy: I see what you are saying, and I agree. <u>On the other hand</u>, it could be that Dog is happy to be alone, but wants to be a good friend to Magpie and help her.

Mr. Cook: <u>Could it be that</u> Dog is *both* caring and sad? Characters are sometimes more than one thing.

Ms. Johnson: That makes sense. Him being sad can <u>connect with</u> our first idea about him being caring but also lonely. He is lonely and he knows what it's like to be sad (since he is blind in one eye), and maybe that is why he is so caring. <u>For example</u>, when Magpie says she will never fly again and Dog says, "I know." He understands her pain.

Give children a moment to debrief with their partners. Then explain that when they use thought prompts to talk or write about an idea, the idea deepens.

"Take a moment and talk to the person beside you. Partner 1, talk about the thought prompts you spotted in our conversation. Partner 2, talk about times you saw us staying close to the text." I gave the children a moment to talk and then reconvened the class.

"Readers, I hope you saw that we used prompts to push our thinking and to help us talk longer and deeper about our first ideas. We also cited particular parts of the story to make sure our thinking was grounded in the actual words and details of the story. When we do these things, we end up growing thoughts that surprise even ourselves!"

It is easy for your minilessons to get into a rut, with each day's lesson involving you demonstrating what you'd do on your text and then scaffolding the kids to do the same on their text. Today's simulation of a book talk is one of about a score of ways to bring in some variety. Take note, because when you develop your own minilessons, you'll find that having a list of ways to vary them is helpful. Remember, novelty ignites interest. The sheer fact that this is a new configuration will draw kids' attention.

Notice that here and nearly always, before we ask children to observe something instructional, we highlight what it is we hope they notice and set them up for the work they will soon be doing in response to what they see.

Your examples, such as this, scaffold students so that when they are asked to talk and write about this text—or another one—a day or two from now, they'll have more to draw upon. This is a good thing because you are making it easier for students to think in interpretive ways and therefore to do work with your support that they could not have easily done on their own. Providing—and then removing—scaffolds is an important kind of teaching.

Notice that almost every minilesson contains debriefing after the teaching, and usually the teacher steps back to name what he or she has done that is transferable to another text and another day. In this instance, the children do this work.

ACTIVE ENGAGEMENT

Set children up to carry on the book talk with their partners, using thought prompts to refer specifically to the story. Then have them continue this work in writing.

"So that was a bit of our book talk. Instead of analyzing it, this time pretend you are part of the conversation and continue it—only you'll be talking just with your partner. Continue to use the thought prompts and refer specifically to the story, just as we were doing." I put a copy of the text on the overhead for all children to see and then ushered them to begin talking. I listened in on one set of partners.

Jessica said, "I agree with Mr. Cook that Dog can be both lonely and caring. For example, like he said, he waited a long time for Magpie to wake up so he could take care of her and be with her. It must be lonely to live in a cave all by yourself."

Alex said, "Yeah, and it doesn't even seem like a nice place! It is all burnt (Alex points to the picture) and "charred," with ashes and stuff. Everything looks dead."

Jessica then said, This makes me realize something about the next part of the story. Dog asks Magpie to hop on his back and they go to the river. It's like they are making a partnership. Magpie says that she can be Dog's missing eye and he can be her wings. This connects to everything! It helps Magpie not be sad and it helps Dog not be lonely."

I called for the children's attention. "Can I stop you?" I asked, and waited until I had everyone's attention. "Remember that these conversational prompts also work for writing! Once you've written one idea, you can extend it using one of these prompts."

LINK

Remind children that they can always use simple prompts to extend their thinking.

"So, readers, today and always, when you say or jot thoughts about a story, it is important to push yourselves to revise those first thoughts until they become your best thinking. One way to do this is to use prompts to nudge yourself to say (and think) more. Make sure that as you do this, you are going back to the text and finding specific places that give evidence for your thoughts, so the ideas you come up with aren't just floating in the air but are tied firmly to the text. Today the prompts will help you extend your first thoughts about the text you chose yesterday. Keep the list with you, and whenever you write or talk about texts, use them to extend and revise your first thoughts. It's more interesting to dig deep, so I'm pretty sure you'll end up using these all the time and inventing more of your own."

By asking children to extend a conversation that was already well underway, you provide them with a running start.

Children may ask you whether they should speak and write about characters from books in the past or present tense. They will wonder whether it is better to say, "Dog was lonely" or "Dog is lonely." Generally, when writing about character traits, readers use the present tense: In the story "Fox," Dog is lonely until he meets Magpie.

Elaborating on Theories about Characters

WHEN YOU AND YOUR COLLEAGUES plan for today's (and every day's) teaching, look over your records to see what you have been noticing about your students' work so you can use small groups and conferring to provide help that is tailored to their needs.

For example, you can expect that some children will list rather than describe their ideas about a character, and many of them will merely name one character trait after another. You'll probably want to carry *Fox*, or another short text the students know well, with you as you work with students. Be prepared to demonstrate the way a person needs to think hard as they reach for the words that precisely describe a character's trait. Sophia writes this about "Eleven" (see Figure 3–1).

> Eleven
> my character is Rachel
> She feels weird (not eleven)
> She feels bad when she wore the sweater
> She hates her teacher.

FIG. 3–1   Sophia's entry merely lists character traits.

It's a brief entry. On the other hand, Sophia does seem to be reaching to say something that she recognizes doesn't fit easily into words. She claims that Rachel, the main character in "Eleven," feels "weird." The important thing is that Sophia seems to grasp that "weird" isn't sufficient, and so she clarifies by saying that Rachel doesn't feel eleven. In an instance like this, support the student's effort to find the words that hit the nail on the head and encourage her to work longer at doing this. What *does* Rachel feel? Encourage children like Sophia to speak in whole sentences and to be explicit. She'll feel better if you equip her with words like "I imagine that she is thinking . . . "

MID-WORKSHOP TEACHING   Developing Powerful Thought

Before stopping the class for a mid-workshop teaching point, I noticed Angelina's entry summing up Clover, a character in Jacqueline Woodson's *The Other Side*. "Writers, can I interrupt?" I asked the class and waited until I had their attention. "Class, I want to show you the smart work Angelina just did. In her entry, she doesn't ramble from one idea to another idea to another. She puts forth one idea, one claim, and then—here's the big thing—*she takes the time to develop that idea*. When writing about ideas, it can help to zoom in on a single idea that you want to advance, and then develop that idea by citing a bunch of parts of the text that go with it. Angelina did that." Angelina read her entry to the class.

(continues)

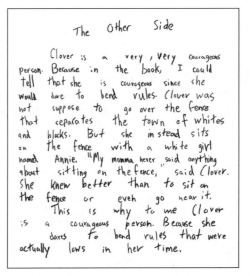

> The Other Side
>
> Clover is a very, very courageous person. Because in the book, I could tell that she is courageous since she would dare to bend rules. Clover was not suppose to go over the fence that separates the town of whites and blacks. But she instead sits on the fence with a white girl named Annie. "My momma never said anything about sitting on the fence," said Clover. She knew better than to sit on the fence or even go near it. This is why to me Clover is a courageous person. Because she dares to bend rules that were actually laws in her time.

FIG. 3–2   Angelina advocates for her claim, then expands on her idea.

(continues)

The Other Side

Clover is a very, very courageous person. Because in the book, I could tell that she is courageous since she would dare to bend rules. Clover was not supposed to go over the fence that separates the town of whites and blacks. But she instead sits on the fence with a white girl named Annie. "My momma never said anything about sitting on the fence," said Clover. She knew better than to sit on the fence or even go near it. This is why to me Clover is a courageous person. Because she dares to bend rules that were actually laws in her time.

"Writers, you might try elaborating on an idea like Angelina just did. If you are game to do this, find a thought you recorded that seems sort of powerful to you, and make a box around it." I gave them a few seconds. "Sometimes, you find a thought that is *almost* powerful, but not quite. You can rewrite your thought to make it more powerful.

"Now copy that thought onto the top of a new page in your notebook and use your thought prompts to elaborate on it. You might start with 'This is important because . . . ,' and then after a while write, 'This connects with . . .' Write fast and furiously for a few minutes."

Somewhere you'll see that when children go to write about a character, instead of thoughtfully selecting some particular descriptors that seem previously right for a character, they run through a giant list of terms that can be loosely be regarded as synonymous of each other. Ali, for example, jotted a list of descriptors for Lupe. She wrote that Lupe is insecure, unconfident, eager to please, worried, anxious, and hard working.

In a notebook entry, Ali seems to brainstorm a host of terms that could possibly describe the character Lupe. (See Figure 3–3).

When I looked at Ali's work, I realized that she, like others, was struggling to shoehorn a complex character into a single descriptor. Her long list was Ali's way of resisting reducing Lupe to a mere label. But she hasn't actually succeeded in capturing the true impression she had of Lupe. I encouraged Ali to give up on the lack of finding a term or two or three that captured Lupe, and to write in whole sentences, whole thoughts, even whole paragraphs.

> I think Lupe had, before, put herself down. But now, she will try to prove herself wrong.
> This is important because she was insecure. She thought badly of herself. She thought she was only a brainy person. But she was good at things.
> It doesn't matter if you can't do it, it matters what's on the inside. Even though she wasn't good she was nice and good on the inside. "She tried again and again." This shows that she doesn't give up. She works and works at a goal. She won't disappoint herself.
> This takes a lot of self-confidence and courage. She tries to believe in herself.

FIG. 3–3 Ali's revised entry shows her reaching for significance.

Once children have made their claims—about, say, a character's traits—you'll want to show them that writers then choose ways to elaborate. It often works for children to provide examples of this trait while using transitional phrases such as "In the beginning of the story . . . Then in the middle . . . Finally, at the end of the story . . . For example . . . And another example of this is . . . " Notice that in this instance, you are providing the writer with a structure that supports elaboration.

Elaborating on Central Ideas

Suggest that when zooming in on and developing ideas, it is best if the ideas are central to the text, realizing however that the truly central things are sometimes whispered, not announced.

"I wonder if any of you have ever taken a photograph and decided one portion of that photograph was really important. If a photographer looks at a picture and decides that the tree in the upper right-hand corner is important, he can zoom in on and enlarge just that one tree. In the same way, literary essayists look over all that they have written about a text and ask, 'Is one portion of this writing especially important and central to the text?' You did this just a few minutes ago with your own writing.

"When you make decisions about what is important, it helps to ask, 'What is important *to this text*?' The important aspects of a text may not hit you over the head right away. Logan Pearsall Smith has said, 'What I like in a good author is not what he says, but what he whispers'" (Burke, p. 89).

Suggest that finding what is whispered in a text involves being willing to let go of one's first interpretation. Noticing parts that don't fit with that first idea is a way to outgrow rather than close in on that first idea.

"Literary essayists look for parts that seem to whisper something different than your big idea about the text. Here's the important thing. If you notice the parts that don't fit with your initial idea, you can let those parts help you revise your idea.

"Let's think about *Fox* for a moment. Earlier, Jessica and Alex were talking about how they think Magpie is the kind of character who always sees the negative side of things—that really, she is a pessimist. So many parts of the text fit with this idea—the way Magpie reacts to her burnt wing, the fact that she doesn't want Dog to help her, the way she crawls under the shadow of a rock and tries to melt into the blackness. But as a close reader, I want to ask, 'What parts of the text *don't* fit with this?' and push myself to understand why."

Demonstrate with the class text and then ask them to try.

I flipped through the first pages of *Fox*, looking for a part that seemed to contradict my idea. "Aha, here we go. In this scene, Magpie is joyously flying on Dog's back. She even says, 'FLY, DOG, FLY! I will be your missing eye, and you will be my wings.' This scene doesn't seem to support the idea that Magpie is a pessimist, someone who always sees the negative side of things, does it? Talk with the person beside you, and here is your challenge. Will you try to figure out how this part that doesn't fit with our first idea about Magpie might deepen or change our thinking about her?"

After a moment or two, I called the children back together. "Do you see that by looking at one part that doesn't fit, we can totally reshape our idea about a character? This is hard work, and I heard many of you grappling with Magpie's personality. Judah was saying that perhaps Magpie has not lost all her happiness, that she still has a little bit of joy inside of her. Max thought that perhaps Magpie isn't a pessimist at all. Instead, maybe she's just very scared, but Dog makes her feel safe and strong."

Channel students to try to apply this work to their own texts.

"Right now, would you take a few minutes and try this with your own text? What part of *your* text doesn't seem to fit with your idea? How might that part change or deepen your thinking? You might draw a line under your entry from today and then start anew, writing to explore new possibilities."

I gave children four to five minutes to write silently before calling them back together as a group. "Writers, the work you are doing is so important, so key, to this unit. Your entire literary essay will be based off of one idea, and you want that idea to be as complex and true as possible. One way you can always deepen your thinking about a text is by asking, 'What part of the text does *not* fit with my idea?' and then letting that part help you revise your thinking. Let's add that to our 'Ways to Push Our Thinking' chart."

You will see that when children talk with each other, they often say, "I agree with that." Ask children to restate the exact part of the idea they agree with. This gives them practice talking about ideas and allows them to listen for and work together to find the words that carry ideas. It also helps children feel comfortable disagreeing a bit, as debate sparks great conversation. Give them words for such discussion, such as "On the other hand, could it be that . . ." or "I partly agree, but in one way, I think differently because . . ."

The work children do in class discussions, small-group talks, and partnerships on the set of texts the class is analyzing provides invaluable support, because the class will have opened up many of these texts. Each child will be able to approach his or her writing with lots of ideas about the text.

BRING MORE OF THE TEXT TO READING RESPONSE

When you write about texts, you often reread all the notes you've written and box a line or a passage that feels to you to have potential. Then you copy that onto the top of a fresh sheet of paper and assign yourself the job of expanding your first idea, using prompts or any other strategies you know. Tonight, select an idea that is worth expanding as the focus of your work for the next few days. Try to stay with that idea for a little while—write lots and lots about it. Reread the text and find more sections that connect with your idea, then write about them. Give examples of your idea. Use prompts to nudge yourself to say more. Then, like you did in our share today, ask yourself, "What part of the story *doesn't* fit with this idea?" You may find that all of this leads you to revise your original idea, and that'd be incredibly exciting.

Finding and Testing a Thesis

IN THIS SESSION, you'll teach students that writers select ideas to craft into theses. You'll show writers ways to question and revise their theses, making sure these are supported by the whole text.

GETTING READY

✔ Mentor text, *Fox*

✔ Your own notebook that captures the class's thinking about *Fox*, or this same thinking on chart paper, to share with the class (see Teaching)

✔ "Possible Thesis Statements" list about the mentor text, written on chart paper (see Teaching)

✔ "How to Write a Literary Essay" chart (see Teaching)

✔ "How Can I Support My Thesis Statement?" list (see Mid-Workshop Teaching)

✔ Chart paper and markers

✔ Three booklets, each one with your thesis statement written on the front in a box followed by one of your supporting reasons (bullets) underneath it, with at least several blank pages (see Share)

✔ Blank booklets, three for each student, that have a box and bullet on the front page for students' thesis statements and supporting ideas (see Share)

I REMEMBER WELL the analytical papers I was asked to write when I was a young girl. I bought myself several packets of index cards, took the bus into the city of Buffalo, made my way to the library, and spent days recording my data about my assigned author. I measured my progress by the growing height of my stack of index cards.

When children in today's world are asked to write academic papers, the challenge has far less to do with collecting data—that they can do with one click—and far more to do with synthesizing the information they collect. Starting today, children will no longer collect assorted ideas about the text they've chosen. Instead, they will invest themselves in shaping, organizing, drafting, and revising entries that elaborate on a single thesis that they propose. The entries they develop around this thesis will be raw materials for the first of three literary essays they'll write in this unit.

As you approach this session, you and your students will bring prior knowledge from previous cycles through the writing process to help them write and develop theses. You may want to look back over some of that work and pull out relevant charts and mentor texts, so you can help students remember and draw on that knowledge today. (When children are in their fourth unit of study, they are also in their first, second, and third units of study.)

Specifically, you can hope that students will bring to this session an understanding of the relationship between the thesis, the supporting ideas, and the evidence they bring into their essays. Today we hope each student selects a thesis that is interesting to him and defensible with evidence from the text. Then you'll help students shift back-and-forth between crafting a thesis and imagining the possibilities for how that thesis will unfurl into an arguable essay.

COMMON CORE STATE STANDARDS: W.4.1.a,b; W.4.4, W.4.5, W.4.8, RL.4.1, RL.4.2, RL.4.3, SL.4.1, L.4.1, L.4.2, L.4.3.a

Finding and Testing a Thesis

CONNECTION

Celebrate the writing and thinking your writers have generated thus far in the unit. Remind children of earlier work they did with theses and reasons.

"Writers, your notebooks are brimming with ideas about the short text you've chosen to study. You've each got reams of ideas about a text—whether it is 'Eleven' or *The Other Side* or 'Gloria Who Might Be My Best Friend.' Today I want to remind you that in the end, you need to decide on *one central idea* for your essay. Fred Fox, a famous speechwriter for President Dwight Eisenhower, once said, 'You ought to be able to put your bottom-line message on the inside of a matchbook.' He was talking about a speech, but he could have been talking about a literary essay or a short story or a memoir or any text at all. As a writer, and particularly as an essayist, you need to be able to name the one crystal-clear idea you want to convey to your reader.

"A while ago, you looked over all that you'd written and selected a seed idea for your personal essay. You rewrote it as a thesis statement and then framed your essay using boxes and bullets. Writers do similar work when writing literary essays. You first find a big idea that is really important to you, and then you write a thesis."

❖ **Name the teaching point.**

"Today I want to teach you that when you are writing a literary essay, as when you write a personal or persuasive essay, you find your seed idea—your thesis—by first rereading all your related entries and thinking, 'What is the big idea I really want to say?' Sometimes it helps to gather a bunch of possible theses about a text, then to choose one."

TEACHING

Demonstrate selecting a thesis by returning to the work the class has done with the mentor text, *Fox*, rereading entries and underlining possible seed ideas.

"People who are writing literary essays often cull great stuff—perhaps by underlining or starring lines in notebooks or by copying over the best stuff they've collected. Sometimes it helps to make a special page full of drafts of possible

Notice that we can't ramble on too long about what the students have been doing. It is tempting to do so because this is a way to orient ourselves before plunging on, but kids will listen more to new information, anecdotes, and stories than to generalizations about what they have already been taught. So if you are recapping, try to make that work a bit interactive ("Let me read over a list of things I hope you have learned. Give me a thumbs up if you feel you have mastered the things on my list or a thumbs down if you haven't yet practiced an item on my list.") And it is not always wise to recap in the connection; sometimes we bring in new information, as in this example. Minilessons, in general, need to be far more densely packed than many people realize.

Visual cues and props can make a big difference in our minilessons, and I haven't emphasized them enough. In this instance, for example, I held one of the working folders we'd used from the earlier essay unit so that as I mentioned boxes and bullets, the object—in this case the folder—nudged children to recall the entire process they experienced in that unit.

thesis statements. Then it is typical to spend time—at least half an hour—drafting and revising those rough-draft thesis statements until you find something that feels right.

"We've been studying *Fox* together, so it makes sense that we practice this work off that text first, and then you can do this on your own with the short text you have been studying. Let's return to our entries and ideas about *Fox*, and as we do this, ask, 'What is the main thing we really want to say?'"

Sitting in the front of the children, I opened up my notebook and displayed it, saying, "This is what I've written, mostly sparked by conversations we've had together." I skimmed the entries for a moment, circling a few bits, with children watching as I underlined, as below.

> At the beginning of the story, Magpie is hurt and Dog comes to her rescue. He carries Magpie gently in his mouth. <u>This shows he is trying to help her, not hurt her</u>. Dog carries Magpie to his cave and takes care of her burnt wing. <u>Dog really wants to help Magpie</u>. He helps her wing get better and then he tries to help her spirits get better.
>
> Magpie does not want Dog's help, but Dog keeps trying. <u>This shows that he doesn't give up easily</u>. He tries to cheer Magpie up by telling her that he is blind and life is still good. But Magpie can only focus on the fact that she will no longer fly. For some reason, <u>she won't let Dog help her</u>.

As I looked over the entry, I voiced over my thinking process. "I'm looking in my notebook for *ideas*, not for facts. This means I'm looking for things that we've thought up by ourselves and that aren't actually stated in the text. Are you spotting anything?" I underlined an idea I found. "Ah, there's an idea!" And I continued on.

Then I paused and said, "I've got a couple of thoughts—they sort of go together and overlap—and I'm going to try a few ways of saying the big thoughts I have." I took up my pen and jotted (on chart paper) some possible thesis statements.

Possible Thesis Statements

- Dog wants to save Magpie.
- Dog tries to help Magpie in different ways.
- Magpie doesn't appreciate Dog's friendship.

Demonstrate testing a potential thesis by asking some key questions, and show that you then revise the thesis statements based on what you learn from doing this.

"After I've drafted a few possible theses, I look these over, sort of weighing whether any of them seem okay. I first reread each and ask, 'Does this opinion relate to more than one part of the text?' Often this question leads me to revise the draft of a thesis so that it stretches like an umbrella over the whole story."

This one short text threads through many minilessons because the children have enough shared knowledge of the text and our work with it that I do not need to do a lot of reminding and summarizing; instead, I can spotlight each new point I want to make.

It is unlikely that you will have captured all the class's thinking about Fox *in written form. So much of the whole-class thinking work you and the children have done has been verbal, or scrawled quickly into your own writing notebook. In preparation for today, you'll want to decide how you will make the past few days' ideas visible for children. I've decided to showcase the class's thinking by putting a few pages of my own notebook on the document camera, having prepared it beforehand to ensure it included enough of the class's thinking to draw from. You could do this just as easily with chart paper and a marker, however.*

You'll notice that my ideas are flawed. It is important to model in ways that expose difficulties so you can address those difficulties. My list reflects the kinds of trouble that kids get into when they do this work.

This is unbelievably powerful. Try it yourself. You will find that very often the ideas you develop about a story relate only to one part. They are ideas like this: "In this story, the main character learns that . . . " A claim such as that pertains to the second half of the story (as is common) and needs to be revised: "In this story, the main character wants . . . and finds it when he learns that . . . " Or "In this story, the main character changes . . . from . . . to . . . "

"Let's test this thesis:

- Dog wants to save Magpie.

"If we think of examples to support this, do they come from the whole story? What do you think? Turn and talk."

The children talked, and then I asked Charlie to report on what he and his partner had said.

"We thought that this is mostly about the first part of the story, where Dog carries Magpie in his mouth and that we should go back to our idea about Dog being caring, because then we can say all the caring things he does in the story. So then maybe our thesis could be 'Dog is a good friend to Magpie.'"

Wanting to extrapolate the main point, I said, "So one way to test and revise a thesis is to ask, 'Does this opinion relate to more than one part of the text?' Another way to test a thesis is by considering whether the thesis is really supported in the text. Is there enough evidence?" I revealed the "How to Write a Literary Essay" chart, with the additional bullets added.

How to Write a Literary Essay

- Grow ideas about a text.
- Use thought prompts.
- Ask questions of the text.
- Pay attention to the characters in a story, especially noting their traits, motivations, struggles, changes, and relationships.
- Find a big idea that is really important to you, then write a thesis.
- Test out your thesis by asking questions.
  - Does this opinion relate to more than one part of the text?
  - Is there enough evidence to support it?

"If I make the thesis 'Dog is a good friend,' then I can show how one reason I think he's a good friend is because he is caring." I jotted this on a new piece of chart paper in a boxes-and-bullets format. "There are a lot of examples in the text to show that he is caring! I'd want to think about another reason I think Dog is a good friend. What made me start to think this? Let's look back at our ideas from earlier." I put our idea sheet back up for all the children to see.

At the beginning of the story, Magpie is hurt and Dog comes to her rescue. He carries Magpie gently in his mouth. This shows he is trying to help her, not hurt her. Dog carries Magpie to his

There are a number of reasons each thesis needs to pertain to the entire text. First of all, when children are writing thesis statements about very short texts, if the thesis pertains to only one portion of the text, it will be almost impossible for the child to garner enough support for the thesis. The texts are too sparse! Then, too, I am steering children toward writing interpretive essays, and this means I am hoping they consider lessons they can learn or messages they can carry from the text. An effective interpretation of a story requires that the reader take into account the most important features of the complete text, including the first and the second halves of the text, certainly, and including a great many smaller features as well.

~ How to Write a Literary Essay ~

- Grow Ideas about a text.
  - Use thought prompts.
  - Ask questions of texts.
  - Pay attention to the characters in a story, especially noting their traits, motivations, struggles, changes, and relationships.
- Find a big idea that is really important to you, then write a thesis.
- Test out your thesis by asking questions.
  - Does this opinion relate to more than one part of the text?
  - Is there enough evidence to support it?
- Collect Evidence.
  - micro-stories
  - quotes
  - lists
  - examples
- Unpack the evidence by telling the reader what it shows, using prompts like:
  - This shows that...
  - This is evidence that...
- Add transitions to glue the evidence together.

This is a great deal of important material to convey simply through talk, so at this point I added to the anchor chart I'd introduced at the start of this unit. Notice that I don't take the time to write these in front of the class.

cave and takes care of her burnt wing. <u>Dog really wants to help Magpie</u>. He helps her wing get better and then he tries to help her spirits get better.

Magpie does not want Dog's help, but Dog keeps trying. <u>This shows that he doesn't give up easily</u>. He tries to cheer Magpie up by telling her that he is blind and life is still good. But Magpie can only focus on the fact that she will no longer fly. For some reason, <u>she can't let Dog help her</u>.

Children began pointing and climbing onto their knees as they spotted new ideas. "We talked an awful lot about how Dog doesn't give up, about how he keeps trying to make Magpie happy. That would work, wouldn't it?" I added the next reason for our opinion to our chart.

> Dog is a good friend.

- Dog is a good friend because he is caring.
- Dog is a good friend because he doesn't give up on his friend.

Debrief the teaching for the children.

"So, writers, when we are looking to develop a strong thesis, there are two things we can do. First, we look back at our notebook entries and begin to list a few possible theses. Then, we test our theses by checking to see if they relate to more than one part of the text and then by asking, 'How would I support this?'"

ACTIVE ENGAGEMENT

Set children up to try this work using their own short story.

"Let's try this with your stories now. Will you take a moment and flip through the writing you've done over the past few days? Just as we did a moment ago, star or underline places where you see ideas—ideas that might become a thesis for you later." I moved around the rug, helping children to do this work and voicing over a few pointers. "Don't forget, you are looking for *ideas*, things the text did not tell you but that you thought up on your own." And a minute later, "No idea is too big or too small. You never know what might make the perfect seed for your essay."

Pay especially close attention to this instruction, because helping children write effective thesis statements and supporting ideas is far more complicated than you might imagine. Hopefully, the teaching seems simple and clear now—but the trail of thought leading to this point has been quite complicated and challenging!

After calling the children back together, I ushered them into part two of today's work. "Right now, will you decide on one idea that stands out to you, one that feels important, and jot that down on the next page of your notebook?

"Try working with your partner, testing out your theses using our list of ways to support thesis statements to help you." I pointed to the "How Can I Support My Thesis Statement" list. I listened in as children did this work in pairs and then asked for their attention.

LINK

Recap that writers reread notes and entries about the text, select theses, then revise their theses by asking questions of them.

"So, writers, today and whenever you write a thesis for a literary essay, look over the ideas you've collected about the text and select one. And then remember that writers test out their possible theses in the ways you just experienced."

Students need to believe that readers can come away from texts with different understandings, so long as sufficient evidence in the text exists to support them. Imagine how productive and provocative their writing will be if they have the chance to share and argue those understandings.

Whenever possible, I want to end a minilesson by reminding children of the array of options available to them so they learn to be the job captains of their own writing. In this link, though, I lay out the steps students need to take today during writing time since their thesis will be the foundation on which they will build their future writing as they gather evidence for their essay.

The Small Size of a Thesis Makes It Perfect for Learning about Revision

WHEN YOU CONFER WITH YOUR CHILDREN keep in mind that you are teaching them to reread their own drafts as well as to write. You want them to be able to discern problems in their writing so they can work with independence. One way to do this is to teach them to check for some of the most common problems that essayists are apt to encounter. For example, today you are helping writers tackle one such common problem. Let them know that it's always a good idea to check to be sure they're writing a clear thesis. The thesis is like an engine—it propels the essay forward.

Children often encounter difficulties imagining the paragraphs they could write to support their theses, and these difficulties should prompt them to revise those thesis statements. Judah, for example, boxed these ideas in his notebook as possible theses (see Figure 4–1).

Realizing that it would be hard to write supporting reasons for many of these, Judah settled on this more modest possible thesis.

> Lupe works hard to overcome her difficulties.

MID-WORKSHOP TEACHING   Deciding on Your Boxes and Bullets for an Essay

"Writers, can I stop you for a moment? I've watched and talked with many of you as you try out various thesis statements and supporting ideas. I've noticed that many of you are struggling to uncover the ways you might support a particularly powerful thesis, and so I'm going to introduce you to a few methods literary essayists often use.

"When imagining the ways you might support a thesis, there are a few go-to structures essayists use. You might remember some of these from our personal and persuasive essay unit." I quickly jotted down on chart paper some ways students could support their thesis statements.

> How can I support my thesis statement?
>
> With reasons
>
> With kinds or ways
>
> With times when

> With evidence of how it is true for one character, then for another character
>
> With evidence of how it is true at the beginning of the story, then at the end of the story

"Earlier, when thinking about our thesis, 'Dog is a good friend,' we listed some reasons we think this is true. But I could also try different kinds of supports. For instance, I could list *ways* that Dog is a good friend: He cares for Magpie's wing; he cares for Magpie's feelings; he offers Magpie a home. Or I could try to see how my thesis is true for one character and then another. In that case, I'd write about how Dog is a good friend to Magpie and then how Dog is a good friend to Fox. Do you see how one thesis can turn into a whole host of different essays?

"In the time that remains today, try out a few different possibilities for supporting your thesis statement. I'll ask you to decide on your thesis and supporting ideas by today's share, when we set up our systems for collecting evidence."

Lupe wanted to prove to herself that she was as good as the other girls.

Lupe was insecure.

Even though she wasn't good, she was nice and good on the inside. She tried again and again. this shows that she doesn't give up.

Lupe is very caring. She is good on the inside. She doesn't need to be on the outside too.

I used to think Lupe was a goody-goody two-shoes. She got all of those awards and seemed so perfect. I realized she isn't perfect. She has to work and practice like everyone.

FIG. 4–1   Judah's boxed ideas

I helped her learn that writers are expected to add the trimmings.

Lupe, the protagonist in Gary Soto's short story, "The Marble Champ," works hard to overcome her difficulties.

Then Judah began to imagine how her bullet points might go. Did she want to write about the *kinds of work* Lupe does? To write about the *reasons* Lupe works so hard to become a marble champ? Or did she just want to provide examples—which would have been a much simpler option. Elaborating on *the kinds* of hard work, or the *reasons for* her work, would require Judah to develop supportive ideas. Here is Judah's next draft of her thesis (see Figure 4–2).

This thesis set up the reason-based (idea-based) topic sentences that Judah then developed: Lupe overcomes her difficulties through hard work; Lupe also overcomes her difficulties by believing in herself. Notice that in each of her subordinate points, Judah presents an idea (not just an example) and in each one, she repeats the stem of her thesis.

The fact that Judah realizes on her own that it would be hard to write supporting reasons for many of these thesis statements suggests that I have helped her develop the eyes to see potential tough spots of her own writing.

As you confer with students, bear in mind that it is far easier for a youngster to develop an essay by citing lots of parts of the text that illustrate the one central thesis. It is another step forward for that child to think about how those parts of the story illustrate the central thesis, categorizing them under subordinate ideas. Parker, for example, had written this when I pulled a chair alongside him.

In the short story "The Marble Champ" by Gary Soto, Lupe learns to overcome her difficulties by working hard and believing in herself.

FIG. 4–2   Judah's draft thesis statement

I think Gloria is the type of character who makes friends easily because she and Julian became friends quickly.

Parker had rewritten his thesis a few times and starred "Gloria is the type of character who makes friends easily." In an effort to produce supportive ideas, he'd written:

For example, she tried to teach him something fun.

Another reason how she makes friends easily is that she made some funny jokes.

Finally, they made wishes which they weren't allowed to talk about.

When I conferred with Parker I reminded him that in the personal and persuasive essay unit, he'd worked on "boxes and bullets." That work involved taking an idea, a thesis, and then attaching reasons to it, using the transition word *because*. I showed him what the template might look like for his current work.

Gloria is the type of character who makes friends easily

- because A,
- because B,
- and most of all, because C.

Teachers, I'm teaching Parker to write a literary essay that is structured in a boxes-and-bullets fashion. This is the most common structure for an essay, and it's one that children know well from their prior essay writing.

When he started again, Parker wrote:

Gloria is the type of character who makes friends easily
. . . because she tries to teach Julian something fun.

I could have pointed out that actually, his first "reason" is truly an example. Instead what I said was that the reason needed to be big enough so that it could be an umbrella over more than one piece of evidence. "It will be hard to fill a whole page on this one reason—Gloria makes friends easily because she teaches Julian something fun." I told him. Parker quickly revised his thesis so that it started:

Gloria makes friends easily
because she does fun things

I nodded and said, "So you have your first reason," and I read it aloud to him. "Gloria is the type of character who makes friends easily because (1) she does fun things.'" I then asked, "And what's the next reason?" and then to prime the pump I reread what he'd written. At that point, Parker was off and running (see Figure 4–3). "Because she makes funny jokes?"

Teachers, it is important to know when it is time for you to exit a conference. You'll want to look for signs that the writer is starting to grasp what you have taught. Don't stay too long and don't aim for the student's first independent efforts to be flawless. Accept approximation. Otherwise you teach dependence and your conferences last too long.

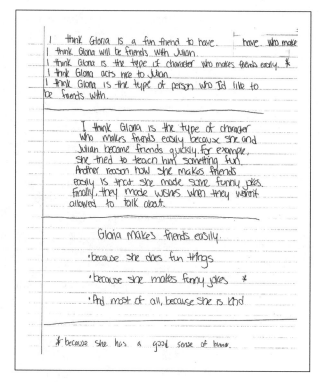

FIG. 4–3 Parker working on his thesis and reasons

Developing Systems to Collect Essay Materials

Congratulate children on their work with thesis statements, and remind them that they need to set up a system for collecting and sorting the evidence they'll gather to support their thesis statements.

"Today marks a momentous day in our unit. Drumroll please." I clapped my hands on my lap to create the sound of a drumroll and encouraged the children to do the same. Then I said, "Today, you have settled upon your thesis and supporting ideas, and you are about to collect evidence and begin drafting.

"Writers have all sorts of ways to celebrate the choosing of a thesis. I often open up a fresh box of pens, giving myself the treat of a brand-new one. Other writers switch to new writing spots or pull out a fresh stack of their favorite paper. Another writer I know cleans her desk so her space is clean and tidy for the new stage in her writing process. The rituals don't matter so much as getting ready matters. As a writer, it is important for you to anticipate what you'll need next and then set yourself up to do that.

"During our earlier essay unit, you each developed your own systems for developing an essay. Some of you collected supportive stories and quotes and thoughts on half-sheets of notebook paper that you stored in folders (one for each of your supporting ideas), and some of you did the same sort of collecting in little booklets (again, one for each of your supporting ideas). Others of you collected your ideas in your writer's notebook and then duplicated those pages in the end so you could scissor them apart.

"If you have a system that works well for you, you can, of course, use that. But because writing literary essays is new (and I know how much sorting and cutting and pasting it will involve!), I'm recommending that you all use booklets for the first round of essay writing. I'll show you how a booklet can be particularly helpful for collecting the quotes and stories you'll need to prove your thesis.

Introduce booklets as a system to collect and organize writing. Demonstrate how booklets work using your own as an example.

"Let me show you my booklets." I showed children the cover of my first booklet. "On the cover of each booklet, there is a box, and inside that box I have written my thesis and first supporting idea—my first bullet." I read it aloud.

Dog is a good friend

- because he is caring.

"Do you notice in my first bullet, I included the words from my box, 'Dog is a good friend' at the beginning?" Writers call this the stem of their thesis, and it is important to write it before each new supporting idea. That way, we make sure to always hold in our mind the *whole* idea that we are trying to support.

"After that first page is a lot of paper, so that I can collect and try out different ways the information can go."

I flipped through the blank pages and said, "This is the end of booklet one. Now let me show you booklet number two." I showed the class that, again, on the cover there was the stem of my thesis and my second bullet. I read it aloud.

Dog is a good friend

- because he doesn't give up.

I flipped through the blank pages of the second booklet, to show them all the space available for writing and revising evidence. Then I picked up the last booklet and again talked through the words on the cover.

Dog is a good friend

- because he sees the good in people.

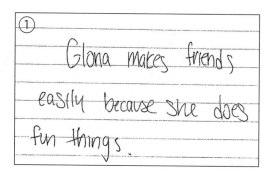

① Gloria makes friends easily because she does fun things.

② Gloria does fun things
- she does cartwheels.
- she looks at robin eggs.
- she plays games.
- she makes kites.
- she makes wishes.

Gloria makes friends easily because she does fun things. She doesn't sit around and play dolls but she likes to do cartwheels and teach people how to do them. She is really good at cartwheels and Julian who isn't could learn from her on how to do them. She makes it seem fun. She also wanted to play games with Julian. She is up for anything. But the most fun thing she does is show Julian to make a wish kite. These are all the things that Gloria does that show why she makes friends easily.

Quote:

"I know the best way to make wishes."

"The kite stayed up for a long time."

③ Gloria also does fun things like look at robin eggs. Gloria is the kind of friend who will do what someone else suggests. Julian said, "I know where there's a bird's nest." Gloria was like great let's go see the nest. Maybe she didn't even want to or wasn't interested but I don't think so. She likes to do fun and different things. She doesn't do girl things but things that are things boys like. She seems like she is open to doing anything and that makes her a fun friend to have. So now I'm realizing it isn't just that Gloria does fun things but she will try anything. Friends who will try anything are the best kinds of friends. Gloria seems to me to be a risk taker.

④ When Julian and Gloria make the wish kites they are having fun and enjoying eachothers company. Julian was so curious and excited to make them. He said, "I didn't know what she was planning. but I went in the house and got pencils and paper." You can tell he is enjoying himself because he gets the pencils and paper so they could write their wishes. He also shows he is having fun because he eagerly ties his wishes to the kite. He also believes or maybe wants his wishes to come true.

FIG. 4–4   Parker's first booklet

"Writers, each of these booklets allows me to gather information that will help me write my first draft. They allow me to add more pages or take away a page and revise it as I am collecting material for my first draft. So take three booklets as I pass them out, and begin right away setting up your booklets so that tomorrow you can begin gathering the evidence for each bullet or subsection of your essay. But, of course, if you have a system that works well for you, you can use that instead."

CRAFTING THESES QUICKLY USING A TEMPLATE

Think of a fairy tale you know well. For now, let's take "Little Red Riding Hood." Quickly write the story line. Remember that it helps to think of the main character, what he or she wants, what gets in the way, how this is resolved.

Now think, "What might this story really be about?" or "What life lessons does the character learn?" For "Little Red Riding Hood," you might write, "The story is really a reminder that evil lurks along our pathways, and we need to be less naïve, more suspicious."

Tonight try using this template to produce an instant thesis about a fairy tale you have in mind: "Some people think (the fairy tale you've chosen) is a story about (story line), but I think it is also a story about (life lesson the character learns)." For example, my Little Red Riding Hood thesis might be "Some people think "Little Red Riding Hood" is the story of a girl, dressed in a red hood, who wants to give cookies to her grandma but instead is nearly eaten by a wolf. I think, however, this is also a story of a girl who goes into the woods thinking she knows more than her mother, and nearly dies as a result.

Using Stories as Evidence

IN THIS SESSION, you'll teach students ways that essayists select mini-stories as evidence to support their ideas.

GETTING READY

✔ Charts from the *Boxes and Bullets: Personal and Persuasive Essays* unit, available for students to refer to during the minilesson

✔ "How to Write a Literary Essay" chart (see Connection)

✔ "How to Angle a Story to Make a Point" chart (see Teaching)

✔ Mentor text, *Fox*

✔ Transition words chart from Session 11 of the *Boxes and Bullets: Personal and Persuasive Essays* unit (see Share)

✔ "When You Want to Give an Example" chart (see Share)

THIS SESSION IS THE FIRST IN A SEQUENCE of lessons that remind students of the ways they can gather evidence to support each of the supporting ideas (or reasons for their opinion) in their literary essay. It is fitting that the first method for collecting evidence involves children rereading the stories they are writing about to locate key moments, then retelling and using those moments to support the ideas in their essays. They'll be retelling those moments to explore their relationship to the central ideas in the text. This is one of several ways youngsters will learn to shift between abstract ideas and concrete details.

Throughout the year, your children will have written about emblematic moments in ways that convey big meanings. My stories about seeing my father leave early on Christmas morning to serve waffles at the hospital or sailing with him at the end of the summer and learning about his excitement over the prospect of returning to work convey both my appreciation for his commitment to his work and my own youthful yearning to carve out a meaningful place for myself in the world. Stories can be powerful vehicles for conveying big ideas. It makes sense, therefore, for readers to collect stories that represent ideas that seem to them to be central to texts.

You may need to reteach lessons from the earlier units to remind your students to bring to this unit what they know about writing effective stories. Above all, they will need to be reminded that there is a giant difference between merely summarizing an event and storytelling that same event. Although there are appropriate times to summarize within an essay, today you will emphasize the value of storytelling key moments from a story. A big part of this will be helping students to draw on all they know about angling a story to illustrate an idea.

COMMON CORE STATE STANDARD: W.4.1.b,c; W.4.3.a,b; W.4.9.a, RL.4.1, RL.4.3, RL.4.4, SL.4.1, SL.4.4, L.4.1, L.4.2, L.4.3.a, L.4.6

Using Stories as Evidence

CONNECTION

Remind children that when writing personal and persuasive essays, they collected evidence to support each of their topic sentences. Suggest that they'll need to do that also when writing literary essays.

"Writers, you'll remember that during our essay unit, after you wrote your thesis statements and planned your supports for your thesis statements—your reasons—you each became a researcher, collecting the evidence that would allow you to make your case. So it won't surprise you to hear that you need to do similar work now. In fact, you can look back on charts from the essay unit and remind yourself of materials you collected then to back up your supporting ideas—your topic sentences. Many of you will decide that one of the best ways to provide evidence for the supporting ideas in your essay is to select moments in the story that capture the idea you are putting forward." As I spoke, I unveiled our anchor chart, with the new bullets added.

Interestingly enough, in our minilessons, we as teachers are constantly required to do just what we're teaching children to do. That is, we are frequently called upon to retell a story, angling it to make one point or another. We therefore have a repertoire of strategies to bring out our angle (or our interpretation). For example, we may highlight the point we want to make by mentioning counterexamples, saying something like, "Donald Crews didn't write about his whole summer down south—no way! Instead, he wrote about just one episode on the train tracks." This is a technique children can learn to use as well. Children can also angle their stories by starting with an overarching statement that orients listeners: "Listen to what I do." "Notice especially . . ." Children, too, can learn to preface their stories with comments that establish their angles.

How to Write a Literary Essay

- Grow ideas about a text.
  - Use thought prompts.
  - Ask questions of texts.
  - Pay attention to the characters in a story, especially noting their traits, motivations, struggles, changes, and relationships.
- Find a big idea that is really important to you, then write a thesis.
- Test out your thesis by asking questions.
  - Does this opinion relate to more than one part of the text?
  - Is there enough evidence to support it?
- Collect evidence.
  - micro-stories

✤ **Name the teaching point.**

"Today I want to remind you that when you are telling a story in the service of providing evidence for an idea, you need to angle that story to highlight the way it supports and connects to your thesis."

TEACHING

Demonstrate that before a literary essayist can tell a story to illustrate a topic sentence, he or she must reread the text and identify bits that could serve as evidence.

"Usually you will have grown your thesis by looking closely at moments from the text. To help others see your convincing evidence, you essentially need to take your reader by the hand, bring him or her to the same moments that you studied, and help the reader come to the conclusion you came to." I revealed the following chart.

> **How to Angle a Story to Make a Point**
>
> - Begin the story by repeating the point you want to make.
> - Use words from the text.
> - Mention what the character does <u>not</u> do as a way to draw attention to what the character <u>does</u> do.
> - Repeat the key words from the big idea/topic sentence often.

"As you can see from our chart, there are a few ways writers do this. When you want to angle a story, you can begin the story by saying the point you want to make, mention what the character does *not* do to draw attention to what he or she does do, and repeat your key points again and again. For example, let's take our bullet, or reason: Dog is a good friend because he sees the good in others. First, we need to think, 'What moments in the story led me to this conclusion? What moments illustrate this point for other readers?'"

Using a document camera to show an enlarged version of *Fox*, I quickly skimmed the first part of the book, adding stars in the margins of the text whenever I found a potential story. The children joined in identifying that the passage in which Dog meets Fox is one that illustrates well Dog's tendency to see the good in others.

I let children know when the teaching point contains a reminder of something they learned earlier. Obviously there will be times when we teach children to use a strategy they learned earlier, and there is no reason to pretend differently. Ideally, we will add a new layer of complexity, as I try to do in this instance.

How to Angle a Story
to Make a Point

- Begin the story by repeating the point you want to make.
- Use words from the text.
- Mention what the character does <u>not</u> do as a way to draw attention to what the character <u>does</u> do.
- Repeat the key words from the big idea / topic sentence often.

If you don't have access to a document camera, then you'll want to use either a chart-sized version of the first portion of Fox or individual copies for each child.

Ask children to watch as you tell one portion of the text as a story. Highlight the steps you take.

After settling upon this passage, I said to the children, "Let's write the story of this first bit of evidence together so that I can show you how to angle it. You can then practice using the same techniques to write a second moment that illustrates this idea about Dog.

"I find it helps to reread the text and clarify the timeline of what happened. When we are working with a short story, finding and storytelling small moments from a text can be a challenge because often you are zooming in on a teeny tiny part of the story and telling it in a really stretched-out way. For example, the episode in which Dog saw the good in Fox only took a tiny bit of time in real life. I'll really need to stretch it out so that it works as a story. I might tell about how first," and I put one finger up, "Fox comes to the bush. And then," I put up a second finger, "Magpie is scared but Dog says, 'Welcome. We can offer you food and shelter.'" I put up a third finger and continued. "Then, Fox compliments Dog and Magpie on their running. Finally," I put up a fourth finger, "Dog beams with excitement.

"But here is the thing—I don't just tell what actually *did* happen first, then next, then next. The challenge will be to tell this in ways that pop out the fact that Dog sees the best in others.

"I'm going to try my story again. But this time I'm going to begin by saying the point I want to make." I wrote-in-the-air:

> *Dog is the kind of character that sees the best in others. For example, one day, a fox came to the bush where Dog and Magpie lived. Fox moves through the trees sneakily, like a tongue of fire. Magpie trembles at the sight of him. But Dog doesn't see the bad in Fox.*

I looked at the chart. "I can use words from the text and I can also mention what Dog *didn't* do to highlight what he did do. Let's see."

> *Dog does not tremble like Magpie. He is not scared by Fox's haunted eyes. Instead, he is excited that Fox has come to visit their cave, and Dog welcomes him in for food and shelter.*

"And then, of course, I want to repeat my idea, what I'm trying to show." I picked up my pen and quickly added:

> Dog only sees the good in Fox.

Invite youngsters to help you debrief, extracting the sequence of what you have done to tell an angled ministory as evidence for one of your claims about the text.

"Will you tell your partner what you saw me do just now? You might think specifically about the ways I told the story to bring out my idea about Dog. And be sure to use our chart to help you name some of what you saw." I allowed the children a few minutes to talk and then called them back together. "Chloe, what did you and your partner notice?"

Chloe began, "You made the fox sound really scary." I interjected, "Yes, good observation." I looked out at the children. "But *how* did I do this?"

When children retell portions of a novel to make a point, the text itself is long enough that it's not challenging to cull a sequence of events. When writing about a very short text such as Fox, however, the entire text is so abbreviated that writers must really zoom in on micro-events to extract a sequenced story. But a sequence is necessary to create a story.

You might be saying to yourself, "Wait a minute. This is an inquiry. The children are supposed to notice what the teacher is doing and name it for themselves!" And you'd be right to point this out. I do take the liberty of naming the moves I make, showing the children how I consciously implement as many of the strategies as possible. I am guiding children to notice certain things. Then too, I am harnessing the power of repetition. By hearing the strategies repeated again and again, I hope children will have ready access to them and that the strategies will become second nature to them as they get to work on their own stories.

Raffi added on, "You used words from the text like *haunted eyes*."

I signaled for others to add on. "And you did that thing about saying what Dog didn't do. You said he didn't act scared like Magpie," added John. "Yeah, you wrote that instead he said 'Come in! Welcome!'" added Parker.

"So, writers, what you are noticing is that I told this story in a way that really *showed* what I most wanted to say, and I did that by using strategies from our chart. I began by saying the point I wanted to make, I repeated the point often, I used words from the text, and I even said what Dog *didn't* do to highlight what he did do."

ACTIVE ENGAGEMENT

Tell children you plan to collect a few stories to support each topic sentence, and ask them to do the same with their own texts.

"Okay, writers, who's ready to try this using their own stories?" The children nodded and raised their hands, and I began again. "First, you'll need to find a part of your story that fits with your first bullet, or reason, written on the first page of your first booklet. For example, Celia is going to go back to 'Gloria Who Might Be My Best Friend' and look for a small part of the story that illustrates her first bullet, 'Julian and Gloria are going to be best friends because they get along.'"

The children took a moment to locate a mini-story. As they worked, I voiced over. "You are probably asking yourself, 'What part of the story *best* shows this part of my thesis?' When you are ready, put a circle around the part of the story that you'll use to support your thesis." When children were ready, I called for them to begin telling their stories. I coached them as they retold. "You just told a bit about what happened in the story. Don't forget, repeat your idea often!" And later, "What could the character have done but didn't do? What did he do instead?

"Writers, all eyes on Celia. She is going to tell a mini-story that highlights Julian and Gloria getting along. Let's listen to see if Celia was able to bring out that they get along."

Celia took a big breath, and began.

> Julian and Gloria are going to be best friends because they get along. For example, on the day that Gloria moved onto Julian's street, she asked him if he could do a cartwheel, and then she turned and did two perfect cartwheels in a row. Julian didn't admit he couldn't and tried really hard to do exactly as Gloria had done, but he fell over. He wasn't very good, but Gloria didn't laugh or brag that she was better. Instead, she said that cartwheels took a lot of practice. There was no teasing or bickering—just two friends getting along.

I said, "Thumbs up if you think Celia's mini-story brings out that Julian and Gloria get along." Many thumbs went up, and I noted who didn't think Celia had told an angled mini-story.

If you feel your children would profit from extra support during the active engagement, you could retell only two thirds of a story and then ask them first to retell the story you've just told and then to continue, adding on the rest of the story. This, of course, would provide them with much more scaffolding than the request to proceed in a similar way, retelling an entirely new small story.

When retelling a sequence of events to make a particular point, children are apt to abbreviate the start of the event instead of starting the story at the climax, because it is usually the section that most pertains to the idea the child wants to advance. I try to remind children that even mini-stories must have a beginning, a middle, and an end.

I deliberately call on Celia here because I know she's fairly adept at this, and I want her to provide yet another demonstration. If none of your students are able to angle their stories well enough that their work can become a demonsration, you can provide a second demonstration yourself.

LINK

Remind writers that essayists collect mini-stories to advance their point, collecting several stories for each booklet—or topic sentence—within a single day.

"So, writers, you already know that when you are writing an essay you need to fill up your booklets with evidence to support each of your topic sentences, and you already know that essayists often collect stories as evidence. Today you've seen how writers of literary essays reread, finding portions of the text that can be told as stories, and then how they angle those tiny stories to support the point they want to make.

"Today I know each of you will collect several stories. You'll likely be able to collect a few stories for each of your booklets. The challenge will be to angle those stories to highlight the idea you are advancing, just as Celia did in her story about Gloria."

Just before sending them off to work, I remind children of the productivity goals for today.

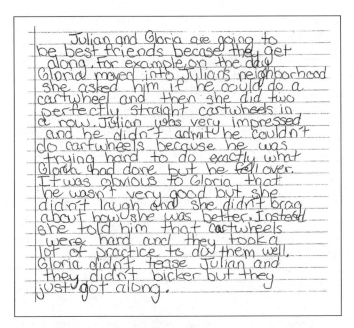

FIG. 5–1   Celia's work after the minilesson

Collecting and Angling Stories to Support Ideas

TODAY'S MINILESSON TEACHES A CHALLENGING CONCEPT. Chances are that you notice students struggling a bit during the active engagement section of the mini-lesson. Whenever this is the case, your teaching needs to become especially forceful. For this reason, you'll probably want to conduct table conferences today. You may not have the luxury of being able to invest lots of time in research. You can count on the fact that children will profit from help, and you can anticipate the sort of help they'll need.

For starters, children will need help seeing the micro-stories they can extract from these short texts. For example, if a child is writing about "Eleven" and wants to make the point that Rachel is silenced by Mrs. Price, she is apt to see only one possible story that might illustrate this, and that story encompasses the whole text of "Eleven." (Mrs. Price says she's seen Rachel wearing the sweater. Mrs. Price doesn't listen to Rachel's protests and moves on to math. Mrs. Price makes Rachel put on the sweater. Mrs. Price acts as if it is no big deal when the sweater turns out not to be Rachel's.)

You can show children that they can also regard "Eleven" as containing several differ-ent episodes, each of which shows Mrs. Price's disregard for Rachel. For example, early in the story Mrs. Price asks whose sweater it is, and even when Rachel sputters, "Not mine," Mrs. Price listens to Sylvia and not Rachel. There are other micro-stories. A bit later, Rachel tries to protest, but Mrs. Price turns to math as if the sweater question is now resolved. Even though Rachel is about to cry, Mrs. Price doesn't notice.

Then, too, children will need help retelling a sequence of actions as a story. Many will be apt to cut to the chase, summarizing rather than storytelling the event. For example, a child might write:

> When Rachel tried to tell Mrs. Price the sweater wasn't hers, Mrs. Price ignored Rachel.

"Writers, can I stop you for a moment? What you've all come to realize today is that the point you want to make alters the way that you tell a story. When parts of a story match your thesis, you stretch out those parts.

"You already know that details are everything, but the point is that you retell details from the story that connect to and provide evidence for your topic sentences and thesis. If you are writing a story and want to show that a place is gloomy, and meanwhile you see that the author has described the place by saying that dark storm clouds hung low, you'd mention that detail."

You will want to let this writer know that he has just summarized—or told—rather than spinning a story—or shown. Although essayists *do* sometimes summarize perti-nent bits of a text to defend a point, a wise writer recognizes the difference between a summary and a story and can produce either one.

Above all, children will need help angling their stories. A great way to build this skill, and most writing skills, is with repeated practice and revision. In this case, that will mean trying their angled story a few times. Remind kids that this is the reason they have all those pages in their booklet—for practicing and playing and trying things different ways! Each time they write, help them pause to look at what they've written, make a plan for how it could be even better, and then in their next revision try to write that better version.

Children (and teachers!) should not think of revision just as something that they save for the end of the writing process, but something that they can use before they draft to help them develop the important parts of their essay. It can be emotionally difficult for students to make significant changes once they have a full draft in their hands, and one way to ease this difficulty is to have much of the revision happening earlier in the process, when the essay still feels flexible and open to change.

When I got to Harrison's table I walked around, looking over the shoulder of each child so I could read what they'd written so far. I noticed that most of the children had made passing references to sections of the text that supplied their ideas but they had not seemed to read those passages closely, or to think and write analytically about them. They merely said, "This part goes with my idea" without helping readers understand that the passage illustrated the claim.

Don't hesitate to ask a cluster of children to stop what they are doing to watch you work with one child. For example, I asked children to watch while I worked with Harrison, who had decided to retell the story of Lupe's dinner conversation to support the idea that Lupe overcame her difficulties through the support of her family. The excerpt from "The Marble Champ" that Harrison wanted to story-tell goes like this.

> *"I'm going to enter the marbles championship."*
>
> *Her father looked at her mother and then back at his daughter. "When is it, honey?"*
>
> *"This Saturday. Can you come?"*
>
> *The father had been planning to play racquetball with a friend Saturday, but he said he would be there. He knew his daughter thought she was no good at sports and he wanted to encourage her. He even rigged some lights in the backyard so she could practice after dark. (Baseball in April, Soto 2000)*

Harrison had initially written:

> For example, one dinner Lupe asks her father to come to the marble competition. "When is it?" her father asks. She said, "This Saturday." The date wasn't good for him but he decided to come anyway.

I said, "Harrison, when I reread my stories to check whether I've angled them to support my thesis, I do this: I underline the parts of my rough draft story that directly show my big idea. Right now, could you underline the parts of your micro-story that show that Lupe overcame her difficulties through the support of her family?"

Harrison reread his writing and didn't underline anything. Then he said, "I don't know what part to underline." I asked Harrison to read each line and then stop and ask, "Does this show Lupe's family being supportive?" I turned to the rest of the group and asked them to give a thumbs up or down as Harrison reread each line, registering their vote. When Harrison finished reading, he realized that neither he nor his classmates had given a thumbs up sign to show that yes, this supported his claim. Harrison paused and said, "I get it. I need to add on to the part about the dad switching his plans to support her." In the end, this is what Harrison wrote.

> Lupe overcomes her difficulties through the support of her family. For example, one dinner, Lupe asks her father to come to the marble competition. Her father drops his fork and drops into deep thought. He had finally planned to spend that very day playing racquet ball, his favorite activity. But he looked into Lupe's eyes, thought about how important it was that she was risking entering a sports competition, and announced he would be there. Lupe grinned.

I debriefed for the observing children. "Do you see that after Harrison realized that his point wasn't clear, he revised his writing? This time he added what he believed the characters were thinking and made sure that the micro-story goes with his claim—his idea." Then I asked each of them to reread their writing line by line, pausing to ask themselves, "Does this show my idea?" I explained to them, "This will help each of you to make sure your micro-stories, your elaboration, matches your idea." I sent them all back to work, reminding them that it may take them three to four tries.

Connecting Stories to Big Ideas

Show students the work of a classmate, highlighting how that child moved seamlessly from storytelling to exposition.

"You already remember from our personal and persuasive essay unit that to use a story as evidence for an idea, it is important not only to angle the story, but also to unpack it. Let's look back at Julia's personal essay to remind ourselves how she did this so expertly. Remember, her idea was that you should seize opportunities to be courageous. Watch how the stories she includes in even just the first part of her essay all go with that idea. Here's what she wrote in that paragraph." (See Figure 5–2.)

> A lot of times in a lifetime you have a chance to be courageous. And when that comes to you, use it. One day, in November, my science teacher had a snake in a glass cage.
>
> "Cool!" everyone said aloud.
>
> "No." I moaned secretly.
>
> After class, my science teacher made me stay and at least touch the snake. I was so scared I could feel my heart pulsing in my chest.
>
> "You can't run from your fears—you have to face them," he said. I touched the snake gently.
>
> "It doesn't seem too bad," I thought to myself. And after a good fifteen minutes, I ended up holding the snake! Mr. Dutt passed away just a few weeks later and I was glad I had the chance to learn that important lesson from him.
>
> When you use your time in the best way possible, you use it courageously.

"Do you notice the way Julia told her story in way that popped out the point she is trying to make, but then she also told that point? She came right out and said it. You learned earlier that essay writers show *and* tell."

> A lot of times in a lifetime you have a chance to be courageous. And when that comes to you, use it. One day, in November, my science teacher had a snake.
>
> "Cool!" everyone said aloud.
>
> "No." I moaned secretly.
>
> After class, my science teacher made me stay and at least touch the snake. I was so scared I could feel my heart pulsing in my chest.
>
> "You can't run from your fears" he said. "You have to face them."
>
> I touched the snake gently. "It doesn't seem too bad," I thought to myself. And after a good fifteen minutes, I ended up holding the snake!
>
> Mr. Dutt passed away a few weeks later and I was glad I had the chance to learn that important lesson from him.
>
> When you use your time in the best way possible, you use it courageously

FIG. 5–2 This start to an essay from an earlier unit shows Julia using evidence to support a claim—work that can transfer to literary essay.

Give children a few moments to try this work with their own stories, restating the main point at the end of one or two.

"Right now, will you pull out one or two of the mini-stories you wrote today? You have probably shown your reader why the moment is important. Now *tell* your reader what you hope this moment shows. Start by saying something like 'This shows that . . .' or 'This is evidence that . . .'"

I added a bullet to the chart from our last essay unit with our new sentence starter.

When you want to give an example:

- An example that shows this is . . . or this shows that . . .
- For instance . . .
- One time . . .
- This is evidence that . . .

Raffi turned to Marie and read his mini-story.

Gabriel is more caring than he thinks. Even though he's sitting on the stoop thinking about running away and living alone, as soon as he hears a cry he got up and started to look. When he heard it again, he walked faster. Some people would just ignore it and keep worrying about themselves, but Gabriel didn't even think about doing that. He just jumped straight up to help.

After a second, he paused and then added,

"This is evidence that . . . Gabriel is caring even though he acts at first like he's just tough."

After a couple minutes of listening in and noting which students found quick success with this and which would need more practice, I called their attention back to me. "Remember that it is important to be using all you know to constantly revise your writing about the evidence. Tomorrow, as you continue writing, remember to make sure that you don't just give examples from the story to support your idea but that you come right out and *tell* your reader what you think and what the story is evidence for."

STUDYING A LITERARY ESSAY

When writing a literary essay, it helps to be able to imagine the sort of text you're hoping to make. For homework, then, study Jill's essay on "Eleven."

Literary Essay on "Eleven" by Sandra Cisneros written by Jill

In my life, not everything ends up like a fairytale. I like to read books where characters are like me. They don't live fairytale lives. We have the same kinds of problems. Many people read Sandra Cisneros's essay "Eleven" and think it's about a girl who has to wear a sweater she doesn't want to wear. But I think the story is about a girl who struggles to hold onto herself when she is challenged by people who have power over her.

When Rachel's teacher, Mrs. Price, challenges Rachel, Rachel loses herself. One day Mrs. Price puts a stretched-out, itchy, red sweater on Rachel's desk saying, "I know this is yours. I saw you wearing it once!!" Rachel knows that the sweater isn't hers and tries to tell Mrs. Price, but Mrs. Price doesn't believe her. Rachel reacts to Mrs. Price's actions by losing herself. "In my head, I'm thinking . . . how long till lunch time, how long till I can take the red sweater and throw it over the school yard fence, or leave it hanging on a parking meter, or bunch it up into a little ball and toss it over the alley?" This shows that Rachel loses herself because she's not listening to her teacher, she's dreaming about a whole other place. It is also important to see that Rachel has all this good thinking about the sweater but when she wants to say the sweater isn't hers, she squeaks and stammers, unable to speak. "But it's not," Rachel says. "Now," Mrs. Price replies. Rachel loses herself by not finding complete words to say when Mrs. Price challenges her.

When Rachel's classmates challenge Rachel, Rachel loses herself. Sylvia Saldivar puts Rachel on the spot light when she says to Mrs. Price, "I think the sweater is Rachel's." Sylvia is challenging Rachel, she is being mean and she makes Rachel feel lost. Rachel cries to let her emotions out. Rachel feels sick from Sylvia. Rachel tries to cover herself up by putting her head in her sleeve. Tears stream down her face. She doesn't feel special like it's her birthday. Instead she feels lost in Sylvia's challenge.

In "Eleven" Rachel is overpowered by both Mrs. Price and Sylvia Saldivar and this causes her to lose herself. I used to think that when people turn eleven they feel strong and have confidence but I have learned that when your eleven you're also 10, 9, 8, 7, 6, 5, 4, 3, 2, and 1.

Read and reread Jill's essay. Try to let it mentor you by studying the way her micro-stories illustrate her big idea. You might start by circling Jill's thesis statement and her topic sentences. Notice where they are in her essay. Then you'll want to notice the way in which everything she writes is channeled to support the thesis and topic sentence. Notice the specific word choices she makes to help her angle her micro-stories to illustrate her big idea. And notice that after Jill tells a story from the text, she writes a sentence discussing how the story addresses her topic sentence. This sentence begins, "This shows that . . ."

Finally, look again at the micro-stories you wrote today and revise them, using what you learn from Jill's essay to help you. Be sure that, like Jill, you include a sentence that discusses how your evidence addresses your topic sentence. Your sentence, like Jill's, can begin, "This shows that . . . ," and it needs to refer back to the topic sentence.

Citing Textual Evidence

IN THIS SESSION, you'll teach students that writers use direct quotes to support their claims about a text. You'll teach them ways writers are discerning, choosing only the quotes that best support their ideas.

GETTING READY

✔ Students' booklets, to be brought to the carpet, along with a pen or highlighter

✔ "How to Write a Literary Essay" chart (see Teaching)

✔ Three quotes from the mentor text that could support one of your reasons, written on separate pieces of chart paper. We use the following sentences for our essay on *Fox*:
"And so Dog runs, with Magpie on his back, every day, through Summer, through Winter." "In the evenings, when the air is creamy with blossom, Dog and Magpie relax at the mouth of the cave, enjoying each other's company." "Magpie tries to warn Dog about Fox. 'He belongs nowhere,' she says. 'He loves no one.'" (see Teaching)

✔ "When Choosing a Quote, Essayists Ask . . . " chart (see Teaching)

✔ "Ways to Bring Quotes into an Essay" chart (see Share)

S KIERS HAVE DOZENS OF DIFFERENT WORDS for snow: new, fluffy snow that's perfect to ski on is called *powder*, melting snow that you slip and slide on is *mush*, hard icy snow that will cut your legs if you fall is called *crust*, and so on. Since the quality or type of snow impacts skiers' rides down the slopes, it makes sense that they have all these specialized terms for it. Children will need specialized terms for their essay writing as well. When children first learn to write about literature, they will probably talk often about the need to cite evidence (or examples) from the text. The goal will be to "give evidence." Most of your students will not yet know that, just as skiers might call on a specific set of words and phrases to refer to snow, literary essayists draw on a set of terms to help state claims and make cases in different ways. Literary essayists have a vocabulary—and a system—to help them incorporate evidence from a text into an essay.

In the preceding session, children learned that they can find bits of a text that illustrate the idea they are advancing and then retell those bits as micro-stories. Today you'll help children learn that as literary essayists, they have a palette of options for referring to the text under study. They will sometimes choose to tell a story to make a point, but other times they'll quote a section of the text to provide evidence, using the exact words of the author. Quoting not only helps to bolster the essayist's claim, but it also works to enrich the essay with the beautiful language the author has used. It is almost as if the essayist is saying, "I cannot say this better myself, so let me tell you what the author has said, or how this part of the story goes, to show you what I mean." Quoting a text is also another way youngsters learn to shift between abstract ideas and concrete details.

COMMON CORE STATE STANDARDS: W.4.1.b,c; W.4.9.a, RL.4.1, RL.5.1, SL.4.1, SL.4.2, SL.4.4, L.4.1.e,f; L.4.2,a,b,c; L.4.3, L.4.6

Citing Textual Evidence

CONNECTION

Contextualize today's lesson by helping children understand the power of quotes to express ideas.

"When you graduate from high school, there will be what is called a yearbook that will contain a photo of each person in your graduating class. You may have seen your mother or father's yearbook. Traditionally, right under each person's photo, there is a quote—a sentence that comes from a book or a song or a poem—that captures the essence of that person.

"Sometimes the quote will be a beautiful saying about friendship or about the joy of working hard or the importance of family. For an athlete, the quote might be, 'It's not whether you win or lose, but how you play the game.' For someone with a big imagination, it might be 'If you can dream it, you can do it.'

"The tradition could be different. The tradition could have evolved so that people put a little picture in that space in a yearbook, or a list of accomplishments. Instead, the tradition is to include a line or two of words that say something just right about you. If we were making a yearbook right now, what quote would go under your picture?" I left a pool of silence. "Any of you have an idea?

"I'm talking to you about quotations because as you get older, you'll find there are more grown-up expectations on you and your writing. And one of those will be an expectation that you include more direct quotations in your writing. I'm pretty sure that if you were to write a story about something your family did together, you'd include the exact words that some of your family members said to each other. Using exact quotes makes a story come to life. So it shouldn't be surprising to you when I say that as you move toward middle school and high school, it becomes just as important, when writing about texts, to directly quote those texts.

"It goes without saying that choosing the quote is a really big deal—whether it is for your yearbook photo or for your literary essay."

> ◆ COACHING
>
> *There are lots of ways we could talk about quotations without leaving the terrain of writing about literature, but part of the challenge is to keep your teaching lively. Bill Zinsser, the author of* On Writing Well, *says the most important quality of good nonfiction writing is surprise.*
>
> *Of course, we shamelessly take every occasion we can find to cheerlead some of the values that matter to us—a beautiful saying about friendship or about the joy of working hard. We play the violin for the importance of family as well.*

✤ **Name the teaching point.**

"Today I want to teach you that essayists work hard to find 'just-right' quotations to include in their essays. A passage is 'just right' for citing when it provides strong evidence for a claim, making readers say, 'I see what you mean.'" As I spoke this last part, I unveiled our anchor chart with this new bullet added.

How to Write a Literary Essay

- Grow ideas about a text.
  - Use thought prompts.
  - Ask questions of texts.
  - Pay attention to the characters in a story, especially noting their traits, motivations, struggles, changes, and relationships.
- Find a big idea that is really important to you, then write a thesis.
- Test out your thesis by asking questions.
  - Does this opinion relate to more than one part of the text?
  - Is there enough evidence to support it?
- Collect evidence.
  - micro-stories
  - quotes

~ How to Write a Literary Essay ~

- Grow Ideas about a text.
  - Use thought prompts.
  - Ask questions of texts.
  - Pay attention to the characters in a story, especially noting their traits, motivations, struggles, changes, and relationships.
- Find a big idea that is really important to you, then write a thesis.
- Test out your thesis by asking questions.
  - Does this opinion relate to more than one part of the text?
  - Is there enough evidence to support it?
- Collect Evidence.
  - micro-stories
  - quotes
  - lists
  - examples
- Unpack the evidence by telling the reader what it shows, using prompts like:
  - This shows that...
  - This is evidence that...
- Add transitions to glue the evidence together.

TEACHING

Recruit children to help you weigh and choose between several possible quotes that could serve as support for your thesis about the book *Fox*. Explicitly teach two considerations you take into account when selecting citations.

"So in my essay about *Fox*, my thesis is that Dog is a good friend. We found a lot of evidence of that, didn't we? Remember in *Strega Nona*, how Big Anthony's house overflows with magic pasta? In the same way, *Fox* overflows with passages that support the idea that Dog is a good friend. The important thing is always to weigh which of the quotes provides the strongest evidence for our ideas. I've hung a chart that I think will help us." I unveiled the following chart.

> ## When Choosing a Quote, Essayists Ask . . .
>
> - Can I point to <u>specific words</u> or <u>actions</u> that support my bullet?
> - Can I explain <u>exactly how</u> these words or actions support my bullet?

"Let's start by looking at some of the quotes I found to support my first bullet, or reason: 'Dog is a good friend because he is caring.'" I showed children three quotes I'd copied onto separate pieces of chart paper (so that I could move their order around and remove some once they were eliminated from consideration.) "Let's weigh which provides stronger evidence."

- "And so Dog runs, with Magpie on his back, every day, through Summer, through Winter."
- "In the evenings, when the air is creamy with blossom, Dog and Magpie relax at the mouth of the cave, enjoying each other's company."
- "Magpie tries to warn Dog about Fox. 'He belongs nowhere,' she says. 'He loves no one.'"

Explain and demonstrate how you go about selecting between a number of possible passages that you could cite, including showing how you use the questions mentioned above.

"What I do is, I just reread the passages I could cite, thinking, 'Which would be the strongest? Next strongest?' Will you look with me and give me a thumbs up when you've decided?" I then read each one in turn to myself, mulling over the candidates. As I did this, I narrated my thought process, saying things like "That one looks really good—wait, I should read through all of them before I decide," and "Hmm, that's a good sentence, but let me check my claim again to see if it matches."

Mess up, deliberately, so you can show students how you check your decisions. In this instance, discover that actually, the words on the cited passage didn't exactly make the point you wanted to make.

By now, most of the kids had their thumbs up, so I numbered them myself, ranking, "In the evenings, when the air is creamy with blossom, Dog and Magpie relax at the mouth of the cave, enjoying each other's company" as the strongest piece of evidence.

"This looks like pretty strong evidence for my thesis," I said. "It shows that they're relaxing and enjoying each other's company, so they're being good friends to each other. Thumbs up if you agree that this is the strongest support for our bullet." Some, but not all, thumbs in the room went up.

"Not everybody agrees, which reminds me that instead of just jumping to the conclusion that this statement works the best, I should ask those questions about it that I'd suggested you ask as well."

A minilesson is always meant to spotlight a specific skill, showing how to do that skill. This means that the author of the minilesson always needs to decide what to skim past and what to teach in detail. Notice here that the passages have already been collected, and they are listed on chart paper. That part is backstory, occurring off stage before the drama of this minilesson begins.

Weighing or ranking evidence forces children to parse and analyze the quotes against each other to determine which are the strongest. A good essayist tosses aside the weakest evidence.

You'll notice that I attempt to make the process visible for children. As always, to do this, I slow down a process that actually happens quickly, under the radar. I make a show of thinking aloud, hoping to convey to children that this is not an easy, one-step process. Then too, I hope children will learn a thing or two from the questions I ask myself and the ways I try out many possibilities before settling on one quote.

One of the things to notice is the way that a chart threads its way through a minilesson and, indeed, through a unit. If we want charts to become part of kids' repertoire, we need to make sure this happens.

> **When Choosing A Quote, Essayists Ask . . .**
> - Can I point to <u>specific words</u> or <u>actions</u> that support my bullet?
> - Can I explain <u>exactly how</u> these words or actions support my bullet?

"Let me first reread the quote to underline specific words." I read aloud, "In the evenings, when the air is creamy with blossom, Dog and Magpie relax at the mouth of the cave, enjoying each other's company."

"What should I underline? Hmm, the words show they're enjoying each other's company, but actually, hold on. My bullet is 'Dog is a good friend because he is caring.' I'm actually not sure that this part where they're enjoying each other's company proves that Dog is caring. Uh-oh! This isn't really very strong evidence for my first bullet after all!" I moved the quote off to the side.

Then I went back to my quotes and sorted them again, more quickly this time, narrating my new choices. "This last quote on the list shows what *Magpie*, not Dog, does. So that definitely doesn't show that Dog is a good friend because he is caring. How about this one: 'And so Dog runs, with Magpie on his back, every day, through Summer, through Winter'? The specific words that support my bullet are 'every day,' and they support the bullet because Dog is doing what makes Magpie happy every single day, even when it's cold and he probably doesn't want to, because he is caring."

Debrief in ways that are transferable to another text and another day.

"So, as you can see, even a few minutes of working to sort quotes is helping us learn so much about how to find effective quotes. It helps to weigh which is best and to make sure there are specific words or phrases that match your bullet—your reason—and that you can explain how the passage supports your overall thesis."

ACTIVE ENGAGEMENT

Set students up to choose quotes for their own literary essays, repeating the same process you demonstrated to find the best supporting evidence.

"So that you get a chance to practice weighing possible quotes, selecting one that best makes your case, why don't you take one of the bullets from your essay and quickly skim your text to find and underline a few quotes that you might use as evidence for one of your bullets. Then, ask yourself those two questions," I pointed to them, "so that you can choose from among the quotes the one you think provides the strongest evidence. After a few minutes, you will have a chance to share your thoughts with your partner."

While students started this work, I moved among them, keeping an eye out for students who seemed as if they'd benefit from small-group instruction after the minilesson. As I did this, I also voiced over, saying things like, "As you underline,

Almost always, when wanting to show students how to do something, it helps to mess up and self-correct because this allows for more explicit instruction.

If children are quoting whole paragraphs of text from the stories to support their claims, you may decide to teach the ways to use only exact, meaningful quotes to support their arguments. When children are first learning to quote, they may be tempted to replace their own writing with large portions of the text they're writing about. Explain that using quotes often involves going back to the text and taking just bits of it to support, not replace, your argument. Often this involves a bit of summarizing, interspersed with portions of quotes.

64

think to yourself, do you need all of that quote or only part of it?" "Great, a lot of you are already weighing your second quote." And "Ooh, I see Parker looking up at the chart! Don't forget to say *why* you think the quote supports your idea."

Seeing that most of the students were almost ready, I invited them to turn and talk. The children talked for a minute or so, explaining and justifying the choices they'd made.

LINK

Send writers off to work, reminding them of the full array of potential activities they can be deciding between.

A few minutes later, I called them back together, saying, "So, writers, today some of you might still be filling your booklets up with angled stories. Others of you will be ready to start collecting quotes that support your bullets, or reasons. When you are doing this, remember that you don't have to settle for just any old quotes. You can choose really effective ones! One good strategy is to start by choosing a handful of possible quotes for each bullet and then to pick the best ones by thinking about which give the strongest evidence for that bullet and why."

Evaluating Evidence for a Claim

WHEN YOU DO SOME QUICK ASSESSMENTS DURING THE MINILESSON, this allows you to intervene more efficiently to provide some children with the leg-up that they are going to need. During the minilesson, you found that some children would benefit from hands-on practice evaluating evidence for a claim. If you pull those children into a small group, you can use the students' own work as a forum for teaching. For example, you can start by writing one student's bullet onto a Post-it and then creating two columns under that Post-it: one labeled "supports" and one, "does not support." If you or the writer jots a few quotes from the story onto additional Post-its, those can then be categorized into the proper category, asking the students to discuss which category each quote fits. After students have the hang of doing this, you can divide the categories into: "strong support," "some support," and "no support."

As you confer, consider the problems kids are getting themselves into, and when you find a fairly widespread problem, use that as your mid-workshop teaching point. Jessica, for example, had found evidence to support her point: "Gabriel is lonely because he doesn't have company at home." The evidence was this sentence: "On the stoop of a tall building of crumbling bricks and rotting wood sat a boy." The problem was that the fact that Gabriel sat apart from the rest of the group didn't seem to prove her bullet.

I asked Jessica why she had chosen that quote, and she happily started to explain, "Well, okay, so Gabriel is sitting on crumbling bricks and rotting wood, and that probably means his family is poor. And if his family is poor, they probably work a lot of hours to try to make money, so they probably are pretty tired at the end of the day and they don't have time to hang out with him. And he probably can't have friends over because he's too embarrassed about how his building is all falling apart and everything, so that would make him extra lonely when he's at home."

I complimented the way she had stuck to her bullet, focusing her thinking around ways to support her idea and not letting herself get distracted or off-topic in her thinking. "But can I give you a tip?" I asked, and she nodded.

Making Sure Evidence Speaks for Itself

"Writers, can I have your eyes and ears? Jessica and I were just talking, and we just realized that sometimes you find a passage from the text that can, in a way, sort of, kind of, be used to support a claim. For example, you *might* be able to stretch things to say that the passage that describes Dog and Magpie relaxing in the mouth of the cave *sort of* supports the reason that Dog is a good friend to Magpie because he's caring. After all, Dog wouldn't sit with Magpie if he didn't care for her, and being a caring friend is linked to caring for someone, in a way, kind of.

"But if it takes a whole lot of explaining and fancy footwork to show that a passage from the text illustrates a concept, then that passage is not the best possible one to cite. So, writers, right now, can you look back at the quotes you've chosen to support your bullets and check to make sure they are strong enough evidence that they don't require a whole boatload of explaining?"

I told her, "When writers look for effective quotes, they try to find ones that don't need a string of *maybes* and *probably statements* to explain why they support the bullet. Your explanation for why the sentence matches your reason had a lot of steps where you were guessing, and they were guesses that made sense, not just random crazy guesses. But still, someone else could say that maybe his family isn't poor, maybe they just live in an old house. Or maybe they are poor because they don't have jobs at all, so they have lots of time to spend with him. And if they said that, you wouldn't be able to prove them wrong. So, when explaining why a quote is effective, one *maybe* or *probably* is fine, but having a whole series of them should caution you that maybe you've strayed too far into guessing. Can you find another quote to use as evidence that you could explain without needing so many *maybes* or *probably statements*?"

After a moment of looking, Jessica decided on "His name was Gabriel and he wished for some company" as more effective evidence that Gabriel was lonely at home. I gave her a thumbs up, and she copied it into her booklet for later use.

Transitional Phrases for Introducing Quotes

Show students that they can introduce quotes into their texts in a variety of ways by offering them many different options.

"You've been doing delicate, careful work, finding and selecting quotes. They're like jewels because they add so much sparkle to an essay. And like jewels, part of the work is to build a setting for each quote so that you show it off in your essay. Many of you have a phrase that you use as a setting for each of your quotes. Each time you want to reference the text, you say the same phrase to lead into the quoted passage—like perhaps you say, each time, 'In the text, it says . . .' That's a great setting for a quote.

"But here is the thing. You seem much more professional if you don't use the same setting for each quote since each quote connects to what you are trying to say in a different way. So while 'In the text, it says . . .' should be in your list of options, it makes a big difference if you have a few other options as well." I revealed a chart of transitional phrases and asked one child to read it aloud while giving children a minute to read it over.

Ways to Bring Quotes into an Essay

- In the text, it says . . .
  (In the text, it says, "And so Dog runs . . . ")
- Give a mini-summary to set up the quote.
  (After Magpie discovers that running feels like flying, it says, "And so Dog runs . . . ")
- Tell who, from what text, you are quoting and what that character is aiming to do, and then add his or her exact words.
  (The narrator in Fox conveys the setting by saying . . .)
  (Dog, the main character in Fox, shows his love for her by saying . . .)
- Use just a few words in the middle of a sentence.
  (Dog does what makes Magpie happy "every day" for months!)

---

*✲ Ways to Bring Quotes ✲✲ Into an Essay

* In the text, it says...
  (In the text, it says, "And so Dog runs..."

* Give a mini-summary to set up the quote.
  (After Magpie discovers that running feels like flying, it says, "And so Dog runs...")

* Tell who, from what text, you are quoting and what that character is aiming to do, and then add his or her exact words.
  (The narrator in FOX conveys the setting by saying...)
  (Dog, the main character in FOX, shows his love for her by saying...)

* Use just a few words in the middle of a sentence.
  (Dog does what makes Magpie happy "every day" for months!)

Ask students to try out the transitional phrases you've given them with their own quotes, sharing how they might introduce quotes in their essays.

"Right now, in your booklets, try out one of these strategies for setting a quote into your essay. Be ready to share your work in a minute!"

A minute later, I conducted a symphony share, tipping my imaginary baton toward one student, then another, starting with a few students whose work would, I knew, be exemplary and set the tone for the others.

Celia read, "Julian tried a cartwheel and fell over. He was embarrassed. He looked at Gloria to see if she was laughing but she wasn't. 'It takes practice,' she said."

John was next. "In the text, Clover says, 'I wonder why that girl always sits on that fence.'"

Then Emily read, "The narrator showed that Lupe did not give up by saying that Lupe 'tried again and again.'"

After a handful of kids had shared, I addressed the group again. "There are lots of other ways to set a quote into an essay. If you invent another way, would you add it to our list of possibilities? And remember that as you get older, you are going to be expected to quote directly from texts that you read—and that will add as much to your essays as quoting from characters, or making people talk, has added to your stories."

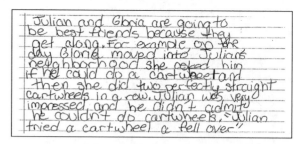

FIG. 6–1 Celia adds a quote.

USING QUOTATIONS AS EVIDENCE

Read Jill's essay again and notice that she has used a quotation that is a complete sentence—it doesn't rely on Jill's words to prop it up. It stands alone, even though it has ellipses showing that a section of the sentence has been left out. Jill could have *instead* written with a partial quote, lifting just a phrase from "Eleven," like Rachel thought it was disgusting to put on a sweater that was "full of germs" that weren't even hers. That phrase, *full of germs*, isn't a full sentence. It is just a few words that support Jill's claim. As you saw today in our share, essayists use both kinds of quotations.

Tonight, take a few of the quotes that you have copied into your booklets today. For each quote, try at least two different possibilities for how you could put it into your essay. At least one should use the full quote, with a sentence before or after to set it up or explain its importance, and at least one should use just a few words of the quote, like the "Eleven" example above.

Session 7

Using Lists as Evidence

WHEN THIS NATION WAS YOUNG, rhetoric was part of each school's core curriculum. Children grew up with as firm a foundation in oration as in multiplication. In school, they learned to articulate their ideas loudly and clearly, using their voices to gather and command attention and to rally listeners to action. And now, in the age of the Common Core State Standards, there is a heightened awareness that students must not only write well, but also speak well.

In the past, children delivered their essays at speaking contests and learned to write in ways that would appeal to the ear. Perhaps for this reason, parallelism is a crucial part of many essays—and many speeches. Think of the greatest, most memorable speeches you can, and you'll probably find yourself remembering lines that were repeated: "Ask not what your country can do for you. Ask what you can do for your country" and "I have a dream."

Essay writing remains inexorably linked to public speaking. "As new weight is given to the presentation of knowledge and ideas, students will increasingly be asked to write in ways that are memorable and powerful for both a reader and a listener."

Today's work with lists invites children to use the parallelism of the list structure to bring rhetorical power to their writing. This session also invites children to write with attentiveness to sound as well as to meaning.

IN THIS SESSION, you'll teach students that writers not only use stories and quotes as evidence, they also use lists to support their claims.

GETTING READY

✔ "How to Write a Literary Essay" chart (see Connection)

✔ Song snippets from www.jango.com (see Connection)

✔ Song lyrics (see Connection)

✔ Student's essay that includes several different lists (see Teaching)

✔ Your own essay on the mentor text, with a sample sentence that could be the start of a list (see Active Engagement)

✔ Students' booklets, to be brought to the meeting area for the share

COMMON CORE STATE STANDARDS: W.4.1.b,c; W.4.9.a, RL.4.1, SL.4.1, SL.4.3, SL.4.4, L.4.1.d,f; L.4.2, L.4.3

Using Lists as Evidence

CONNECTION

Put today's minilesson into context by saying you'll teach students about a third ingredient they can put into their essays. Along with stories and quotes, they can write with lists.

"Writers, you've already learned about two things you can put into your essays—mini-stories and quotes. Today I'm going to remind you about a third ingredient. (I feel like we're making pizza and I'm teaching you the different toppings—tomato sauce, pepperoni, and cheese.) From your study of personal and persuasive essays, you should already know that in addition to writing with stories and quotes, you can write with lists!" I unveiled our anchor chart, with this new item added.

◆ COACHING

Connections that begin with reviewing the work that the class has been doing are important but can be dull. The reference to pizza makes this connection more memorable for children. If I felt my students weren't engaged in my lessons I could have asked, "Doesn't it feel like we're making pizza?" That would invite a response from them. Sprinkling in little ways for children to be more active is important.

How to Write a Literary Essay

- Grow ideas about a text.
  - Use thought prompts.
  - Ask questions of texts.
  - Pay attention to the characters in a story, especially noting their traits, motivations, struggles, changes, and relationships.
- Find a big idea that is really important to you, then write a thesis.
- Test out your thesis by asking questions.
  - Does this opinion relate to more than one part of the text?
  - Is there enough evidence to support it?
- Collect evidence.
  - micro-stories
  - quotes
  - lists

~ How to Write a Literary Essay ~

- Grow Ideas about a text.
  - Use thought prompts.
  - Ask questions of texts.
  - Pay attention to the characters in a story, especially noting their traits, motivations, struggles, changes, and relationships.
- Find a big idea that is really important to you, then write a thesis.
- Test out your thesis by asking questions.
  - Does this opinion relate to more than one part of the text?
  - Is there enough evidence to support it?
- Collect Evidence.
  - micro-stories
  - quotes
  - lists
  - examples
- Unpack the evidence by telling the reader what it shows, using prompts like:
  - This shows that...
  - This is evidence that...
- Add transitions to glue the evidence together.

"And the good news is that you already know a lot about lists. Do you know the Charlie Brown sayings? Happiness is a warm puppy. Happiness is learning to whistle. Happiness is two kinds of ice cream. Happiness is . . . what?

"Or do you know that song from *The Sound of Music,* about a few of my favorite things?" I began singing the first verse to them. Or Pink's song, 'Perfect,' has a repeated refrain so it's a bit list-y. How does it go?" I started in on the first line of the chorus, and quickly the students joined in.

"As a writer, it is your job to ask, 'How did authors do it?' I mean—we could look around this room and list stuff we see: I see desks, chairs, a rug, books, papers. Somehow, I don't think the list we just wrote will be one that millions of people know by heart. What's so special about the Charlie Brown list, the *Sound of Music* list, and the list in the refrain of 'Perfect'? What makes a list effective?

"You already know that in a list, there are words that repeat: '*When the* dog bites, *when the* bee stings.' There are also, usually, teeny tiny details: Happiness is *a warm puppy*."

✦ **Name the teaching point.**

"But today I want to teach you that lists, like songs or poems, are written for both the ear and the heart. They need to sound good *and* mean a lot. Writers say them aloud as they write to make them sound good. And the writers think, 'How can I bring together a surprising combination of items so that the whole list makes an effect on the reader?'"

TEACHING

Point out that lists are powerful, so they are best used to emphasize important ideas.

"Because lists are powerful, you wouldn't want to include lists in your essay that are about tangential, unimportant things. You might want to list all the ways that Dog is a good friend. This way, your list would help you to further the point you wanted to make, providing evidence for your claim."

Give an example of a child who used lists in several ways and places within an essay, suggesting how the lists were made as well as sharing the finished lists.

"In Celia's essay about the story 'Gloria Who Might Be My Best Friend,' Celia knows that it is important to show that the two characters respect each other to provide evidence for her claim that Julian and Gloria are going to be best friends, so she used a list to emphasize that point. She thought of all the times when they show respect for each other. She then wrote a sentence about one of those times and copied some parts and changed other parts of that sentence to make a short list."

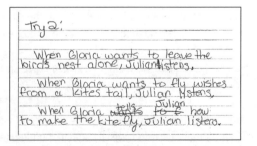

FIG. 7–2   Celia's second attempt at a list

You could also play a snippet of the song. You can get songs from the Sound of Music from www.jango.com

Of course, you'll want to reference a song that is popular with your children. Often song lyrics have a repeating line that ends with a list. You can search online for song lyrics and print them out. Having the lyrics on hand is also good if you are shy about singing in front of your students!

This session introduces a skill that has turned out to be more challenging for youngsters than I ever anticipated. You'll invent your own adaptations.

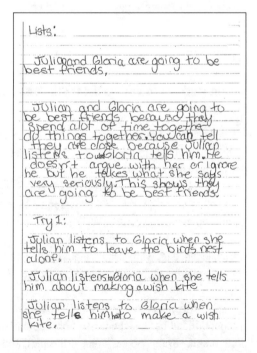

FIG. 7–1   Celia's first attempt at a list

"Celia also wanted to show that the two children do lots of things together, which is her next bullet, so she wrote a list about that. Again, she sort of made a pile of examples of things they did together, and then Celia wrote a first sentence and worked from there, repeating a lot of the sentence, trying to make it sound right. In the end, she wrote:

> Gloria and Julian peek at the bird's nest together, get red Kool-Aid mustaches together, fly a kite together, and wish to be best friends together.

Debrief by emphasizing the process of writing a list.

"The trick to writing lists within your literary essay, then, is to first decide on what the message is that you really want to say, and then collect tiny specific examples that will provide evidence for whatever it is that you want to say. Then start writing, usually writing a whole sentence about the example that comes first in the book. After you write that first sentence, read it aloud to yourself and try to figure out how to turn the one sentence into a list that sounds good.

"For example, this sentence conveys an important idea—that Gloria is happy when she is with Julian—which is another reason that supports the claim that Julian and Gloria are going to be best friends."

> *Gloria seems happy to be seeing a bird's nest with Julian.*

"We could then collect other tiny examples of what makes Gloria happy when she is with Julian and just say the starting phrase (Gloria seems happy . . .), then add one tiny example and then another."

ACTIVE ENGAGEMENT

Recruit students to write a list for the essay on the class mentor text, scaffolding their work in writing the first sentence.

"Now, let's try out how this would go for our Fox essay. One of our bullets, or reasons, is 'Dog is a good friend because he doesn't give up on his friends.' Let's try to build a list to support the claim that Dog is a good friend because he doesn't give up on his friends.

"Let's all think for a bit and when you have an idea put your thumb up." I waited until about half the class had their thumbs up and then I asked, "Will someone start us off with one example, and then we'll build off that one example?"

One child piped up with, "Dog is a good friend because he doesn't give up on his friends. He doesn't give up on Magpie when he realizes that she'll never fly again."

"Hmm . . . How shall we write that?" I paused, allowing the children to think along with me and then I wrote. "Dog is a good friend because he doesn't give up on Magpie when he realizes she'll never fly again." I underlined the first portion of it, saying "So we'll repeat this part, and we'll need a list of specific examples that can follow the repeating

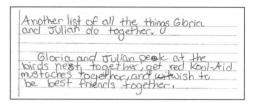

FIG. 7–3   Celia's third attempt at a list

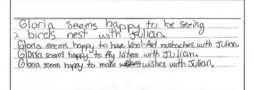

FIG. 7–4   Celia's final and best list

Much of education includes learning to apply what one already knows to new situations. When children learn to plan an essay by considering whether they could support their thesis statement with reasons and evidence, they can apply this to lots of different situations.

part. Can you and your partner brainstorm some examples, and then try saying them aloud, remembering that a good list not only makes sense, but it also sounds good so that it has an effect on the reader?"

Soon afterward I called on some children and before long, we'd constructed the list.

> Dog is a good friend because he doesn't give up on his friends. <u>He doesn't give up</u> on Magpie when he realizes that she'll never fly again. <u>He doesn't give up</u> on Magpie when she sleeps for a week. <u>He doesn't give up on</u> being Fox's friend even when Magpie warns him.

LINK

Remind the students of the options they have when collecting materials to support their thesis.

"Writers, today and whenever you write literary essays, you'll draw on lots of different options as you gather material in your booklets. Some of you may draft and revise stories, rewriting those stories so they are angled to make your point. Some of you will spend time collecting quotes and setting them, like jewels, into your essays. Others of you will try your hand at writing lists for each of your supporting ideas. Or you might even want to look for specific examples to use as evidence. I'm going to add *examples* to our chart as well so you have the full range of your options displayed on our anchor chart."

How to Write a Literary Essay

- Grow ideas about a text.
  - Use thought prompts.
  - Ask questions of texts.
  - Pay attention to the characters in a story, especially noting their traits, motivations, struggles, changes, and relationships.
- Find a big idea that is really important to you, then write a thesis.
- Test out your thesis by asking questions.
  - Does this opinion relate to more than one part of the text?
  - Is there enough evidence to support it?
- Collect evidence.
  - micro-stories
  - quotes
  - lists
  - examples

Asking and Answering Questions on the Page

THE FACT THAT CHILDREN ARE WRITING ABOUT THEIR READING doesn't change the nature of your conferences. You'll still tend to begin the conference by researching what the youngster is already working on for you to decide what aspect of that work you want to support and what aspect you want to extend. When I drew a chair alongside Richard, who was writing an essay on Cynthia Rylant's story "Slower Than the Rest," he showed me his booklet and explained to me, "I am proving that Leo matches the turtle 'cause they are both slow. I'm not sure if it is a summary or a story because it is a little of both." I knew what he was referencing—the story is about a child—Leo—who is a slow learner and about Leo's relationship with a turtle, Charlie, with whom he identifies. Richard showed me what he had written (see Figure 7–5), and I read it, thinking, "What is this young writer trying to do?"

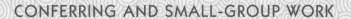

> Leo said that "It wasn't fair for the slow ones." This shows that Leo hates being slow He thinks that it isn't fair for the slow ones. Leo talked about how there are great things about Charlie. He was really saying that even slow kids have things that they are good at. Charlie represented Leo and all of the other slow kids in Leos class.

FIG. 7–5   Richard's notebook entry

MID-WORKSHOP TEACHING   Deciding on the Weak Spots in an Argument and Collecting to Strengthen Those Spots

"Writers, can I have your eyes and your attention please? The writer Philip Lopate said something I want to share with you in his preface to a book entitled *Best Essays of 1999*. Lopate read thousands of essays to select the very best for his anthology, and from all that reading, he learned that very few things can be said about *all* essays. Essays are different, one from another. Some contain long narratives; some take inventory (like a shopkeeper takes inventory of merchandise, listing what he or she has). But Lopate does say that *all* essays are both arguments and collections.

"I've been thinking about that because you guys are natural at doing both things. Just yesterday, you argued very convincingly for an extra-long recess. And you are born collectors—that's clear from the pins and badges on your backpacks.

"Because there are two things all essayists do—collect and argue—and because you are all good at both of those things, I was thinking that you might want to look over the booklets of material you have collected around each of your supporting ideas, and you might want to think, 'What *else* could I collect that might help me make my case?' And you might want to think, 'Have I aced my argument? Have I provided so much supporting evidence that no one would dream of trying to counter my claim?'

"The interesting thing is that actually, arguing and collecting are parts of the same thing. In the end, an essayist is like a trial lawyer like on the TV show *Law and Order* or movies like *Legally Blonde*. You will go before a jury (yours will be a jury of readers), and you will argue for your claim. Adam will argue that Mrs. Price took her fury out on Rachel. Celia will argue that Julian and Gloria are en route to becoming BFFs. Whatever your argument, each of you will need to present evidence to be convincing. To get that evidence, to win your argument, you need to collect: to collect ideas, facts, information, observations. Your time for collecting is almost over. You'll soon be going before your jury. Quickly reread the booklet of material you have gathered in support of each of your claims, and decide where the weak spots are in your arguments, and decide on your plan of action going forward."

I asked Richard what he thought of what he'd written, and he said it was good, but he had more stuff to say and hadn't figured out how to put it—whether it was a list or a summary or whatever. Clearly, Richard was torn between wanting to simply write his ideas and wondering what form or genre he was working within.

"Richard," I responded, "I'm really glad that you are saying to yourself, 'What *is* this that I'm writing? Because you are right that this is not really much of a story, is it? If it was a story, then you'd be telling about what one character did first, next, next—and you aren't doing that, are you? The other thing is that it *does* help to always have a sense of the kind of thing you are writing, because then you can think, 'How does a person do that kind of thing well?' For example, if you were writing a list now, you'd know what makes a good list. So you are right to wonder, 'What *am* I making?'

"And the truth is that you are making something we haven't talked about yet in this class, but it is a kind of writing that essayists do a lot. I think what you are doing is you are having a conversation with yourself on the page. And specifically, you are asking thoughtful questions and then answering them. And to me, it looks like the question you are asking is 'Why did the author put the turtle, Charlie, in the story? What does the turtle have to do with the story about Leo and other slow kids?'

> You might ask, Why did Cynthia Rylant decide to make Leo find a turtle and not a frog? the reason is because turtles are slow animals just like Leo. Cynthia Rylant wanted to use Charlie as a metaphor for slow kids.

FIG. 7–6   Richard is having a conversation with himself on the page.

"That's an important question that a reader can ask: Why did the author do this? And it seems to me that you have asked that question, and you are sharing your answer to it as well. You could even come right out and ask that on the paper: 'Why did Cynthia Rylant decide to make Leo find a turtle?' Essayists do that. They take questions and put them right into their essays." This is what Richard eventually wrote (see Figure 7–6).

Later, when I saw Richard's work, I brought his work to a small group to let them know that conversations with oneself can also go into essays and that it often helps to ask and then answer provocative questions, like "Why might the author have . . . ?"

Reading Lists Aloud

Ask children to practice reading a list they've written to themselves and then to a partner.

"Writers often read their work aloud, so they can hear the words they've written, to hear how they sound—and lists especially are meant to be read aloud. So let's do this share like a symphony. Each of you, and your lists, will be a part of the music we create. So take a second to look through your booklets and find a list you wrote today that you really like.

"First, you need to practice reading one of your lists in your head, reading your list aloud *really* well. You won't want to read it like this." I read the first part of my list very quickly, running the words together as if they were one word: "'Gabriel is lonely when he sits on the stoop outside his building. Gabriel is lonely when he eats his butter sandwich at school.' Instead, I will want to read my list as if the words are worth a million dollars." This time I read my list slowly and rhythmically, giving each word weight.

"Would you work with your partner? Give each other help and advice, so each person's words sound as wonderful as they can be.

"Writers, here's the thing. As you read your list aloud, it very often happens that you find ways to change it so the words sound even better. So read it again, this time with pen in hand, and if you find a way to make the list sound even better, then change it around. If not, move on to another list."

Not only is this share lovely and exciting for students, but it also helps them develop a felt sense for parallelism in structuring language. Developing this felt sense makes teaching parallelism later much easier. Often, powerful language and powerful structures are easier to feel than to explain.

You may find that one child's list resembles another's. This is not surprising, considering they are working with the same short texts.

SESSION 7 HOMEWORK

SAYING ESSAYS ALOUD

Singers warm up by singing some scales. And writers warm up by talking in the voice, the persona, they want to assume. Sometimes before I write a minilesson or a letter to your parents, I practice by saying the words aloud to myself. When you wrote personal narratives, you practiced by storytelling to each other, and now that you will be writing a literary essay, you need to practice by using your professor voice.

Tonight, write your thesis and your first topic sentence. Then use your professor voice to fast-write a little lecture on that topic. Do the same for your second topic sentence. As you do this, pretend you are actually giving a little course on your topics. Bring your papers to school. They will be first drafts of your essay!

Putting It All Together
Constructing Literary Essays

W HEN I WAS YOUNGER, a singing group named the Byrds sang a song—"Turn! Turn! Turn! (To Everything There Is a Season)"—and the refrain talked about the turning seasons and how there is a time for everything.

That sentiment means a lot to those of us who are writers—because in writing, as in farming, there is a rhythm to our work. The farmer plants, waters, weeds, and harvests, and the writer plans, gathers, outlines, drafts, revises, and edits. This ancient rhythm is in our bones; we remember it like a river remembers its seasonal rise and fall.

I hope the rhythm of writing is in your students' bones now as well. I hope that your students remember it and can sense that the time has come to turn, turn, turn. Today you'll help your children perform that miracle of miracles. They'll begin with a pile of notes and that will turn, turn, first into a writer's draft. "Which piece of evidence best matches my claim?" they'll ask. "What stays? What goes?"

From reading over their notes, writers will begin to develop an image of their finished essay, but that image will come also from writers engaging in that special kind of reading that writers do. They'll read the work of another author—one who has written something similar to the essay they'll be writing. As they read, they'll ask, "How has she constructed this text? What has she done with her text that I, too, can do with mine?" And they will annotate that text for themselves.

Throughout the room, your children will tack their material together. With scissors and tape, they'll place one entry next to another, constructing an essay. They have a feel for how to do this by now. It's in their bones.

Today, then, students engage in a hands-on manipulative process of constructing an essay. Soon they'll abbreviate this process, with most of the work happening in the mind's eye. Soon students will go from reading and thinking to outlining and writing an essay. But for now, you support the physical, manipulative process of constructing meaning.

IN THIS SESSION, you'll teach students some of the ways that writers create drafts out of collections of evidence. You'll also teach children ways to study published literary essays to find structures for their own literary essays.

GETTING READY

- ✔ An sample literary essay written by another student, perhaps an older student, or one that you've written, to use as a mentor text (see Teaching and Active Engagement)—one for each student

- ✔ "How to Write a Literary Essay" chart (see Teaching, Active Engagement, and Mid-Workshop Teaching)

- ✔ "When You Want to Give an Example" chart from Session 5 (see Mid-Workshop Teaching)

- ✔ Enlarged copy of the Opinion Writing Checklist, Grades 4 and 5

- ✔ Individual copies of the Opinion Writing Checklist, Grades 4 and 5, one for each student

- ✔ Scissors and tape

COMMON CORE STATE STANDARDS: W.4.1.a,b,c,d; W.4.4, W.4.5, W.4.10, RL.4.1, RL.4.2, RL.4.3, SL.4.1, SL.4.3, L.4.1, L.4.2, L.4.3.a, L.4.6

Putting It All Together

Constructing Literary Essays

CONNECTION

Celebrate that children are ready to construct their literary essays, and remind them that they already know how to check and organize the materials in their folders or booklets.

"Writers, today's the day! Essayists look over all their materials, select the parts that will work best, and then decide how to cut and combine those parts so they fit together to make an essay. Do you remember that when I wanted to write an essay about my father being my best teacher, I reread a story I'd written and chose the parts that especially showed my father being a good teacher?

"Do any of you remember doing similar work—rereading some evidence that you'd collected and thinking, 'If I want to use this story or this example to make my point, which part is especially compelling and convincing?' Do you remember thinking, 'I can cut this passage down because just this one bit relates.' We spent a lot of time, during that personal and persuasive essay unit, underlining the parts of stories, examples, and lists that seemed like they were the best evidence for the case we were putting forward.

"You all know a lot about how writers take raw materials and piece those materials together to form a draft. Before you begin to piece together your essay, let's look at another author's essay and examine how it is constructed."

❖ **Name the question that will guide the inquiry.**

"Today, instead of a regular minilesson, we will do an inquiry. Remember we did this earlier in the year when we wondered what made for good freewriting? Today the question we will be researching is what makes for a good literary essay? And what, exactly, does a writer do to be a powerful essayist?"

It is efficient to recall prior instruction, allowing students to stand on the shoulders of that learning and to connect what they know already with what they are learning. Whenever you can do this, it is wise to do so.

It is a bit hard to rally children to step into the role of being literary essayists. Still, it's important to try to help children know that they are not just producing a text; they are also becoming the kind of person who makes this sort of text.

TEACHING AND ACTIVE ENGAGEMENT

Set up writers to study a mentor text, letting them know that they should be thinking about the inquiry question.

"I'm going to suggest that you do that special kind of reading that writers do before they make a draft, looking over this draft of a literary essay and asking, 'What has she done that I, too, could do?' This essay is written by a sixth-grader, Katherine, and many teachers have said that it is a very effective essay. It is worth studying." I distributed Katherine's essay to each child and displayed an enlarged copy on the overhead projector. "Writers, you'll notice that Katherine has written an essay off of *Fox* also." It will be interesting to study an essay off of a text we all know so well.

"Writers, while I read the essay aloud, notice the different components, or parts, of the essay, labeling what you notice. Partner 1, will you specifically study the bits the author has tacked together to construct her introduction and last body paragraph? And Partner 2, will you do the same for the middle portion of the essay? Think, 'What did the author do that I could try?' and afterward we'll talk about it."

I read with intonation that highlighted the thesis and its relationship to the supporting ideas as well as the link between evidence and an idea. (The emphasis, in the essay below, is our own.) After reading just a paragraph, I paused to say, "Annotate—mark up—your text."

In the book, FOX by Margaret Wild and Ron Brooks, the character, Dog, is a good friend. <u>He is a good friend because he is caring, because he never gives up on his friends, and because he sees the good in people.</u>

<u>One reason Dog is a good friend is because he is caring.</u> Dog cares for Magpie's body when she is hurt during the fire, he cares for her emotions when he tries to cheer her up, and he cares for Fox when he needs a place to stay. At the beginning of the book, Dog is a caring friend to Magpie when her body is hurt from a fire. For example, Dog holds Magpie in his mouth, and his mouth is described as "gentle." Dogs' mouths contain sharp teeth that are normally used to rip birds apart. But Dog instead uses his mouth to carry Magpie to safety. This shows he is caring, not hurtful. Also, the text says "Magpie does not want his help," but Dog stays and helps to tend her burnt wing anyway. All of this evidence shows that Dog is a caring friend.

<u>Dog is also a good friend because he doesn't give up on his friends.</u> Dog tries many times to help Magpie. For instance, when Dog first saves Magpie, they both know she will never fly again. Dog tries to cheer Magpie up by saying, "I am blind in one eye and life is still good." Magpie rejects his kindness by saying "An eye is nothing" and going off to hide in the shadows of the cave. But Dog does not give up on Magpie. Later in the story, when she wakes from her long sleep, he "persuades her to go with him to the riverbank." Magpie sighs because she does not want to go, but Dog convinces her. This shows that he won't give up on trying to make her happy!

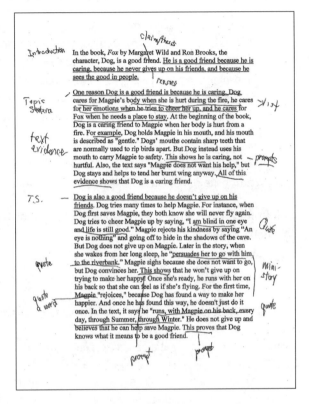

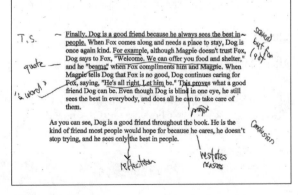

FIG. 8–1   Students annotate Katherine's essay.

Once she's ready, he runs with her on his back so that she can feel as if she's flying. For the first time, Magpie "rejoices," because Dog has found a way to make her happier. And once he has found this way, he doesn't just do it once. In the text, it says he "runs, with Magpie on his back, every day, through Summer, through Winter." He does not give up and believes that he can help save Magpie. This proves that Dog knows what it means to be a good friend.

<u>Finally, Dog is a good friend because he always sees the best in people</u>. When Fox comes along and needs a place to stay, Dog is once again kind. For example, although Magpie doesn't trust Fox, Dog says to Fox, "Welcome. We can offer you food and shelter," and he "beams" when Fox compliments him and Magpie. When Magpie tells Dog that Fox is no good, Dog continues caring for Fox, saying, "He's all right. Let him be." This proves what a good friend Dog can be. Even though Dog is blind in one eye, he still sees the best in everybody, and does all he can to take care of them.

As you can see, Dog is a good friend throughout the book. He is the kind of friend most people would hope for because he cares, he doesn't stop trying, and he sees only the best in people.

Cull from students their observations of the mentor text, marking the component parts of the text (thesis, list, topic sentence, etc.).

I marked my own copy of the essay, signaling that I expected children to be doing the same. After a moment, I channeled students to share and listened in as partners talked to each other.

Richard announced to his partner, "I noticed quotes." Celia nodded.

"Guys, if you look closely at a quoted section of the text, you can notice *how* the author quoted that part," I said.

Soon the children were noticing instances when the cited text was just a word and other instances when it was several sentences. "What ideas do you have for why Katherine would quote the parts that she did?" I asked, and the children launched into a discussion of that. I gestured for them to think more and left to crouch down next to another group.

Collect students' observations.

After a bit, I called the writers back together and asked a few students to say, quickly, what they noticed.

Harrison shared, "I noticed that the essay included a list." When I gestured for him to elaborate, he read from the essay, "'Dog cares for Magpie's body when she is hurt during the fire, he cares for her emotions when he tries to cheer her

Of course, literary essayists often structure essays differently than this one. For example, essayists often entertain points of view other than their own, writing—"Some might argue differently . . ."—and then providing a counterargument. Then, too, essayists often compare and contrast one text to other texts or to life. The actual components you teach aren't especially crucial, and I encourage you to make your own decisions. And make your own sample for children to study!

up, and he cares for Fox when he needs a place to stay.'" And then he added that he noticed that Katherine included important, not unimportant things, in the list.

Interested, I said to the rest of the class, "Thumbs up if you noticed that too." and as students put their thumbs up, I murmured, "I'll label this part of the essay with the word *list*," and then I said, "Are there other lists?" and scanned the paper.

After deciding that no, there weren't other lists, I gave a marker to half a dozen other students, asking them to jot what they noticed in the margins of the essay. Soon the essay bore the labels of text evidence that matched reason, topic sentence(s), mini-story, quote, thesis statement, elaboration, and conclusion. We also added to our "How to Write a Literary Essay" anchor chart by including how a writer unpacks her evidence for a reader.

Teachers, notice that I have decided to have students share their ideas, which I know can consume a lot of time. My biggest priority is to protect writing time, so I make a big effort to keep the discussion focused.

How to Write a Literary Essay

- Grow ideas about a text.
  - Use thought prompts.
  - Ask questions of texts.
  - Pay attention to the characters in a story, especially noting their traits, motivations, struggles, changes, and relationships.
- Find a big idea that is really important to you, then write a thesis.
- Test out your thesis by asking questions.
  - Does this opinion relate to more than one part of the text?
  - Is there enough evidence to support it?
- Collect evidence.
  - micro-stories
  - quotes
  - lists
  - examples
- Unpack the evidence by telling the reader what it shows, using prompts like:
  - This shows that . . .
  - This is evidence that . . .

~ How to Write a Literary Essay ~

- Grow Ideas about a text.
  - Use thought prompts.
  - Ask questions of texts.
  - Pay attention to the characters in a story, especially noting their traits, motivations, struggles, changes, and relationships.
- Find a big idea that is really important to you, then write a thesis.
- Test out your thesis by asking questions.
  - Does this opinion relate to more than one part of the text?
  - Is there enough evidence to support it?
- Collect Evidence.
  - micro-stories
  - quotes
  - lists
  - examples
- Unpack the evidence by telling the reader what it shows, using prompts like:
  - This shows that...
  - This is evidence that...
- Add transitions to glue the evidence together.

LINK

Send writers off to make a plan for how their essay will go and then write a draft.

"Before Katherine wrote her essay, she wrote a quick outline that she followed as she wrote. She sketched out how her essay would go, jotting key words such as *introduction*, *thesis*, *new paragraph*, *topic sentence*, *list from page 3 of booklet*, or *example from page 2 of booklet*.

"The start of her outline for her essay looked something like this."

Introduction:
Thesis
Body paragraph 1:
   Topic sentence
   List from page 3 from my booklet
   An example with a quote p. 2
   Write more about it (prompts)

"So, writers, once you have your essay planned, spend the bulk of today writing your draft. Remember always that one way you can get ready to draft is to read the work of other writers, asking, 'What has she done that I, too, could do?'"

Making Parts into a Cohesive Whole

D ON'T BE SURPRISED IF YOU FEEL you have to hustle among your children today, helping them plan their outlines and draft their essays. You'll want to remind children to draw upon prior experience with personal and persuasive essays. You might say, "Remember, you have to make sure that your evidence actually matches your reason." Or "If it is hard to find a way to use some writing you've done in your draft, it might be that your writing is great but that it doesn't advance the claim you are putting forward in your essay. It can be a great bit of information and yet not 'go.'"

In addition to saying prompts and reminders to the whole class, you can also influence what the whole class does by identifying selected students who are doing what others could be doing and then making a fuss over them. For example, you might hear a student saying aloud a planned paragraph, trying the information following one sequence and then another. "I look at the way Jessica is rehearsing how one of her body paragraphs might go. She's saying the paragraph in one way, then in another way. I bet that will make her writing stronger."

Chances are good that some of your students will need help letting go of some of the evidence they've collected. Sometimes students think that the longer the essay, the better it is, but actually they can include so much elaboration that their major points get overwhelmed. "Choose the most compelling, best-written material," I might say. "Decide which evidence will be especially convincing."

As you touch base with one table full of youngsters after another, be on the lookout for writers who find it difficult to outline their planned essay. If a few children are belaboring the outline, you may decide to help them produce one quickly, because the last thing you want is for energy for the draft to be detoured into the outline. You might say to a small group of children, "Read over what you collected for your first body paragraph and star the best-written material from the collection. Now label the things you have starred, #1, #2, and so forth, based on the order in which you plan to write that material. That'll work fine as an outline." No matter what, you won't want the process of making an outline to require more than five minutes or so of a writer's time.

MID-WORKSHOP TEACHING Piecing Together Evidence

"Writers, a predictable problem that writers encounter when they draft is how to piece together their evidence. Harrison and I were just talking about transitional words like *Another example . . .* , *Not only did she . . . but she also . . .* , *Furthermore . . .* that helped him move from one piece of evidence to another. I remembered this chart on transitional words and phrases that helped us." I held the chart up and read it to the class.

When You Want to Give an Example

- An example that shows this is . . .
- For instance . . .
- One time . . .
- This is evidence that . . .

"So, writers, remember, you can use this chart for help with elaboration or transitions as you write your drafts today. And I'm going to add to our 'How to Write a Literary Essay' anchor chart so that we don't forget that essayists glue their evidence together using transitions. Remember, time is ticking away, so push yourselves to get as much done as you can on your draft today."

(continues)

When children are cutting and pasting pieces together from across their booklets to make their body paragraphs, it is predictable that they won't use transitional sentences to flow from one piece of evidence to another, or from a list to a micro-story. Therefore, you'll need to show them how to write sentences that link their bits into a cohesive whole.

You may choose to carry Katherine's essay with you as you confer and work with small groups. You can bring the essay out to help students by suggesting they study her first body paragraph. Ask them to look for and underline the transitional words she uses. Explain to these writers that transitional words and phrases smooth the connections between thoughts. Readers don't feel tossed from one idea to the next. Students could also make a list of transitional words or phrases (*otherwise, so, therefore, on the other hand, but,* and *however*). Remind them of transitional words or phrases they used in this unit and in the personal essay unit (*for example, another example, one time, for instance, in addition to, another,* and *this shows that*). Then have the children look at their own writing and revise by adding those very important transitions.

<u>One reason Dog is a good friend is because he is caring</u>. Dog cares for Magpie's body when she is hurt during the fire, he cares for her emotions when he tries to cheer her up, and he cares for Fox when he needs a place to stay. At the beginning of the book, Dog is a caring friend to Magpie when her body is hurt from a fire. For example, Dog holds Magpie in his mouth, and his mouth is described as "gentle." Dogs' mouths contain sharp teeth that are normally used to rip birds apart. But Dog instead uses his mouth to carry Magpie to safety. This shows he is caring, not hurtful. Also, the text says "Magpie does not want his help," but Dog stays and helps to tend to her burnt wing anyway. All of this evidence shows that Dog is a caring friend.

Rereading as a Means to Revise and Then Setting Goals

Advise children of some predictable problems writers encounter when constructing essays. Ask children to help each other reread and revise with their checklists as guidance.

"Would you and your partner look at first one person's writing and then the next person's writing? Reread the sections that you assembled today and, as you read, check for a couple of the predictable difficulties that essayists often get themselves into.

"First of all, sometimes essayists find that they have collected so much evidence that each paragraph in their essay could be three pages long! Harrison, for example, has at least two pages of evidence showing that Lupe overcame her difficulties through hard work. If you're in Harrison's predicament, you can be very selective, choosing only the most compelling evidence.

"Meanwhile, however, keep in mind that you can write several paragraphs to support one of your ideas. So Harrison's thesis is that Lupe overcomes her difficulties through hard work and support from her family. If he wanted to do so, Harrison could write one paragraph showing that Lupe got support from her family early on, and then another paragraph showing she got support again later. Or Harrison could tell in one paragraph about the support she received from her father, and in another paragraph about the support she received from her brother. So in the end, you may have two or three paragraphs supporting each of your topic sentences.

"Then, too, it is important to reread a draft checking for clarity. A stranger should be able to read the essay and understand it. Sometimes, for example, a reader will be

The Opinion Writing Checklist, Grades 4 and 5 can be found on the CD-ROM.

Opinion Writing Checklist

	Grade 4	NOT YET	STARTING TO	YES!	Grade 5	NOT YET	STARTING TO	YES!
	Structure				**Structure**			
Overall	I made a claim about a topic or a text and tried to support my reasons.	☐	☐	☐	I made a claim or thesis on a topic or text, supported it with reasons, and provided a variety of evidence for each reason.	☐	☐	☐
Lead	I wrote a few sentences to hook my readers, perhaps by asking a question, explaining why the topic mattered, telling a surprising fact, or giving background information. I stated my claim.	☐	☐	☐	I wrote an introduction that led to a claim or thesis and got my readers to care about my opinion. I got my readers to care by not only including a cool fact or jazzy question, but also figuring out was significant in or around the topic and giving readers information about what was significant about the topic.	☐	☐	☐
					I worked to find the precise words to state my claim; I let readers know the reasons I would develop later.	☐	☐	☐
Transitions	I used words and phrases to glue parts of my piece together. I used phrases such as *for example, another example, one time,* and *for instance* to show when I was shifting from saying reasons to giving evidence and *in addition to, also,* and *another* to show when I wanted to make a new point.	☐	☐	☐	I used transition words and phrases to connect evidence back to my reasons using phrases such as *this shows that . . . .*	☐	☐	☐
					I helped readers follow my thinking with phrases such as *another reason* and *the most important reason.* I used phrases such as *consequently* and *because of* to show what happened.	☐	☐	☐
					I used words such as *specifically* and *in particular* in order to be more precise.	☐	☐	☐

unclear over the pronouns. 'Who is *he*?' the reader might wonder. Every writer needs to be able to shift from writing to reading, to reread your work looking for places that will be confusing, and then to revise those places for clarity.

"And, lastly, writers, you can also check your essay against the fourth- and fifth-grade Opinion Writing Checklist that you are very familiar with now, since you used it during our personal and persuasive essay unit. Remember that as you continue to draft and revise your essays, you should be thinking about all the qualities of this genre that your readers will expect you to have in your writing.

"So, writers, take some time to reread your own and each other's work, checking to be sure you've selected the most compelling and pertinent evidence, written in well structured paragraphs, that you've been clear, and that your writing has the qualities of opinion writing that are on our checklist. Then you'll spend some time alone setting goals for the work you will do tonight to revise your draft so that you can come in tomorrow with your essay finished and so that it represents all that you know how to do. Please make sure to write these goals and include them in your essay folders."

SESSION 8 HOMEWORK

REVISING FOR STRENGTH AND CLARITY

Tonight you have an opportunity to revise the draft that you assembled in school today. Revise it first for power. You are writing an essay that aims to be persuasive. You'll be most convincing if every portion of your essay is fresh, new, and compelling. So read over the bits of evidence you've collected, and decide whether some sections of it seem redundant or unnecessary. Do what any skilled writer would do—and cross those out. Then look at the evidence that is compelling and convincing enough to remain in your essay, and think, 'How can I make this even stronger? Even more convincing?' Finally, double-check your draft for clarity. Ask someone from home to listen, and read your draft aloud. Notice where you stumble as you read or when your words no longer feel like they are reaching your listener. Revise these places, aiming to be precise, clear, and convincing!

Writing to Discover What
a Story Is *Really* About

IN THIS SESSION, you'll teach students that writers seek out patterns in their books or short stories, using those patterns to develop ideas about the story's theme or message.

GETTING READY

✔ Students' short stories that they wrote their essay about in Bend I or old favorite books they have read that they want to write about, to be brought to the meeting area for the minilesson (see Teaching)

✔ List of question prompts to get children thinking about a pattern in their text, to be read aloud by a student (see Teaching) and then written on chart paper for the whole class (see Active Engagement)

✔ "Writing to Think about a Message or a Theme" chart (see Share)

COMMON CORE STATE STANDARDS: W.4.1, W.4.7, W.4.8, W.4.9.a, RL.4.1, RL.4.2, SL.4.1, L.4.1, L.4.2, L.4.3, L.4.6

THIS SESSION OPENS A NEW BEND in the road of the unit. You start the minilesson by letting youngsters in on the plan. "So far," you say to them, "you've done great writing work. But writing literary essays requires not only great *writing* work, but also great *reading* work." Then you tell your students that the best way for Katherine—the young author of the essay that has been a mentor for your students—to lift the level of her essay is not to improve her writing, but to improve her thinking about her book. "Dog is caring," you say, "is not the kind of idea that will make people stop in their tracks and say, 'Whoa.'"

With that, you launch a small sequence of work that aims to teach youngsters the power of higher-level interpretive reading. Ideally, your real point in the writing workshop is to encourage youngsters to transfer their interpretive reading comprehension skills from the reading workshop into the writing workshop. But there will be some classrooms in which children's comprehension is mostly literal. You try, therefore, in these two brief days, to give kids a bit of an experience reading interpretively. That is, you are teaching kids that readers don't just gulp down a text. Readers also pause to think, "So what is that text saying to me?" And that thinking can spark the ideas that eventually undergird writing about reading.

I recently watched a child come to the end of his novel, snap it shut, and sling it onto the bookshelf. "I'm done," he said. "I've read sixteen books. I've got to put another star by my name." Before Derrick raced off, I asked what he thought of the book. "Umm . . . ," Derrick said. He hastened to reassure me. "I read it, I promise," he said. "I just don't remember it."

Too many children are growing up believing that comprehension is an optional "bonus" to reading. I hasten to tell them that if they have neither a memory of the text nor new ideas as a result of their reading, then they haven't really read the book at all. "Reading," I tell them, "is thinking, guided by print. Reading is response. Reading is your mind at work."

Once children begin to think about texts, they tend to think about characters, inferring their character traits. That is a step in the right direction, but we (and the Common Core State Standards) ask far more than this, and children are ready for more. This session, then, challenges youngsters to think more deeply and more interpretively. This involves nudging youngsters to think not only about particular parts of the text, growing ideas that are rooted to a chapter, but to develop ideas that relate to the text as a whole. Again, once children think interpretively, they'll want to reduce an entire novel to a theme that could fit inside a fortune cookie. This session challenges them to push beyond that, growing ideas that are multileveled.

"You are teaching kids that readers don't just gulp down a text. Readers also pause to think, 'So what is that text saying to me?' And that thinking can spark the ideas that eventually undergird writing about reading."

Writing to Discover What a Story Is *Really* About

CONNECTION

Explain to children that this bend will be different than the first. They will write a second literary essay but this time will focus on raising the level of their theses.

"Writers, in the first portion of this unit, you learned a lot about how to write the component parts of a literary essay—how to angle stories so they support a claim, how to collect examples and shape them into lists, how to select quotes that make your case. Now we are starting on a new bend in the road of this unit, and my job is to help you write literary essays that are a giant step beyond any you've ever written.

"I have some writing tips up my sleeves, but what I mostly want you to know is that the quality of a literary essay comes not just from the *writing work* but also from the *reading work* you do. The strongest literary essays advance provocative, surprising, insightful ideas about a text.

"Think about the essay Katherine wrote that we studied earlier. It is a *really* well-written essay. Katherine supported her main claim with small stories and tight lists and carefully selected quotes, and she wrote inside a crystal-clear structure. The easiest way for that essay to be strengthened is not more writing work, but more reading work. The idea, the thesis, she advances—'Dog is a caring friend'—is perfectly okay, but it is not the sort of insightful, provocative idea that stops people in their tracks and makes them go, 'Wow.'

"Today and tomorrow, I'll show you some ways to lift the level of your thinking about texts. I'm going to help you develop more complicated and sophisticated ideas."

❖ **Name the teaching point.**

"Today I want to teach you that to grow and write about ideas that are central to a text, writers sift through everything that happens, looking for deeper patterns—patterns that may not immediately meet the eye. If there is a pattern of friends betraying each other repeatedly, or of relationships ending, or of people being marginalized—of anything—the writer asks, 'What is this story really saying about that?'"

I've always thought it is helpful for people—for us all—to know the bigger goals that we're aiming toward. For that reason, I want kids to be in on the design of a unit of study, grasping the way bends in the unit are planned.

When I describe literary essays in this way, I am angling children toward writing interpretive essays. By channeling them to look for patterns in stories, I'm directing them toward the work that high school educators refer to as literary interpretation.

TEACHING

Explain that writers notice underlying patterns in a text. Help children grasp this sort of thinking by engaging them in figuring out the pattern in a series of numbers and then in *Fox*.

"Thinking about the patterns that underlie a book is not easy work. The writer needs to think, 'What *could be* the pattern?' and try on one answer, another, and another. So to think about the patterns that underlie the story in *Fox*, you need to think, 'What keeps happening a lot?' You aren't thinking about the specific characters—Fox and Dog and Magpie—so much as about how this is a story about persons, about friends. So you think, 'What do the friends in this story (or the characters in this story) keep doing?'

"Let me help you get into the swing of thinking about the underlying patterns. There is a big test that students take to get into college. When I took that test—the SAT test, it is called—it contained a kind of question that I called the *pattern question*. The test makers would give students a series of numbers or pictures, and the students would need to figure out what pattern lay under the row of numbers or pictures. If a student did this well, he or she would be able to figure out what came next in that row of numbers or pictures.

"Are you ready to try one of those pattern questions? (Remember, this tests *college-aged* kids, so you are not supposed to be able to figure this out. But miracles happen, so here goes.)" Then I revealed these numbers, written on chart paper:

1, 2, 3, 5, 8, 13, 21 . . .

"What number comes next? To figure that out, you need to figure out how this system gets the next number—how the pattern goes. Turn and figure it out together."

The room turned into an uproar, and I voiced over, saying, "To figure this out, remember, the trick is to study the pattern between the numbers. Once you've found the pattern, the whole set of numbers will make sense!"

After a bit, I intervened to ask if any student had figured this out. Soon the class was talking about how when the first two digits are added, they equal the third digit: $1 + 2 = 3$, and how when the second and third digit are added, they equal the next digit, and so on.

Channel students to transfer the thinking about pattern work they just did with numbers to the text the class has been reading, noting the reoccurring actions and thinking, "What is the author saying about this pattern?"

"It's not easy to see patterns that are sometimes right there before your eyes. It takes looking and looking again. Once we do see a pattern that explains how things go together, that pattern makes everything click together.

"Let's try to figure out the underlying patterns with *Fox*. I usually start by recalling the actual plotline of the story, and as I do that, I'm thinking, 'What keeps happening?'" I ran through the plot on my fingers, as if mulling it over in front of the kids.

Dog saves Magpie.

Magpie refuses Dog's help and wants to be left alone.

Magpie and Dog get back together and Dog helps her fly.

Fox comes.

Magpie is at first scared of Fox but then goes off with him, abandoning Dog.

Fox abandons Magpie.

"What issues or events or feelings keep occurring again and again? What are you thinking? Turn and talk."

After a bit, I called on Charlie, who said, "Magpie keeps being with Dog and then not: yes/no, yes/no. She likes him, she doesn't like him, yes, no."

I nodded. "I noticed that too. There are a lot of friends rejecting each other. Magpie tries to reject Dog when she is hurt. And she really rejects him when she goes off with Fox. And she is not the only one who does that rejecting. Fox rejects her, too. And you could also say the book is about friends rejecting each other because there is a character who *doesn't* reject anyone, right? Dog accepts them all. So I think we could say that one pattern we see in this book is that some friends keep on rejecting each other, and other friends are true-blue.

"Each of you has brought a text you love. Some of you have a favorite novel of all time; some of you have one of the short stories that a friend of yours wrote about last week. Whatever you have brought, right now, will you think about a pattern you see in that text, about something that keeps happening a lot?" I gave the children a moment to think about this. "Tell the plot across your fingers, and think of what happens not as this person or that one, but as people who are doing these sorts of things." After a moment of silence, I said, "Thumbs up if you have thought of a pattern for your text." Most children signaled with thumbs up.

Help youngsters know that once a writer identifies a pattern, the next question to ask is "What is the text saying about this pattern?" Provide a sequence of questions one can ask to do this thinking.

"Let's think why the author has written a story that contains the pattern we're seeing, okay? I've given Anthony a list of ways to coach us to think about this question. He'll call out a prompt, and let's all think of this, based on our books, okay?"

Anthony read, "So what pattern do you see in your book that you want to think more about?"

Teachers, it's important that children who are writing about novels are writing about novels they have already read. The novels should mean something to the children and they should remember them really well.

I said to the class: "Answer that in your mind," and gave them time to think. Then I said, "I'm thinking about the fact that some friends in *Fox* keep on rejecting each other, accepting each other—on and off again."

Anthony read, "Can you describe some times when that pattern reoccurs?"

I said to the class, "List times across your fingers when you see your pattern, and I'll do that too." I did that thinking quietly.

Anthony read, "What do you think the author is saying about that pattern?"

Again I signaled to the class that we needed to think about this, and I did, silently. After a bit I wrote in the air, saying, "Maybe this story is saying that some people are always looking for better, better, better friends, and always giving up on one friendship to try to get a better one." Then I jotted my thoughts in my essay folder.

Anthony read, "Can you say more?"

Again, I jotted my thoughts as I wrote-in-the-air. "It could be that the author is saying that if you are always making and rejecting friends, that can end up being a hard way to live your life because you can end up feeling alone."

Debrief in ways that remind students of the big work—the main goals.

I shifted from the role of writer to that of teacher. "I'm hoping you have learned that to write literary essays that are a giant step ahead from what you've written so far, it will help if you focus on the reading work that makes for an insightful essay. The best way to improve essays that are your own version of Katherine's essay on 'Dog is a good friend' is to develop more insightful ideas about the story and to get thesis statements that are more interesting to your readers.

"One way to do that is to think about the plot of the story, to think about what the patterns are that underlie the plot, and to ask, 'What might the author be saying about these patterns?' I hope you have seen that when you do that sort of thinking, you won't know the answer. You speculate. You mull."

ACTIVE ENGAGEMENT

Orchestrate the students so that some of them write-in-the-air, following the sequence of questions you just suggested to help them grow insightful ideas about texts.

"You guys already started doing this. Will you take a quick second and bring your mind to that question again: 'What pattern underlies my story?'"

I gave the children a moment to think about that again. Then I said, "Partner 1, will you take Anthony's role and coach Partner 2 to write-in-the-air, thinking just as I did? I have Anthony's prompts written up here, but you are going to have to listen carefully and to figure out how to time these prompts. You ready? Partner 1, read off the first question!"

Teachers, another option is to write on chart paper for all children to see. I opt not to do this for the sake of time. My primary goal is for children to hear the free-floating nature of my writing, and jotting quickly in a notebook or folder allows me to move fast and cover more terrain. After the lesson, when time is not of the essence, I'll take this freewriting and chart it for children to reference in the days ahead.

Questions to help us think, "What is the text saying about this pattern?"

- What pattern do you see in your book that you want to think more about?
- Can you describe some times when that pattern reoccurs?
- What do you think the author is saying about that pattern?
- Can you say more?

As I crouched among the students, I heard Partner 1 say, "What pattern do you see in your book that you want to think more about?" And then "Can you describe some times when you see that pattern reoccur?" And "What do you think the author is saying about that pattern?"

Alex had chosen *Crow Call*, by Lois Lowry. He flipped through the pages of the book with his partner. "There is a pattern like when she buys the big men's hunting shirt and when she blows the crow call with her dad. Both times go with how she is trying to be just like her dad. So I guess that's a pattern: trying to be like her dad. I'm not sure what Lowry is saying about it, but um . . . ."

I spoke into his conversation. "I love that you aren't stopping just because you aren't sure. Later, when you get your pen, you can write, 'Maybe Lowry is trying to say . . . .' Then you can write, 'Or maybe she is trying to say . . . .'"

LINK

Prepare children to go off and write-to-think, using writing to identify and think about patterns in their texts.

"Remember that whenever you want to deepen your ideas you can look for a pattern across a text and then write to discover what the story is really saying about that pattern. We've done this thinking with one pattern in a text, but there are always many patterns that one can identify and think about.

"Let's shift to do this important thinking by writing, because even more insightful ideas come out of the tips of your pens when you get those pens moving. Alex, you'll probably write to discover what Lois Lowry is *really* saying about the ways Liz is trying to be like her dad. The rest of you, get started too." Once I saw children deeply involved in this writing, I signaled for them to return to their seats.

As you help children interpret texts, it is important to remember that there are different schools of thought in the world of literary criticism. Some people argue that by close reading, a student can detect the author's message. Others, and I count myself among them, believe that texts do not carry a single message. Texts aren't fortune cookies that can be cracked open to reveal a single moral. I believe that by close and responsive reading, readers co-construct meanings. I'm convinced that readers will not (and should not) all arrive at the same meaning for a text, because reading involves integrating all that we know from the text and all we know from our own prior reading and prior experiences. Although I do not believe there is any single message encoded into a story, I am not uncomfortable suggesting that children read closely, trying to ascertain what an author has tried to convey. With older children, I reword this, asking them to attend to what the text says, because often the author is not accessible. But with upper-elementary children, I try to help them reach toward an understanding of what the author might be saying; in doing so, I avoid channeling them toward a single consensus about "the author's meaning," because this can close down conversation and thoughtfulness.

Whichever school of thought you represent, it is important that children learn to read closely and to bring their own constructive minds to the job of asking, "What's this story really about?"

Celebrating Successes, Anticipating Struggles

YOU MAY FIND YOURSELF SAYING, "This is hard for my kids." Don't assume that hard is bad. The message of the nation's effort to adopt and implement the Common Core State Standards is that students do need to be challenged to do harder work than they are accustomed to doing. If you don't get overwhelmed by the fact that they'll struggle a bit, you'll probably find that your children are game to do ambitious work and that they'll learn in big strides because the work does challenge them.

On the other hand, when work is uphill, it is important to guard morale, to rally energy, and so we want to encourage you to look for triumphs that you can celebrate. For starters, you might assign yourself the job of reading student writing, looking for bits to celebrate.

It is impossible to overemphasize the importance of pointing out places where a child has written powerfully. If a youngster has come up with an insight that stops you in your tracks and makes you go, "Wow," be sure to tell the child this. For example, perhaps you will decide to simply circulate around the room, making little check marks beside instances in which a child's writing is more insightful than usual. "Bravo!" you can whisper. "That's such a fresh, original idea!" In this way, you can let a child know when she has used a powerful word or image or insight. Sari wrote that Zachary, a child in a divorce story, feels *hopeless*. I pointed to the term and said, "That is such a powerful word! You've said something really strong here." Sari was so fueled by my recognition of what she had done that she ended up rereading her entire entry, erasing some of her other words and substituting more powerful synonyms. I could have taken this a step further and used Sari's work as an occasion to teach the whole class the importance of selecting precise terms.

Then, too, if a youngster uses a conversational prompt to extend his thinking, you can help that student comprehend the power of the transitional phrase he has just written. If he has written, "Jenny lies in bed thinking about the boar, loose in the woods. I *realize* . . . ," you can point to the phrase *I realize* and say, "Wow! I can't wait to read what new thought comes to you, what the idea is that you realize about this story. It

MID-WORKSHOP TEACHING Remembering to Move Up and Down the Ladder of Abstraction

"Writers, do you remember back in the personal and persuasive essay unit when I talked to you about Roy Peter Clark and 'going up and down the ladder of abstraction'? At the top of the ladder, Roy Peter Clark wrote about 'eternal grief.' At the bottom of the ladder, he told the story of interviewing parents whose teenage daughter had died twenty years earlier. When their daughter had been alive, if she was out for an evening, they'd always left the porch light on 'til she got home. Since she died twenty years ago, that family has left their porch light on, continuously. Including that detail is writing at the bottom of the ladder of abstraction.

"I'm telling you this because you guys need to be writing at both the top of that ladder and the bottom. When you are at the top of the ladder," I waved my hand above my head as I had for them in the personal and persuasive essay unit, "you are writing about big ideas like friendship. At the bottom of the ladder," here I brought my hand down, "you write about Dog carrying Magpie gently in his mouth, noting that word *gently*. You write about details.

"What I want to remind you of now is that when you get going on a big idea about your book, remember that big ideas are carried by tiny specific ideas. And Richard Price has said, 'The bigger the idea, the smaller you write.' It wouldn't have worked for Roy Peter Clark to write about eternal grief and to illustrate that idea by writing just about a family who has been sad for many years. It was the specific detail of that porch light, turned on, shining continuously for twenty years, that brings home the abstract idea.

"So be sure that you shift from the top to the bottom and back. If you are writing at the top of the ladder, shift to the bottom. If you are writing about the concrete, detailed specifics of your story, shift to the top of the ladder and write about big ideas."

is so exciting to see brand-new ideas emerge!" In that way, you can help the child understand the meaning of a phrase that he could otherwise use in a rote fashion. React similarly if a child writes, "The important thing about this is . . . " Tell the child you can't wait to see what it is she selects as the most important thing, and act as if that choice is a weighty one!

When I praise the strong aspects of what a child has done, I try to be very specific and to name what works in a way that can provide guidance for another day when the child is writing about another topic. For example, Harrison wrote the following about "Flyte," by Angie Sage (see Figure 9–1).

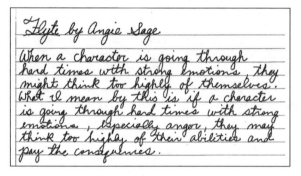

Flyte by Angie Sage

When a character is going through hard times with strong emotions, they might think too highly of themselves. What I mean by this is if a character is going through hard times with strong emotions, especially anger, they may think too highly of their abilities and pay the consequences.

FIG. 9–1 Harrison's notebook entry

I pointed out to him and to others that Harrison had used a strategy that could help them all as readers. "I love the way you are grasping for just the right words to express your idea," I said to Harrison. "It is true that authors often need to try out a few different ways of saying something before they get it just right."

With this support to goad him on, Harrison continued working with zeal. Not surprisingly, as he wrote, his ideas morphed into new lines of thinking. He began writing about how one character, Simon, is angry and jealous. Harrison contends that those feelings make Simon "think too highly of himself." (See Figure 9–2.)

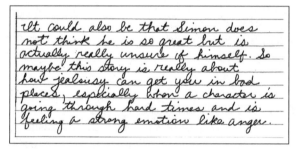

He wants to prove that he is better or just as good. Simon says that its not fair that their long-lost brother who has barely even studied Magyk is so good and ruined Simon's life goal. It was Simon's dream to learn all about Magyk and be Marcia's apprentice.

FIG. 9–2 Harrison continues to explore his ideas.

But the exciting thing was that as Harrison wrote, his thinking changed. While that is not necessarily a mark of an effective finished essay, the goals when writing to learn are entirely different. For now, the intention is for Harrison to write in ways that spark newer and deeper thinking, so it was a good thing to see this emerge on his paper (see Figure 9–3).

It could also be that Simon does not think he is so great but is actually really unsure of himself. So maybe this story is really about how jealousy can get you in bad places, especially when a character is going through hard times and is feeling a strong emotion like anger.

FIG. 9–3 Harrison's ideas grow interpretive.

When a child's thinking changes—celebrate. When he begins to think more deeply, and in more complicated ways about the mix of motivations behind a character's actions—celebrate. Your youngsters are doing complicated work, so they'll need to feel that their risk taking, their messy ideas, their out-on-thin-ice conjecturing, are all being done in a safe and supportive environment.

Using Sentence Starters to Develop New Thinking

Let writers know they can use general prompts to jump-start their thinking. Ask them to try it.

"Sometimes, when you are trying to grow ideas, it can feel like you've run out of steam. I've compiled a list of prompts that I find helpful at those times." I revealed the following chart.

Writing to Think about a Message or a Theme

- I learned from (the character, the event) that in life it is important to . . .
- Even if . . . you should . . .
- This story teaches us not only about . . . but also about . . .
- When I first read this story I thought it was just about . . . but now that I think more deeply about it, I realize that it is really about . . .
- Something that's true in this story that's also true in the world is . . .

"Return to the entry you were just working on. Try out a few of these starters to see if you can get new ideas rolling. If one sentence starter doesn't work or you don't like the ideas you are developing, just skip a line and start anew!"

As children wrote, I coached in, reminding them of a few key things. "Don't forget to say your idea in a couple different ways. Try a few different prompts on the same idea. You might be surprised what you come up with." Then later, "If you find you've written a lot of high-up-on-the-ladder kind of stuff, climb back down the ladder and try to ground your idea in some concrete details."

Teaching your students to entertain provocaative, significant questions about a text is worthwhile work, because in real life there are no questions at the ends of chapters. Skilled readers need to be able to generate as well as to muse over questions.

After a few minutes I called the children back together, praising their willingness to write freely and tenaciously.

> Some people are lonelier than others. Take this character, Gabriel, who's lonely. Some readers who read <u>Spaghetti</u> think it's about a boy name Gabriel who finds a cat, but I think it is about a boy who finds his goal in life; to have a companion. In the beginning Gabriel is pretty quiet and keeps to himself. In the middle Gabriel starts to appreciate having a companion. In the end he enjoys having a companion.

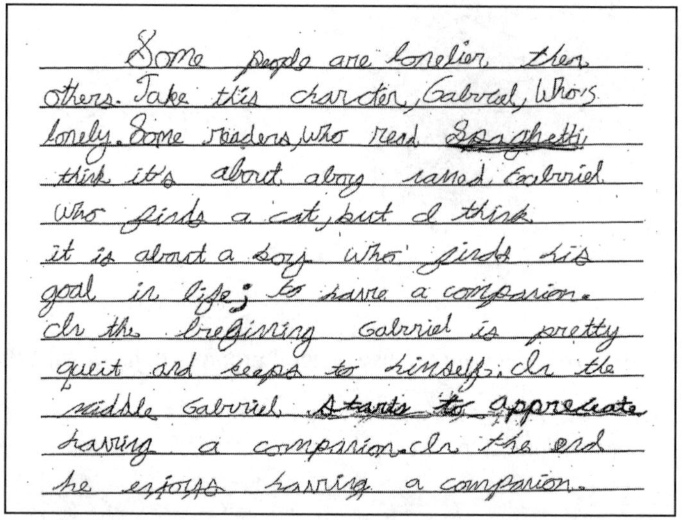
Some people are lonelier then others. Take this charcter, Gabriel, Who's lonely. Some readers who read Spaghetti think it's about a boy named Gabriel who finds a cat, but I think it is about a boy who finds his goal in life; to have a companion. In the beginning Gabriel is pretty quiet and keeps to himself. In the middle Gabriel starts to appreciate having a companion. In the end he enjoys having a companion.

FIG. 9–4 Raffi writes about "Spaghetti" by Cynthia Rylant.

SESSION 9 HOMEWORK

FINDING ELUSIVE MEANING IN TEXTS

For homework tonight, look back at the text you're studying, and this time pay attention to a part of the text where nothing much happens. Ask yourself, "Why is this section of the text here?" Don't settle for "Who knows?" as the answer. There must be a reason—so speculate. Ask, "Could it be . . . " and then say, "On the other hand . . . " Entertain the question! See if you find any larger patterns that this part might connect to.

As you do this, you may find that you come up with several central ideas. Good readers generate lots and lots of ideas about a text's larger meaning.

Session 10

Adding Complexity to Our Ideas

WHEN WE ARE YOUNG, there is a certain simplicity to life. Talking to strangers is bad. Eating your vegetables is good. Crossing the street alone is bad. Listening to your parents is good. There is a simple code to live by, and the weight of the world's more complex issues falls on the adults around us.

As we grow older, though, the complexity of the world slowly makes its way into our consciousness. Black and white yield to shades of gray. Things become more complicated. Nothing exemplifies this more in childhood than time spent on the playground.

I'll never forget the sunny, September morning in my childhood when Elena joined our third-grade class. Elena, who owned all the "wrong" clothes, talked about My Little Ponies and Strawberry Shortcake, and had the bad habit of falling asleep at the most inopportune times. No one would play with her, and I'd watch her sit quietly by herself in the play yard corner. I received all sorts of advice: "Stick up for her, stand by her side," my parents would say. "Stay out of it or you'll get teased too," my friend Jill would say. The truth of the matter was, I had happened onto one of life's gray areas. There was truth to what my parents suggested *and* what Jill warned. No perfect solution existed.

You can be sure that your students have experienced similar moments on the playground or in the cafeteria. The simple world they once knew is slipping away slowly, giving way to a more realistic, yet profoundly more complex reality.

Today, you will teach children that in books, as in life, nothing is ever black or white. As they develop ideas about their stories, they need to take complexity into mind, creating ideas that are more multifaceted and true to life.

IN THIS SESSION, you'll teach students that essayists look at all sides of a text and form complex ideas, adding depth to their writing.

GETTING READY

✔ "Tips for Developing More Complex Ideas" chart (see Teaching)

✔ "To Develop Complex Ideas" chart, to be written with students during the Teaching

✔ Sample student writing with instances of *maybe*, *but*, and *also* or other transition words that take the writer on new paths of thought (see Mid-Workshop Teaching)

✔ "Possible Templates that Can Support Thesis Statements for Literary Essays" chart written on chart paper, and individual copies for each student (see Share)

COMMON CORE STATE STANDARDS: W.4.1.a,b; W.4.5, RL.4.2, SL.4.1, SL.4.4, L.4.1, L.4.2, L.4.3.a

Adding Complexity to Our Ideas

CONNECTION

Tell children that they have learned one way of developing strong theses but that writers have another.

"I have to admit I've been holding something back from you. There is a writing lesson—a life lesson, really—that I've been wanting to teach you for a while. I've waited and waited. In fact, I'd planned to wait until almost the end of this unit. But the writing you did yesterday blew me away, and I said to myself, 'They are ready.'

"There is an advertisement that says, 'Life used to be so simple' and a picture of a young child. You can look at that advertisement and think it is saying that life was simple when we were little, but really life was never simple. It's just that when a person is young, when a person doesn't yet have the eyes to see many sides of an issue, life can seem simple. But becoming a more mature writer and essayist means becoming someone who has complicated ideas."

❖ **Name the teaching point.**

"So what I want to teach you today is that most things in life are not just one way. Things are complicated. They are not black or white. Essayists know this, and they work hard at seeing the different sides in stories, forming complex ideas about the texts they are reading and writing about."

TEACHING

Explain to children that characters in books, like people, have more than one side. As literary essayists, they need to work to uncover the multiple sides of a character.

"I read a study once about people who are socially smart, which basically means they are good with people. People who are socially smart can see more than one side of a person or an issue. They understand that people are more than one way and that they change. No one is *only* mean or nice. Instead, most people are any number of things, all smushed together. People who understand this also tend to be good readers, because they can understand texts in deeper ways. They wouldn't just say 'Magpie is fickle.' Instead, they'd try to understand Magpie in a more complex way. Why does she keep wanting what she doesn't have? What really drives her? These are questions that strong relationship builders, strong readers, and strong literary essayists, ask."

◆ COACHING

I want to teach children that challenge can be enticing, can be a reward, even!

Teachers, if your reading instruction hasn't delved into this kind of interpretive work prior to now, you might want to channel your students to think in more complex ways about the characters in the novels they are reading. If they are thinking "This character is not just one way. He's complicated," and working to develop nuanced ideas about the characters they find in their reading books, this will support their writing.

Introduce a few ways essayists make their theses more complex, and demonstrate how to take a simple idea and make it more complex.

"As I mentioned earlier, one of the easiest ways to improve Katherine's essay, 'Dog Is a Caring Friend,' would be to bring in a more complicated idea about the text. More complicated ideas take into account more sides of a text, an issue, a person. Sometimes, more complicated ideas are not just about a single character, but about life itself."

Tips for Developing More Complex Ideas

- Understand that things are never just one way—something that seems all good, all bad, is probably more complicated, more many-sided.
- Understand that what things appear to be on the outside is not necessarily what they are on the inside.
- Understand that things change across a story. Characters change. People's responses change. And those changes are at the heart of the story.
- Understand that when a character acts in certain ways, the author is probably trying to show that in life, some people act in those ways.

Tips for Developing More Complex Ideas

- understand that things are never just one way — something that seems all good, all bad, is probably more complicated, more many-sided.
- understand that what things appear to be on the outside is not necessarily what they are on the inside.
- understand that things change across a story. Characters change. People's responses change. And those changes are at the heart of the story.
- understand that when a character acts in certain ways, the author is probably trying to show that in life, some people act in those ways.

"So let's start with Katherine's initial idea: Dog is a caring friend. If we want to develop more complicated ideas about Dog being a caring friend, let's see if one of these suggestions can help us." I ran my finger over the chart.

"This first point seems like it is talking to us. If we want to make the idea that Dog is a caring friend into a more complicated idea, we need to remember that things are never just one way. Will you watch me try to push myself? See if you can notice and be able to say back what you see me doing.

"Okay. So I am supposed to consider that Dog's caring might not be all good. Let me test that thought out. You could say he is *foolishly* caring: he trusts people who shouldn't be trusted (like Fox). Could I say he learns that being all-caring gets you nowhere, because everyone basically stabs him in the back?

"This is hard! I'm thinking back to what I know about Dog to see if that can help me spark some thoughts around the notion that he can't be just one way. I'm remembering his blind eye. Hmm.

"But wait. I *am* getting a little idea. In a way he was blind to let Fox in, and in a way, that blindness ended up hurting Magpie. If Dog had been more observant and thoughtful about Fox, he might have sent Fox away. What about the idea that Dog was a caring friend, but also an unseeing friend?

Writing this, we actually came up with a lot of life lessons that sometimes (in our adult cynicism) seem all too true—none of which would be appropriate to share with kids or are likely the interpretation the author hopes we'll make of this story.

"I think there is evidence for that! Now let me try saying it in different words."

> Dog is a caring friend, but he is not observant.

> To be a good friend, you need to be not only caring but also observant.

> Being a good friend involves not just *blindly* loving someone. It is also important to watch, observe, and understand.

"I will have to think about which thesis is backed up by evidence in this story."

Ask children to name what you have done in a way that can be transferred to other texts and other days.

"Tell your partner what you saw me doing that you could perhaps do with your ideas. Turn and talk."

After the children talked a bit, I asked for them to talk to the larger group and soon collected this list.

To Develop Complex Ideas

- Take a starting idea, and decide you are going to rewrite it.
- Use one of the tips for developing more complex ideas.
- Come up with a bunch of possibilities, including unsupportable ones.
- Go back to the book and think about the specific details of it.
- If you get an idea that is beginning to feel supportable, say it in different ways.

ACTIVE ENGAGEMENT

Set students up to take the simple idea you used during the demonstration and make it more complex, scaffolding their work with class charts.

"Let's try it again. With your partner, will you take Katherine's original idea, 'Dog is caring,' and make it more complex by using one of the other tips for developing complex ideas on our chart? Follow the steps that I have outlined."

I listened in as partners worked together, coaching them to try different versions and reach for more precise, yet complex, ideas. A number of children were stuck, so I voiced over.

"Writers, there are a few sentence prompts that can help you prime the pump of your mind. Try one of these out."

> So and so is . . . on the outside, but on the inside, _____ is . . .

> When I first saw (read about, met) so and so, I thought he was . . . But now that I know him better, I realize that deep down, he's . . .

My ideas about _____ are changing. At first I thought he was . . . but now I'm starting to think he is really . . .

My ideas about so and so (such and such) are complicated. On the one hand, I think . . . On the other hand, I think . . .

"I'll take one of those stems and say it to myself, and it will get me started on my thinking."

I listened as Marie said, "Dog is caring on the outside, but I think deep down he's . . . lonely?" I moved on to overhear others.

Pull the children back together and share a few observations that will benefit the whole class.

"I heard a lot of great thinking. I also heard Celia and Richard say that Dog has two strong traits, not just one. He is caring, but he is also gullible. Marie and Chloe talked about how on the outside Dog is a caring friend, but on the inside he might just be lonely. The interesting thing is that none of us are sure our ideas are right. Like all essayists, we'll need to go back and ask, 'Is this a thesis I can prove?' Often in the midst of trying to prove a thesis, the idea evolves."

LINK

Send students off to think about how they can bring more depth to their writing by writing a more complex thesis statement.

"In today's writing workshop, you'll have a chance to read as well as write. You can write marginal notes some of the time, but write long and strong in your notebook, growing your ideas. Remember, there is nothing wrong with having a simple, one-sided thesis. Those often make for very powerful and clear-cut essays. But if you want to write essays that are head and shoulders above those you've written before, it helps to reach for complicated ideas."

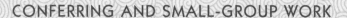

Stretching Initial Ideas

IN TODAY'S CONFERENCES, you'll probably find that some of your writers are struggling to come up with more complicated ideas, especially if they have not had a lot of practice doing this kind of thinking work during their reading workshop. You will want to scaffold students' work today, targeting the writers you think will need some extra support in developing their ideas.

I pulled up next to Brandon, who had written the following (see Figure 10–1) about *Number the Stars* and seemed stuck for what to do next.

> Anne Marie's realizing the world is a big scarey place. In the begining it didn't feel so scarey to help the others. like it would just be a sleepover. I think now Anne Marie is realizing how mean the world can be. so she's kind of growing up.

FIG. 10–1   Brandon's entry

"Brandon, tell me a bit about what you are working on," I began. Brandon proceeded to tell me about his entry, in which he recognized a significant change in Anne Marie's perspective from the beginning to the end of the book. I smiled, glad that he was able to take this first step and deepen his thinking.

"Brandon, I'm impressed with the work you've done here. What I love most is that you've pushed yourself past your initial ideas about Anne Marie's personality and instead focused in on her *perspective*. In this case, you've found that her perspective changes across the book, as a result of her experiences."

MID-WORKSHOP TEACHING
Simple Words that Set Us on New Paths of Thought

"Writers, can I have your eyes for a moment? I've put Max's writing up on the overhead so we can take a look at it. Max was writing to explore ideas in 'Boar Out There' by Cynthia Rylant. Let's take a moment and read it, and then we'll talk about what we see." I read the entry aloud, putting particular emphasis on words like *maybe*, *but*, and *also*.

> I think that Jenny is lonely. <u>Maybe</u> she goes out to find the boar to either befriend him or to show everyone she is brave. Which she is. She is brave to go find the boar. The boar is also brave because he stays there with Jenny without attacking. <u>But</u> he is not all brave because he gets scared when he sees or knows that someone is after him. <u>Also</u> Jenny knows that there is more inside the boar than most people think. Even a wild boar can have a true kind heart inside. People prejudge him, but Jenny knows not to.

"Talk to the person sitting beside you. What do you notice Max did as a writer and a thinker?" I gave children no more than a minute to talk and then pulled them back together. "I heard many of you noticing that Max allows one idea to lead to another and to another. He lets each thought lead to something deeper and better. What is important to notice are the words Max used to help him along. Do you see the way he used words like *maybe*, *but*, and *also*?" I underlined these parts of the entry and reread a bit.

> Jenny is lonely. <u>Maybe</u> she goes out to find the boar to either befriend him or to show everyone she is brave.

"See how he uses *maybe* to propose a possible reason for her loneliness?" I read the next two sentences.

> The boar is also brave because he stays there with Jenny without
> attacking. <u>But</u> he is not all brave because he gets scared when he
> sees or knows that someone is after him.
>
> "Here Max uses *but* to make his idea more complex and multisided. The boar
> is brave, *but* he is also not brave.
>
> "When you find yourself stuck and need an extra push, try using words like
> *also*, *but*, and *maybe* to push yourself into new thinking."

I chose to pursue another line of inquiry, wondering whether Brandon had a sense that Anne Marie's perspective was multifaceted as well. "What about Anne Marie's perspective?" I asked. "You wrote that she sees the world as mean, right?"

"Yes." Brandon nodded vigorously. "She has gotten older and seen a lot more of what is happening. I don't think she realized when she was little how mean people are."

"Do you think they are *only* mean, Brandon? Do you think that is all Anne Marie sees in the world?"

Brandon thought for a moment and then gave me a resounding "No!" He continued, "She sees people helping, like Peter and how Lise helped, and Uncle Henrik."

I seized the opportunity to make my point. "Brandon, developing ideas is a bit like playing those video games you love so much. You need to constantly push yourself to get to a higher and higher level. When you reach here," I put my hand level with my nose, "aim for here," I reached my hand high above my head. "One question that can help you reach higher is 'Is there more to this?' Let's try with your idea about Anne Marie. You wrote that Anne Marie is realizing how mean the world can be. Is there more to what she's realizing?"

Soon, Brandon developed the following idea

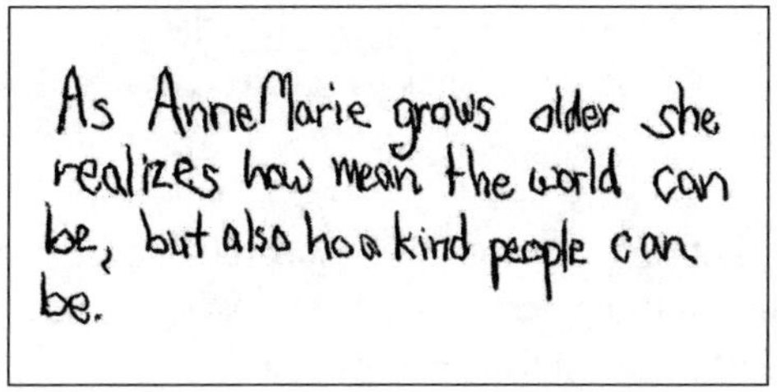

> As Anne Marie grows older she realizes how mean the world can be, but also how kind people can be.

FIG. 10–2   Brandon writes more about what Anne Marie is realizing.

Developing Ideas and Supports

Guide students to find ideas in their writing that will become their thesis statements.

"Writers, your essay folders are starting to fill with new thinking about your favorite texts. You've collected page after page of jots and ideas, and even had the bravery to try out thoughts you weren't so sure about. Because you took risks, you discovered new ideas you never would have found before.

"As essayists, a time comes when you must step back, survey the work you've done, and commit to a thesis worth writing about. Right now, would you find the *seed*, or *idea*, of a thesis?" I gave children a few moments to look at their writing.

"Now, turn to a fresh, clean page where you can try out different wordings for your thesis like we did with our last thesis statements. On this page, you'll try out all the possible ways your thesis and supporting ideas might go. We'll call it our 'try-it,' so write that up on the top and get going!

"I don't see many of you going. Hmm, how many of you think you are ready to do this work right this minute? Thumbs up if you do. Thumbs down if you don't."

A fair number of children signaled that they weren't sure they were ready, so I said, "It looks like I should guide you through the steps. Start by getting out the text you'll be writing about and your ideas on that text. Step one is to find an idea that is important to you and to write it as a thesis. Start right now by rereading and marking an idea that is important to you. If you find two ideas, that is even better, because you will need two for tomorrow's workshop. Go!"

After two minutes, I said, "Just another minute. Talk to someone near you if you need help, because hearing someone else's ideas can sometimes help. For now, don't worry about how your idea is worded."

Possible Templates that Can Support Thesis Statements for Literary Essays

- When I first read this, I thought . . . , but now as I reread it, I realize that . . .

  To many people, this text seems to be about. . . . That makes sense because. . . . But to me, the text is about . . .

- So and so is . . . because of A, B, and most of all, C.

- This text teaches readers that when (times are bad, you are alone—whatever the problem is in the first half the text), then (there will be a friend, things will get better, you can grow stronger from it—whatever the solution is in the second half the text).

  Early in the text, (the characters have this problem).

- Later in the text, (the character learns this).

- My ideas on . . . are complicated. On the one hand I think (A) . . . On the other hand, I think (the opposite of A).

Channel students to take their thesis statements and use a template to frame their thesis and supporting ideas.

After another minute, I said, "Okay, now you need to crystallize your thesis into a claim that you can prove with evidence. To do that, it often helps to plug your ideas into a template, so I'm going to remind you of those. Some of these templates will seem familiar from our personal and persuasive essay unit, and others will be new." I turned a sheet of chart paper over to reveal this list. "You have a few minutes to make yourself a thesis, using the ideas you already came to, and adjusting them to fit into some version of one of these templates. After you have made one, try to make another, because you'll be writing two essays tomorrow. They can be similar to each other."

As children worked, I moved around the meeting area, focusing specifically on helping children develop theses that would easily frame an essay. After a few minutes I asked the children to put a star next to their best two theses. "If you are not completely happy with your theses," I told them, "keep trying to get to something better. I've made a copy of these templates for each of you to have and to tape into your essay folders. They may work throughout your life, so it might help to get used to them! You might try asking your partner to try to come up with words, too, because sometimes having a new brain on something can shake things up enough to make it click into place. Each of you needs to come to tomorrow's workshop with at least two crystallized theses that could be proven with evidence from the text."

> Early in the text Maddie stays silent when the other girls tease Wanda. Later in the text she regrets staying silent. This story teaches us the importance of speaking out when you believe something is wrong
>
> · Early on, Maddie stays silent and lets the other girls tease Wanda so she can fit in
>
> · In the middle of the story she starts to regret the way she treated Wanda and wonders if she was unfair.
>
> · In the end, Maddie regrets her silence.

FIG. 10–3   Parker's template for his essay on "The Hundred Dresses"

SESSION 10 HOMEWORK

LEARNING TO MAKE COMPLEX CLAIMS

Sometimes when you are looking at a menu, it's tempting to try the one or two things that catch your eye first and to stick with those without branching out. But sometimes, the dish you never thought you'd like turns out to be your favorite once you've tried it. So tonight, look again at the menu of templates for thesis statements, and this time try out every single item on the menu. Try to make each thesis better than the last! You might be surprised by which one ends up being the best at expressing your idea. If you are able to draft a thesis for each template, congratulations on being a true explorer!

Flash-Drafting Literary Essays

IN THIS SESSION, you'll teach students that essayists flash-draft essays, getting their thoughts down quickly on paper so they can revise later.

GETTING READY

✔ "How to Write a Literary Essay" anchor chart (see Teaching, Active Engagement, and Mid-Workshop Teaching)

✔ Mentor text, *Fox*, or the book you used for your demonstrations in Bend I

✔ Sample student's essay from Session 8 to use as a mentor, either projected on an overhead or copies for each student

✔ Charts from the unit, available for students to access and blank chart paper (see Teaching and Active Engagement)

✔ Loose-leaf paper for students' flash-drafts

✔ "Ways to Push Our Thinking" chart (see Teaching and Active Engagement)

✔ Small copies of the "How to Write a Literary Essay" chart, one for each student, to be taped to the inside of their essay folders (see Share)

COMMON CORE STATE STANDARDS: W.4.1, W.4.4, W.4.10, RL.4.1, RL.4.2, SL.4.1, L.4.1, L.4.2, L.4.3, L.4.6

WHEN TEACHING SOMEONE TO SKI, you make your way slowly down the mountain together. When the incline is gradual, you say, "Ski to those signs over there, then wait for me." The child skis along, with you a few feet behind. You calculate the risks in the interval between where she is and the appointed meeting spot and think, "She's okay for now," so you ski on in front, coming to a stop beneath the signs. She joins you there, and for a moment you admire the view, and then you ask, "Ready?" and you give her some pointers. "This time, when you want to go slowly, tip your skis to dig your inside edges in, like this," you say, and demonstrate. She emulates you, though you both know it is different once there's some speed involved. "Why don't you ski over to the top of that ridge?" you say.

The fact that you inch down the mountain in that sort of a stop-and-go fashion does not mean that this is your image of proficient skiing! Perhaps you'll make a few trips like that one, but it won't be long before you and the youngster talk at the top of the slope, midway perhaps, and then again at the bottom, with the youngster traveling from one ridge to the next without you defining the pause spots.

In the personal and persuasive essay unit, your children already journeyed down the essay mountain with you asking for frequent stops to regroup and resolve. And they already took the step of traveling the mountain more quickly. Today's session is not the youngster's first or even second experience writing an essay straight through. Still, this mountain is a steeper one than the first, and you've increased your expectations for how the child makes it down the mountain. So you will see that across today, there is a progression from more to less scaffolding.

In just a single day, your children will write two entire literary essays. Both are meant as flash-drafts and the best of the two will be revised in significant ways before it becomes the writer's publication. Knowing that, by the second half of this lesson, try to allow the youngsters to make their way down the slope without much assistance. You'll learn by watching their progress! Expect to learn as much about your teaching as about the learner's strengths and weaknesses.

Flash-Drafting Literary Essays

CONNECTION

Tell youngsters that in life, they'll sometimes be expected to whip up literary essays in no time.

"For the past two days, you've worked to grow more complicated ideas about your texts. Today I want to tell you about one more challenge that you all will face as you get older. There will be times when you are asked to write an entire essay—start to finish—in about ten minutes.

"Ten minutes! The essays you wrote earlier in this unit took us more like ten days. So today I want to teach you how to write flash-draft essays that draw on everything you know about effective essays. I'm going to help you get into your bones all you know about writing essays so that you can do all of that work—writing with a thesis statement and topic sentences, writing with examples, micro-stories, quotes, and lists and so forth—on the run, as you write the essay."

Explain that to teach kids to do this, you'll return to the idea of flash-drafting, helping kids write two flash-drafts in one day.

"To do this, you'll be flash-drafting, like you did earlier this year when you worked as a class on the 'I love ice cream' essay. We called that Essay Boot Camp, so I suppose we should call this High-Demand Essay Boot Camp because you'll again write an entire essay in ten minutes. But this time, (1) you'll write not one but two essays in a day; (2) they'll be literary essays, which are harder than personal essays; (3) you won't all write the same essay, so you won't be able to support each other as you did when you wrote "I Love Ice Cream"; and (4) you'll write one of today's essays without any help from me.

"And meanwhile, your essays will be about the complicated ideas you've been growing over the past few days.

"If minilessons and writing workshops were ski slopes, it's reasonable to say that today would be labeled with a triple black diamond."

◆ COACHING

The job in the connection is to engage kids. We pull out all the stops—humor, drama, pathos, activities. Today we try challenge. The point is to ruffle their feathers, to effectively communicate, "Listen up."

Notice again the assumption that hard is good. You won't find a single place in this series where we say to kids, "Today I am hoping you'll do such and such. It's easy. You'll do it quickly." We do believe that in life, people want nothing more than a project to sink their teeth into. People want work that is good. One of the greatest joys is to work shoulder to shoulder with others, on work that is challenging and important. Best yet is the joy of seeing yourself become palpably stronger, more skilled. So yes, we list all the hard parts of today's triple black diamond trail, doing so with total confidence that the harder the job, the more energy and resolve kids will bring to it.

Notice too that whenever possible, we try to keep the language consistent across units and across years. It is true that every teacher may not like the phrase boot camp—*but we caution you against naming this something else. It is incredibly helpful to kids if each teacher in a school does not invent his or her private language, naming the same thing a score of different names. When that happens, it often takes kids until November to grasp that their new teacher is talking about the same thing as their last teacher, just using different words.*

♣ Name the teaching point.

"Today I want to teach you that to whip up a full-blown, well-developed essay, it is important to remember that if you don't have a dream—a vision—of what that essay should be, you'll never create the essay you imagine. You need to first create an image in your mind of how the whole essay will go."

TEACHING AND ACTIVE ENGAGEMENT

Remind kids of the work they'll do, and what they'll learn. Point them to charts and mentor texts to help them reach that goal.

"Remember, your goal will be to whip up a couple of complete literary essays today—and in so doing, to learn how to do all that you have learned fast, on the run. Before you can do any of that, it will be important for you to have the idea of what you are trying to say. So return to your 'try-it' page and read over the theses you grew."

"Thumbs up if you have at least a very rough draft of a thesis statement in mind." Many children signaled that they did. "If you don't have a dream or vision of how your essay's going to go, how are you going to make the essay a reality? You need an image of what you are working toward, so you can then try to make that dream come true. Look at the anchor chart and the mentor text from earlier in this unit if you need to, to develop an image of what you are aiming to write.

"How many of you think you could write an essay in the next ten or fifteen minutes? Thumbs up if you do. Thumbs down if you're not so sure you're ready. Hmm, not many. There are a lot of skeptics in this class. Don't worry, I'll coach you this first time to help you remember how writers do it. Let's get going!"

Begin coaching students step by step to write a literary essay, starting with the title, author, thesis, and first body paragraph. Push for fast writing.

"Begin by writing the title, the author of the text, and your thesis on the loose-leaf paper I handed out. Katherine's essay can be a model—only, you will use your thesis and your text. Go ahead." A few seconds later I called out, "I need to see all pens moving on the page. Just the title of the book and then your thesis statement. Write, write, write."

I walked around the carpet and announced, "Once you have written your thesis, you know how to start a body paragraph. The topic sentence for the body paragraph will come right from your thesis. Our chart can help you." I recruited two students to write their fast draft on chart paper in front of the class.

"I see many writers already on their first body paragraph. Now I'm sure they are going to add either an example or a mini-story, a quote or a list."

I leaned in and whispered to Celia, "You are stopping too much. Instead of thinking about what you are going to write, then freezing the thought, then recording it, you need to let ideas come to the tip of your pen as you keep writing, even when you are not sure what you will say next. Let your pen go. Think with your pen."

~ How to Write a Literary Essay ~

- Grow ideas about a text.
  - Use thought prompts.
  - Ask questions of texts.
  - Pay attention to the characters in a story, especially noting their traits, motivations, struggles, changes, and relationships.

- Find a big idea that is really important to you, then write a thesis.

- Test out your thesis by asking questions.
  - Does this opinion relate to more than one part of the text?
  - Is there enough evidence to support it?

- Collect evidence.
  - micro-stories
  - quotes
  - lists
  - examples

- Unpack the evidence by telling the reader what it shows, using prompts like:
  - This shows that...
  - This is evidence that...

- Add transitions to glue the evidence together.

Teachers, one of your major jobs as a boot camp instructor is to push your writers to write more than they would have alone and to write faster. So throughout this boot camp you will push that agenda. You are a cheerleader for your children to write fast and a lot in a short amount of time. This experience will convince them that they can do it!

Asking two kids to do this on chart paper is a way of providing extra scaffolding for someone needing that help. If a youngster feels stuck, he or she can essentially adapt what one of the two students are doing.

I spotted a few children using their time ineffectively, and I wanted to make sure that all of the writers knew this was a major time waster. "Writers, don't waste time erasing—cross out if you need to, and move on. Come on guys, let's write long and strong!"

Watch the kids write and tailor your prompts and nudges based on what you see. If they aren't unpacking evidence or citing directly, push for those strategies.

I stood below the "Ways to Push Our Thinking" chart and said, "I'm noticing that many of you are giving examples from your stories, but most of you aren't unpacking how the example shows that the claim is true, so use a thought prompt like, 'This shows . . .' 'This makes me think . . .' 'This proves . . .' 'This is important . . .'" Noticing that a couple of these were not on our list, I added them.

At a key turning point, make sure one of the children who are writing on chart paper does the work you want everyone doing, and call the class's attention to that model.

I stood beside the easel Ali was writing on and said, "Holy moly! Ali is wrapping up her first body paragraph by restating her thesis and her topic sentence. I underlined a few key sentences she'd written.

I then leaned in and put an X about ten lines past where Raffi, Marie, and Tony were writing. I asked them to try to write all the way up to or past the X by the next time I passed by.

Teachers, it is best to not stay seated during the boot camp. Getting up and walking around allows you to support individuals and allows you to note what kids seem to be doing well and what they are not doing so that you can use these observations in your voiceovers.

Teachers, if we want our children to use the charts in our room, then it is important that we take every opportunity to illustrate how useful they can be.

Teachers, sometimes your mere presence makes children work harder because they feel seen. Some learners need more of what I call an "I see you factor." They need to know you are watching and they are being held accountable for doing the work.

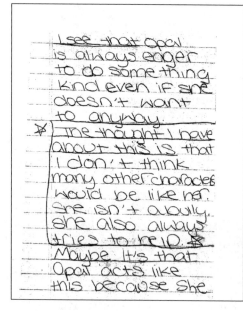
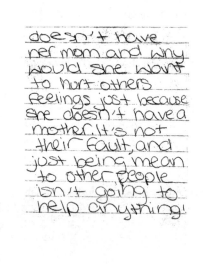

FIG. 11–1 Lu pushing his thinking about Opal from *Because of Winn Dixie* using prompts

I again walked around and whispered to a couple of children to check out what Ali or Max were doing. I said, "See how Ali wrote, 'One example from the text is . . . ,' and then she wrote about that example? You can do that too. A few seconds later I quickly voiced over, "Writers, remember, you have to make sure that your evidence actually matches your reason.

Teachers, when you see a child doing something positive, you'll want to compliment her in a voiceover so that others will hear and pick up on what she has done and do it themselves.

"Writers, make sure you are moving to your second body paragraph. Again, use our chart if you need help with your topic sentence. The topic sentence for this paragraph will relate to a later portion of your thesis. Remember to indent this topic sentence.

"Writers, eyes on me for a second and pens up." I paused and waited for all eyes to be on me. "You can shake your hands out as I talk to you for a second. Here's a tip: a good interpretation is able to be proven across the text, so make sure you reach for examples from all different parts of the text. An easy way to do that is to write, 'For example, in the beginning . . . , For example, later in the story . . . ,' and 'For example, in the end . . . ' Your idea isn't as convincing if you are only able to prove it by citing examples from one part of the story. Let's get back to work."

I could have said something like "Parker went back to a Post-it he'd left in his book, searching for a quote that he can cite. I know he is just about ready to pick his pen up and quote the text, and then he'll talk about the cited section by discussing what it shows."

When time is almost up, push for goal-driven, fast and furious writing.

A minute or so later I voiced over, "Writers, we only have four minutes left. I see that many of you are in the middle of your second body paragraph. Raise your hand if you have gotten at least that far."

Most hands went up. I said, "Impressive!"

I looked around the room, and I could tell my writers were getting fatigued. So I called out, "Let's go, writers. Let your pen fly down the page. If your hand is starting to hurt from writing so much so fast, that is a good sign. Shake it out like this." I illustrated.

I walked around for a bit, coaching individual children to add lists, mini-stories, quotes, and their thinking to their essay. Then I signaled to the children that there were sixty seconds left and that they'd better move on to their conclusion. Most of the children started to write even faster. I called out thirty seconds, and then said, "In ten, all pencils go down, Nine, eight, seven, six, five, four, three, two, one." Most children dropped their pens and pencils and shook out their hands. A few children kept writing, trying desperately to finish.

Debrief by celebrating the sheer volume of students' writing.

"Writers, look how much you wrote in ten minutes. No, really, look at how much you wrote. Look at what you wrote yesterday and compare it to what you wrote today in just ten minutes." I gave them a minute to do that and then said, "Give yourselves a pat on the back."

LINK

Set children up to study what they've done with a partner, labeling the parts of the essay (topic sentence, micro-story, etc.) as they'd done earlier with the mentor essay.

"So, writers, you are going to spend some time working with your partner studying your flash-draft and your first essay and marking up your drafts by noticing the different component parts of the essay and labeling what you notice, just like we did when we studied Katherine's essay. Then you will discuss and jot down on a goal sheet what you will do in your next essay to improve the quality of it and plan for how you will do that work.

"For example, I might notice that in my conclusion I just restated my thesis and did nothing else. One thing I could do is to study what Katherine did in her essay (or study the essays of my classmates) to learn other ways to conclude an essay.

"After about five minutes of partner work, it will be time for you to go back to your 'try it' page and get the next thesis statement you starred and flash-draft it. Let's go off and get to work immediately. I will signal you when it is time to start your next flash-draft."

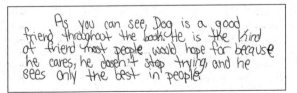

FIG. 11–2   Katherine's ending

I could have said, "Writers, don't forget the power of because. *Writing down the word* because *forces you to say more. So don't just write one* because. *Follow that one with another and another." I would have liked to put a Post-it on the pages of Amelia, Alex, Celia, Chloe, and William's writing that said, "Because . . . Because . . . " I didn't because I saw energy waning and time running out.*

Katherine's ending actually reads like this: "As you can see, Dog is a good friend throughout the book. He is the kind of friend most people would hope for because he cares, he doesn't stop trying, and he sees only the best in people."

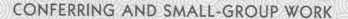

Coaching Writers to See More and Do More to Ratchet Up Their Work

AFTER TODAY'S MINILESSON, students will work together with a partner to review the essay they just wrote, contrasting it with their earlier essay and with the mentor essay. The fact that partners will be doing this work collaboratively means that students' thoughts will be voiced—and easy, therefore, for you to listen in on, to assess, and to coach. You'll want to observe students' assessments of their own and each other's drafts to understand each individual's image of an effective essay. You will probably find that some students can name qualities of good writing and components of effective essays that they haven't yet been able to produce. It can be tempting to be frustrated at them for talking the talk and not walking the walk, but the truth is that it is a big deal for a child to be able to see what needs improving in an essay, even if that child is more able to talk about those improvements than to accomplish them.

When partners are meeting today, one of your main jobs is to help individuals see how they have grown as essayists. Seeing yourself getting better at something always inspires you to do better work. It is like when you are on a diet, hating every second of it, and after a week you get on the scale and you have lost four pounds. Your attitude changes. You don't mind nearly as much skipping dessert because you saw results. So one thing you can do today is to point out to children how much growth you see in their writing.

If the growth since the start of this unit has not been dramatic, then look back to the start of the first essay unit, or to a student's early on-demand opinion writing. Say to the writer, "You used to . . . but now you . . . " Ideally, you will see that this most recent flash-draft is, in some ways, more advanced than the essay the writer worked on across ten days at the start of this unit. If that is the case, you will especially want to celebrate growth and help writers know this means that their trajectory promises a lot more rapid growth. When complimenting growth, be sure you are very specific. How is the thesis statement more advanced? What is it that you notice the writer is beginning to do that is working?

The conferring you will do when children are flash-drafting harkens back to what you did during the first session in the personal and persuasive essay unit and, more

MID-WORKSHOP TEACHING
Flash-Drafting a Second Literary Essay

"Writers, it is time to begin your second flash-draft of the day. Remember what I said earlier: if you don't have a dream—a vision—of what that essay should be, you'll never create the essay of your dreams. You need an image of what you are working toward, so keep your goal sheet next to you, where you jotted down what you wanted to do to improve the quality of your essay a few days ago, and keep the mentor text out on your desk so you can use and refer back to it as you are writing. You might also want to look at the 'How to Write a Literary Essay' anchor chart. Keep all of these in mind as you now flash-draft. Here are a few predictable pitfalls I am noticing."

- Don't stop mid-sentence. Just keep going. Keep your hand moving down that page.

- Don't overwhelm your essay with too many examples, or your point will be lost.

- Don't just plunk an example, quote, micro-story, or list into your essay without explaining why it is there.

"This time, however, you will be in charge of your own boot camp. You'll say to yourself, 'Let's go. Keep writing. No more examples. They are swamping my essay. I need a good quote. I need to write my thinking. I'd better write faster.' Okay, writers, boot camp has officially commenced!"

recently, to your conferring during Session 7 of this unit. In both those instances, students were drafting essays. For today, we strongly recommend that you plan on moving fairly quickly among the writers. This is not a good day to settle in alongside only two or three children. They will all need to feel your presence. And also, they all need a lot of time for writing, so they can't participate in prolonged conversations with you today.

As you move among the writers, notice what they are doing and think of the tips you can give. Sometimes you'll whisper in a tip. Leave a lot of responsibility to the writer. For example, you might say, "I notice that you are giving a lot of examples in a row. Be your own instructor and think about what you could do to fix that." Alternatively, you might say, "Reread your first body paragraph and think about what you need to do to improve that paragraph and do it." Then you'll want to step back and watch to see what the writer does. You can give the writer a thumbs up and then jot down what the writer did in your conferring notes.

You'll also want to encourage children to leave their goal sheets from Session 8 out as they are writing, and their essay plans from the templates in Session 10. Draw on that information as you confer and coach.

You may still find the need to voice over to the whole class a few helpful tips, but try to keep them at a minimum, because you really want the writers to work on getting into their bones all that goes into writing a good literary essay. Too much coaching may foster a reliance on you, and instead you want to provide a temporary scaffold to support this complicated work of essay writing and then remove it so children become more independent and self-reliant.

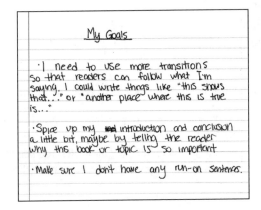

My Goals

· I need to use more transitions so that readers can follow what I'm saying. I could write things like "this shows that..." or "another place where this is true is..."

· Spice up my introduction and conclusion a little bit, maybe by telling the reader why this book or topic is so important

· Make sure I don't have any run-on sentences.

FIG. 11–3   Parker's goals

Choosing an Essay to Revise

Channel children to choose one of their flash-drafted essays to revise over the next few sessions.

"Writers, you have a tough decision ahead of you. You have to look between your two flash-drafts from today and pick the one you think would make for a better literary essay if you worked on revising it over the next few days. One way you can decide which is the potentially better essay is to look at your theses. You need to decide which one will make for the most compelling essay. To make this decision, you need to think about which essay idea is more complex and more true to life, as well as provable.

"Then take the one you have chosen and, using the anchor chart, make a plan for the revision work you will need to do to move this essay from good to great. I have made copies of the chart for each of you to have and tape into your essay folders. Why don't you get at it?"

SESSION 11 HOMEWORK

 ## MAPPING A REVISION PLAN

Tonight, think back over the plans you made during our share and turn those into written plans for revising your essay. You'll want to figure out improvements to tackle first, next, and so on. You may get new ideas and revise your plan as time goes on, but what you come up with tonight should be enough to take you through the next two or three days of writer's workshop, helping you use your writing time as productively as possible.

How to Write a Literary Essay

- Grow ideas about a text.
  - Use thought prompts.
  - Ask questions of texts.
  - Pay attention to the characters in a story, especially noting their traits, motivations, struggles, changes, and relationships.
- Find a big idea that is really important to you, then write a thesis.
- Test out your thesis by asking questions.
  - Does this opinion relate to more than one part of the text?
  - Is there enough evidence to support it?
- Collect evidence.
  - micro-stories
  - quotes
  - lists
  - examples
- Unpack the evidence by telling the reader what it shows, using prompts like:
  - This shows that . . .
  - This is evidence that . . .
- Add transitions to glue the evidence together.

116

Session 12

Beginnings and Endings

JUST AS STORIES OFTEN RELY ON TRADITIONAL BEGINNINGS—"Once upon a time . . ." and the like—so, too, literary essayists can draw on the traditions of their field. When high school and college students are taught to write essays on *Hamlet* and *Beloved*, teachers tell them to begin their essay with a few sentences that situate this essay within its larger context. This is exactly what I do in this minilesson—in fact, in this very paragraph! My writing is shaped like a funnel. First I talk about texts in general, then narrow in to talk about the lessons older children can be taught about literary

"In this session I try to teach children to write opening sentences that situate their essays within larger contexts."

essays. If you keep reading, you'll see that I continue funneling you, my reader, in toward the specific point I plan to make today. Specifically, in this session I try to teach children to write opening sentences that situate their essays within larger contexts.

I also show children that once they've written an introductory passage, it follows that they write a corresponding closing passage. Finally, I invite children to spend any extra moments polishing their essays. They'll especially learn more about making citations and about using the specialized language of literary scholars.

IN THIS SESSION, you'll teach students that essayists think carefully about their introductions and conclusions, giving readers the larger context for their claim in their introduction and leaving their readers with something to think about in their conclusion.

GETTING READY

✔ Opinion Writing Checklist, Grades 4 and 5 (see Connection)

✔ Charts from the unit, for students to reference

✔ Examples of leads written for secondary school essays (see Teaching; see CD-ROM for more essays)

✔ Example of one child's process for writing and revising a lead, using an essay children have studied (see Teaching)

COMMON CORE STATE STANDARDS: W.4.1.a,d; W.4.5, RL.4.2, SL.4.1, L.4.1, L.4.2, L.4.3.a,c; L.4.6

Beginnings and Endings

CONNECTION

Celebrate yesterday's hard work and help writers anticipate and take ownership of the work that lies before them: revision.

"My friend Amanda once climbed Machu Picchu. She told me that as she stood at the base looking up at the majestic mountain that stands 7,970 feet high, she thought to herself, 'There is no way I can climb this.' But Amanda set out on the trek anyway. Out of sheer resolve and grit, she reached the summit. When she looked down at the ground she had climbed, she was in awe of what she had accomplished.

"I tell you this story because at the start of yesterday, when you heard you were expected to write two literary essays in a single day, you probably felt just about like Amanda did when she stood looking up toward Machu Picchu thinking, 'There is no way I can climb that.' But like Amanda, you went forward, with grit and determination, and you did it. You reached the summit. And now, looking back, I'm pretty sure you feel some measure of awe over what you've accomplished.

"I don't think I need to tell you what the work will be that you do today and tomorrow on your literary essays. You've drafted, so now what?"

The students chimed in that now they'd revise, and I gave them a thumbs up. "Look over your essays, and think about the revision work you know your essay needs you to do," I said. As they did this, I voiced over their work, saying, "I'm pretty sure you are recalling our Opinion Writing Checklist, thinking, 'Have I done all the things on that checklist?'" I gestured to it. "And I'm noticing some of you are glancing up at our charts and mentor essays, and some of you are reviewing the revision plan you made yesterday—all wise."

This is overstatement, to be sure, and if your kids didn't blow you away yesterday you will probably want to temper it. There is one thing I really like about it, however, which is that the message continues to be that there are few pleasures in life more satisfying than that of pushing oneself to accomplish a big task. I've recently read about some people who are researching what it takes for kids to succeed in school, and they have found that there are character traits that are every bit as important as study skills. And the character traits they believe matter are not those normally fostered in character education. That is, a good deal of character education spotlights the importance of accepting others, being generous, being polite—and of course those traits matter. But there are others that also matter—ones that schools do not necessarily make a great point of fostering—and they include grit, perseverance, dedication to a task, and a capacity to work hard. This mountain metaphor is one of many ways in which this series values those traits.

Explain that you want to add one more kind of revision to their list, and proceed to explain that essayists often work on the "bookends" of an introduction and conclusion.

I didn't wait for children to be finished rereading before pressing on. "So today you can begin making any of those revisions. I want to add one more item to your list, and that is that I want to teach you to work on your introductory paragraph. That is the paragraph that ends with the thesis statement, which you've all written already. Often essayists do as you've done, and write the body of their essay and only later return to work on the introduction and conclusion that bookend the essay. And there are some techniques that kids learn in high school or college about how to write introductions and conclusions. I thought I'd teach those to you, if you are game."

Set the stage for giving kids a repertoire of ways to start and end an essay by reminding them they already have a repertoire of ways to start a narrative and to write a thesis.

"You already know a lot about how to begin and end pieces of writing. All your life, you've worked on writing the start and finish to stories.

"The other day, you learned a few templates that writers of literary essays often find helpful when they are trying to crystallize their thoughts into thesis statements, and that is a big part of an essay's introduction. For example, you learned that essayists often find it helpful to organize their essay so the essay will take readers on the same journey of thought that the writer once traveled. In those instances, it works to use a thesis that says something to the effect of, 'When I first read this, I thought . . . but now as I reread it, I realize . . . ' 'I *once* believed . . . but *recently* I've come to think that . . . ' or that says, '*Early* in the text . . . *Later* in the text . . . '"

❖ Name the teaching point.

"Today what I want to teach you is this: before the thesis statement literary essayists usually put their particular essay, and/or the particular text they are writing about, into context. They write a generalization about literature, or stories, or life—one that acts as the broad end of a funnel, channeling readers so they are ready for the specific point the essayist sets forth in the thesis statement."

TEACHING

Refer to the panoramic view at the start of some movies and to the way the camera later zooms in on a single character making his or her way through that larger context, to help writers sense the function that lead paragraphs often play in literary essays.

"You know how some movies begin by showing the whole landscape, and then the camera seems to zoom in on some specific place—perhaps a winding country road—and eventually we see an old man cycling down that road. In a similar fashion, literary essays often begin by showing the whole landscape, and then the camera zooms in. When a literary essay begins with a wide view, it often means the essay says something general about how literature tends to go, or about stories, or about life. That big worldview is chosen because it provides a big-picture context for this particular essay, this particular journey down a road of thought."

Tell the story of how one child went about writing the lead to a literary essay. Highlight the steps taken, including asking, "What is my essay really about?" and brainstorming a variety of choices.

"When Jill worked on her essay, she had already written her thesis."

> Many people read Sandra Cisneros's essay "Eleven" and think it's about a girl who has to wear a sweater she doesn't want to wear. But I think the story is about a girl who struggles to hold on to herself when she is challenged by people who have power over her.

"Because Jill wanted to begin her essay as those movies begin—planning the bigger context, then funneling in to this particular essay—she first thought, 'What is the biggest thing I am talking about here?' She knew she couldn't start trying to make some lovely panning shot like in those movies unless she knew the bigger arena in which she wanted to set this particular essay. She knew the essay talked about a girl who struggled to hold onto herself when she is challenged by her teacher, but was she going to pop out the part about how teachers treat kids? How girls think and feel? How people in power treat people out of power? Or something else? Depending on which of these she chose, she would have put her essay into a different landscape.

"Jill decided that she wanted to highlight—to pop out—just the idea *that people in life—all of us—struggle.* Jill gathered a cluster of friends, and together they brainstormed a bunch of possible lead sentences that talk about the big picture of characters and their struggles. They suggested these possible leads":

In the first edition of this book, we displayed some leads to essays that my sons wrote in high school, just to give kids a sense of what leads can do. We've taken them out—they are well beyond the reach of your students—but they may be interesting to you, so bits of them are here in the coaching column, and more are on the CD-ROM.

"The desire for love and for money has motivated much of human history. Western literature is filled with novels that address the conflicting feelings a woman and her family feel when the woman must decide between marrying a man she loves and marrying a man who can provide for her financially. Many of the characters in Jane Austen's novel, Pride and Prejudice, *personify one view or another of the advantages and limitations of marrying for love rather than for money."*

"I am a lacrosse player. When decisions must be made in the heat of a game, our coach has always told us that the worst thing to do is to stall. It is always better to make a decision, however bad it may be, rather than to freeze in indecision. When I first heard this advice, I was skeptical. Now, after reading Shakespeare's Hamlet *and Heller's* Catch-22, *I understand the wisdom of my coach's advice. A bad decision is always better than no decision at all, because every decision leads to some amount of progress, even if the progress comes, as in* Hamlet *and* Catch-22, *from mistakes made and lessons learned."*

- Whenever I watch a movie, I know there will come a part when the music changes and I need to worry about the character. That part is sure to come because in the movies, as in all stories, characters struggle.
- My life is full of problems. Everywhere I turn, it seems that there are problems. When I read stories, I realize I am not alone. Characters in books, too, struggle with problems.
- In school I learn from lessons that teachers teach, but when I read stories, I learn from problems that characters encounter. When I see how people in books face their problems, I become better at facing my own problems.

"In the end, Jill wrote this as her lead."

In my life, not everything ends up like a fairy tale. I like to read books where characters are like me. They don't live fairy tale lives. We have the same kinds of problems. In Sandra Cisneros's essay "Eleven," Rachel has problems like I do. In this essay, Rachel struggles to hold on to herself when she is challenged by people who have power over her.

Debrief, naming the replicable steps that the mentor author took that students could also take, now and often, when writing an introduction to a literary essay.

"Writers, I want to review the steps that Jill used to come up with her introduction, and as I do this, will you start doing those same steps yourself to think about your introduction?" I revealed a chart so that I could touch each point as we reviewed Jill's process.

"First, Jill thought about the general themes her essay addresses. Think what the general themes might be for your essay. Remember, she thought, 'Could this be about how teachers treat kids? How people in power treat powerless people? How girls think and feel?'

"Jill decided that she wanted to highlight—to pop out—just the idea *that people in life—all of us—struggle*, and you'll need to make a choice as well. *Then* Jill generated a list of possible leads and chose the one that best represented what she wanted to say in her essay. You ready to try this?"

If you think your students won't be able to hold on to the steps to writing an introduction, you might want to create the following chart and have it up during the lesson and afterwards.

Steps to Writing a Lead

- List general themes your essay might address.
- Choose one.
- Brainstorm possible leads that pop out that theme.
- Choose one.

ACTIVE ENGAGEMENT

Channel students to think about their own essay by first thinking of the essay's larger landscape. Ask them to work with partners to begin to generate lists of possible leads.

"So quickly, jot a few possible general themes you could say that your essay addresses. In a minute you'll talk to your partner."

After a minute, I said, "Partner 1, tell Partner 2 what you are considering."

I listened as Raffi told Marie the general themes he thought his essay on "Spaghetti" addressed. Raffi said, "My essay could be animals that, you know, change people's lives, help people," he said. "Or maybe, like that a cat can teach lessons, like weird people and things can be teachers." Raffi stopped and Marie gestured to say, "More, more," so he took a deep breath and continued. "Or you could say my essay is about people, characters, who go from happy to sad, who change their attitudes, or who are lonely." I moved on to others, coaching children as I did.

LINK

Remind writers that they now have a process they can go through to write a lead paragraph for a literary essay. Summarize the steps of the process. Then provide students with their options for revision work today.

"So, writers, you'll all be revising today. *One way* to revise is to work on an introductory paragraph. When doing so, begin by asking, 'What general themes might this essay address?' and come up with some options, as we just did. But there are lots of other ways to revise an essay. Right now, list four other really smart sorts of revision work that people in this room could be doing today. Turn and talk." The children talked, and I said, "How many of you will be rereading your essay to make sure you have exactly cited the text, and that you have unpacked those quotes to show how they go with the idea you are trying to make?" I channeled those kids off to work. "How many of you will be making sure that you use a variety of elaborations—including stories, examples, quotes, lists, and so forth?" Again, I sent a few students to work. "How many of you will be working on an introduction?" Many hands went up, and soon the meeting area was empty, so I headed off to help the writers.

If your students are having a hard time writing leads for their own essays, you might enlist the whole class's help to create one for a story children know well. Take a simple childhood tale like "Cinderella" or "Jack and the Beanstalk" and prompt children to think of large, familiar themes. Tell children that the themes of fairy tales are repeated throughout literature. "Cinderella," for example, which explores the notion of good triumphing over evil, and more precisely, someone with little power triumphing over someone with significantly more, is mirrored in The Lion, the Witch and the Wardrobe, Peter Pan, Skinny Bones, Pinky and Rex and the Bully, Dancing in the Wings, *and* The Meanest Thing to Say.

- Adults sometimes teach us to keep quiet and say nothing, even if we disagree with what someone else has done? Really, we should learn to speak up and say our opinions.

- Sometimes it is hard to say what you really think, because you might be afraid that people won't be like you. I think it is better to be yourself and not worry about fitting in.

- Kids all over the world stand by and watch bullies treat other people badly. It's not okay! You need to stand up against mean people.

FIG. 12–1   Parker's introductions for *The Hundred Dresses* that address themes

Addressing Struggles

A S YOU SET OFF TO CONFER, it is helpful on some days to step back and survey your room for signs of struggle. It is important to remember that sometimes children who are struggling need an image of what it might look like for them to do this work. A helpful strategy to draw upon in these situations is writing-in-the-air.

For example, as I looked around the room I saw struggle written all over Tyler's face, so I pulled my chair alongside him. He had in front of him his draft, his revision plan, Katherine's mentor essay, and his copy of the chart title "How to Make a Literary Essay," but he sat immobilized.

"What's up?" I asked.

"When I read my draft, it doesn't sound good. I planned to work on my transitions, but I'm stuck."

"What's giving you trouble?" I asked.

"My big idea is that 'Eleven' isn't really a story. And I'm on the first reason—because it doesn't have a problem and a solution," Tyler said, and read aloud the lines he'd cited as proof.

> Mrs. Price says, "That is enough nonsense. Put the sweater on."
> "But."
> "Now."

As well as:

> When Mrs. Price said, "Of course it's yours. I remember you wearing it,"
>
> Rachel couldn't say anything. Her power was taken away from her.

(continues)

Using the Language of Literary Scholars

"Writers, earlier I mentioned that there are some techniques that kids learn in high school or college about how to write introductions and conclusions, but I'd like to teach you one other trick: Your essay will be more powerful if you use the words of your trade.

"This is true for any endeavor. My niece and nephew raise and breed chickens. They are eight years old—they are twins—but they want to be taken seriously by other poultry breeders so they can purchase good birds from them and sell their birds for a good price. As a result, when Abigail and Hugh write and speak to adult poultry breeders, they use the words of their trade. They say things like this: 'This bird has strong coloring on the undercoat, and its vent is clean and pink.' Or they'll say to a breeder, 'We are looking for a good showmanship bird, one with smooth legs and a good head.'

"If you want your literary essays to be taken seriously, you need to use the words of your trade. The main character, as you will recall, is the *protagonist*. The text is written in the voice of the *narrator*. The start of the story is its *lead*. You might describe a story by speaking of its *setting*, *plot*, *theme*, or *tone*. So one thing you can do is to read over your draft and see if you've used the words available to you, and make sure that you have included the vital information of the text you are studying in your essay—the title, genre, and author's name."

"So why do you think it is hard to combine these?" I asked, but Tyler didn't have an answer.

"Tyler," I said, "do you remember that when I taught you to collect mini-stories that illustrate your big idea, I told you that after you tell the story about one time, then you need to unpack the story, showing how it relates to your big idea? You need to say something such as, 'This shows that . . . ' and 'This is important because . . . ' Well, I'm realizing that I should have taught you that in fact writers 'unpack' almost *any* evidence that they include in an essay, including quotations. I think the reason you are struggling to combine your claim and your evidence is that you haven't really unpacked your evidence yet." He still looked unsure, so I added, "What I mean by 'unpacking' the evidence is that you need to be able to take a quotation from the text (like those you have in your draft), and you need to talk about how that quotation serves as evidence for your claim." Then I urged Tyler to talk to me about how this bit of evidence went with the point that he was trying to make. I reminded him that he could use thought prompts. Tyler read aloud his evidence.

> Mrs. Price says, "That is enough nonsense. Put the sweater on."
> "But."
> "Now."

"This shows she's really mean and gets mad?" he said, his intonation suggesting this was more of a question than an answer.

"Tyler," I intervened, "remember, your thesis is, 'Eleven is not really a story,' and one reason for this has to do with Mrs. Price saying, 'That is enough nonsense.' How does that show that this isn't really a story?"

"'Cause she keeps getting mad at Rachel. She never stops," Tyler said.

"So, Tyler, that is important. I am going to show you how you might write this, but pay close attention because I am going to turn it over to you to continue. The way you'd write this, then, might be like this," I said, and started to write-in-the-air.

"Eleven" is not shaped like a story because stories usually have problems and solutions, and in this text, there are problems but those problems don't have solutions. From the start of the text to the ending of it, Mrs. Price doesn't listen to Rachel.

I paused and asked Tyler to take over. Tyler continued, "Mrs. Price doesn't listen to Rachel ever. This big problem never gets solved. Even in the end of the story, when Rachel tries to say something she only gets to say, 'But' before Mrs. Price cuts her off."

When Tyler was done I said, "So, Tyler, when you go to put bits of evidence together, remember that you need to unpack the evidence. You need to talk about how that particular bit of evidence goes with the main point you are trying to make."

As you survey your room, you might see a bunch of writers who are struggling with the same thing. If so, it would be wise to call them together for a small group. For example, if you see a group of children whose essays tend to be redundant, you may begin the small group by saying that you noticed that many of them are using the same text evidence to support several reasons, while others make the same point over and over with four or five examples. Caution them against these things. Tell children that after they put their pieces together, their challenge is to reread their essays with critical eyes, eliminating redundancy. Encourage children to think about what does and doesn't hold their attention. For example, if a character faced the same challenge over and over, or fought the same battle with the same enemy in every book in a series, they, as readers, would grow frustrated and bored. Remind children that just as they are hungry for new thoughts, ideas, and story lines, so too are their readers wanting to be challenged by new ideas in each paragraph of an essay.

Then ask the writers to reread their essays, trying this out. Spend some time coaching individual children into figuring out how they can fix their essays. End the small group quickly by restating your teaching point and then send them back to their seats to continue with the work you started together. The last thing you want is for your readers to be eyeing the clock as they sit with you. And sometimes less is more.

Writing Conclusions

Tell students that literary essayists craft their conclusions with care. List some choices writers have for their conclusions.

"Something terrible happened to me last night. I was watching a television show—an enthralling one. I kept wondering how it would all come together at the end, and it never did. Suddenly, the words came onto the screen: 'To be continued . . .'

"Has that ever happened to you? It's an awful feeling, isn't it, to be left in the lurch?

"So I want to take a few minutes to remind you that your essays need endings. You'll probably want to try three or four different possible conclusions (just like you often try three or four introductions).

"Remember we learned that literary essayists begin their essays with a generalization about literature or life, to set up the broader context for their thesis. Well, the conclusions you write have a similar job. Literary essayists conclude their essays by reconnecting their specific idea—their thesis—to that broader context and then leaving readers with something to think about, to linger over—to carry around in their minds and perhaps to revisit later on in discussion with others."

"The conclusions you write matter especially because they are the last impression that your readers will be left with. The conclusion puts forth the final thoughts you want to emphasize about the text you have read. Constructing your essay is like constructing a building. All your hard work will be for naught if you have only a strong foundation and sturdy floors, but no roof! So, tonight, you will need to reread what you have drafted today and then make a strong final statement to conclude your journey of thought. Remember that you have choices."

(If you think your students won't be able to hold onto the steps of writing a conclusion, then you might want to create the chart shown at the top of the following page, and display it during the share so children can refer to it as they try to write their conclusions.)

Conclusions

- Reconnect to the broader theme or generalization.
- Make connections to:
  - Your thesis and emphasize why the claim and evidence matter
  - Yourself and the life lesson you learned or realized
  - The author's message
- Leave readers with something to think about.

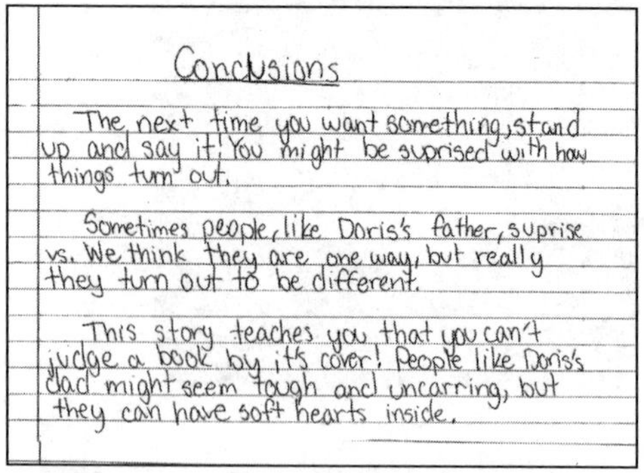

Conclusions

The next time you want something, stand up and say it! You might be suprised with how things turn out.

Sometimes people, like Doris's father, suprise us. We think they are one way, but really they turn out to be different.

This story teaches you that you can't judge a book by its cover! People like Doris's dad might seem tough and uncarring, but they can have soft hearts inside.

FIG. 12–2   Celia's conclusion about *Stray*

CRAFTING CONCLUSIONS

Sometimes you don't know how powerful an idea can be until you see it on the page and it takes your breath away. Tonight, draft a conclusion to your essay. Come up with a few different conclusions that leave readers with a new idea to consider or something to think about. Reread your final paragraph with each of your ending sentence options, and find one that, when you see it on the page, takes your breath away.

Using Descriptions of an Author's Craft as Evidence

PERSONAL ESSAYS, persuasive essays, and literary essays all resemble each other. In each one, the writer articulates a claim and several subordinate ideas. To support their ideas, writers draw on anecdotes, quotations, lists of examples, and so forth. One of the few features that set literary essays apart from other essays is this: literary essayists pay attention to the author's craftsmanship and to the literary devices an author has used. That is, the writer of a literary essay notices not only what a text says, but also how the text creates emphasis and meaning. This work is so integral to a reader's ability to understand a text that the Common Core State Standards dedicate three anchor reading standards to the study of craft and structure. Children are asked to not only interpret words, phrases, and figurative language, but also to analyze the way an author's use of craft conveys an overall meaning. This critical work is brought front and center in today's session.

In this session, you'll teach young essayists that they are wise to notice not only the content but also the craftsmanship of the text under study. The session could introduce a whole series of minilessons (teachers of experienced writers may decide to stretch this one session into several). For most fourth-grade classrooms, however, it's enough to expose children to the notion that they will want to notice how an author uses literary devices to convey the deeper meanings in a text.

IN THIS SESSION, you'll teach students that writers find evidence to support their claims by studying the choices authors make in their texts.

GETTING READY

✔ "Literary Devices that Highlight Meaning" chart (see Teaching and Mid-Workshop Teaching)

✔ Mentor text, *Fox*, or the text you have been using in demonstrations

✔ One page from the mentor text that shows a number of literary devices for the students to mine for evidence (see Teaching)

✔ "How to Write a Literary Essay" chart (see Link)

COMMON CORE STATE STANDARDS: W.4.1.b, W.4.5, RL.4.1, RL.4.4, SL.4.1, L.4.1, L.4.2, L.4.3, L.4.5.a,b,c

Using Descriptions of an Author's Craft as Evidence

CONNECTION

Celebrate all that students have learned and help them understand the importance of having powerful evidence.

"Writers, today is our last day of revision before we move onto another essay. You've drafted, redrafted, and revised, using not just what you learned in this bend but what you have learned across your entire career as essay writers.

"Today I want to add a new strategy to your toolbox. In an earlier lesson we talked about how ideas can be the okay kind or they can be the kind that stop people in their tracks, the kind that make them go 'Whoa.' The same is true for evidence. Your evidence can be the sort that makes people shrug, or it can be the kind that makes people pause, think, and say, 'Hmm, you're right!'"

❧ **Name the teaching point.**

"Today I want to teach you that literary essayists use not only *what* a text says, but *how* the text says it as evidence to support their claims. Writers use the fact that an author deliberately crafts a story—or any text—in ways that highlight the deeper meaning."

TEACHING

Tell the class about a writer who has supported a thesis on a familiar text with an analysis of the author's craft. Recruit the class to try the same work, using this challenge to rally their energy.

"Writers, this morning, in the parking lot, Mr. Burdock and I were talking about you kids, as we always do. We started to talk about the cool work both classes are doing with our class essays about *Fox*. I wanted to tell you about the cool work his kids have been doing.

"While we have been growing ideas about Dog, they've been focused on Fox. Apparently they think Fox is the worst kind of evil—the kind of evil that is charming and enticing, that lures characters like Dog to open their door (and their hearts) to him. They've decided that although he seems charming on the outside, he is really poison. One of their claims, in fact, is 'Fox is poison because he destroys things.'

During the lead of a minilesson, we have a chance to help children recall what we've taught them. The way we recall previous instruction matters, because we can make students feel as if prior lessons contained armloads of hard-to-remember, discombobulated instructions and directions, or we can make them feel as if our teaching had turned the light on in a new space, illuminating the way.

"I also wanted to tell you about the other stuff his kids have been doing that was pretty impressive. Those kids have been trying to find evidence that will stop people in their tracks and make them go 'Whoa.' Not just big ideas that do that—but evidence. Then he said that they thought it was boring to support the idea that Fox is poison by showing where Fox whispers to Magpie, convincing her to leave Dog. Instead, to be really fancy-pantsy, they've been noticing—get this—the way Margaret Wild uses literary devices to portray Fox. Do you want me to tell you what they've noticed, or do you want to see if you can notice this stuff for yourself first?"

Predictably, the kids wanted to do it themselves. "Okay," I said. "I'll just do a tiny bit of this to show you, and then let you try it. What we'll need to do is to reread a part of the text where she might be using words that make Fox seem destructive—that's the claim they need to prove, right? Instead of looking mostly at what Fox is doing, we'll look at the language—and specifically the literary devices—the author uses to portray him. I think you know the common literary devices to be looking for." I flipped the chart paper on my tablet over to show a quick list.

> ### Literary Devices
>
> - Comparisons (metaphors and similes)
> - Sound effects
> - Dialect or words from another language
> - Alliteration
> - Repetition
> - Descriptive words or sentences

Recruit children to study the craftsmanship in your mentor text, showing them that authors often use literary devices to highlight what they want to say.

I put a passage that I knew was worth mining up on the document camera so the children could study the author's language. "So you are going to look to see if Margaret Wild uses one of these literary devices to support the idea that Fox is the kind of character who ruins things." I began reading.

> *After the rains, when saplings are springing up everywhere, a fox comes into the bush; Fox with his haunted eyes and rich red coat. He flickers through the trees like a tongue of fire, and Magpie trembles.*

"Reread it again, with your partner, and underline specific word choices that the author has made. As you do that, think, 'She could have described this differently. Why might she have chosen this word, this phrase?'"

Teachers, of course this lesson could have revolved around finding the literary devices that support our latest interpretation of Dog—the idea that being a good friend involves not just blindly loving someone but also watching, observing, and understanding. But sometimes it is nice to leave something for a bit, so when you come back it feels new and fresh.

You might alter this list to make sure it encompasses the literary devices in the major texts that have been under study in your classroom. Don't avoid a device because the class hasn't studied it. You can tuck in a bit of explanation; human beings learn language by immersion.

Then I said, "I'll start. Watch me do the first bit of noticing, and then you and your partner can try it too. I'm noticing that in this part of the story, the author has chosen to make the weather be just after the rain. I have to pinch myself to remember that stories aren't true. This day did not actually happen after the rain. That was a choice that the author made. Why would she make it after the rain, I wonder? Not rain—but *after* the rain. Hmm." I was quiet, and around me kids' hands shot up. Speaking in a tentative, "maybe" voice, I said, "Perhaps she did that to show that the world is clean, and things are growing. Because she has the little baby trees, the saplings, *springing up*. Not popping up. Springing up. The world feels like spring. Newborn and fragile and full of new life. I'm not sure if any of this will connect to the idea that Fox is destructive, but maybe she'll show him coming into this world in ways that are destructive."

"Writers, tell each other what you noticed me doing to study the author's language." After a minute, I said, "Now you try it. Talk about what else you notice from that same passage."

Soon the kids were full of talk about the decisions the author made when she described Fox as having "haunted eyes" and a "rich red coat," "*flicker[ing]*" through the trees like a *tongue of fire.*"

After a bit, I called on some children to share their observations with the class. The children said that Wild compares Fox to a "tongue of fire," and this probably suggests that Fox is going to destroy the springlike world and all the new things that are springing to life.

LINK

Return to the story of the class that approached texts with the lens of asking, "What literary language did the author use?" And "How does this show what the text is *really* about?"

"Writers, I absolutely adore the conversation that made me outgrow myself, and I am pretty sure you are the same way. The cool thing is that from this day forward with Mr. Burdock, we can look at texts with new lenses.

"I know you already have lots of ways to read texts and to develop and support your own interpretation of the text. Now you have one new method to add to your repertoire. Now you know that it can really pay off for you as a writer to look closely at the way an author has written, at the author's craft.

"Writers, I know you'll be adding literary language to your drafts. But will you also remember to draw on all the work you've learned to do to make you literary essay better?"

As I talked I ran my hand across the chart "How to Write a Literary Essay."

"You'll spend some time rereading your draft and thinking 'What does my draft need?' You might find that you need to collect evidence by adding micro-stories, quotes, lists, and examples and if so, don't forget to also work on the transitions that glue the evidence together. You might find entirely different work needs to be done. You have a lot to do, so let's get right to work."

Of course, the obvious thing to notice in the passage is the author's treatment of Fox. We deliberately don't discuss that because it is the low-hanging fruit, so we leave it for the children, hoping to support their work.

One of the reasons we have chosen this text is because of the rich language and plethora of literary devices. Depending on the children sitting before you, you might choose to focus instead on the way the term haunted *seems to suggest there is something dark inside Fox. Choose examples that are beautifully rich, yet clear enough for your children to grasp.*

If you want to show a second example, you could channel students to study the following passage, in which case they'd probably notice the repetition of the word watching *and the odd juxtaposition of words in the last line, describing the smells that filled the cave.*

> *"In the evenings, when the air is creamy with blossom, Dog and Magpie relax at the mouth of the cave, enjoying each other's company.*
> *Now and again Fox joins in the conversation, but Magpie can feel him watching, always watching her.*
> *And at night his smell seems to fill the cave—a smell of rage and envy and loneliness."*

The work you teach today is important enough to the genre of literary essays that you'll probably want to insist children look at ways an author's craft supplies the text's meaning. This work definitely merits more than a day. Extend the work if you can!

Supporting the Study of Authors' Craft

AS YOU MEET WITH STUDENTS TODAY, you may want to teach them that instead of scanning the text, hoping a craft move or literary device will pop out, saying, "Here I am! Look at me," it can help to take a key passage and think, "I'm *sure* there are literary devices and craft decisions within this paragraph. Let me read very, very closely to find them, and see whether they support my claim." Encourage children in whatever they find. They needn't (and likely won't, in the beginning) find the fanciest, most sophisticated kinds of evidence. A powerful word or sentence may be enough to get them going.

To scaffold this work, you may want to convene a small group and give a short demonstration of how to read closely for evidence that supports your claim.

"Let's pretend that your claim for an essay on 'Eleven' is that Cisneros is celebrating the importance of writing.

"Zoom in on any paragraph. Let's take the top of page 2."

> Not mine, not mine, not mine, but Mrs. Price is already turning to page thirty-two, and math problem number four.

Show children that you squeeze your mind and try to come up with something to say about the way Cisneros has crafted this sentence. Let the children see that you at first feel speechless. "Umm, well, it's long!" Let the children see that you are tempted to brush your first thought aside but resist. "The sentence is not just long; it also has lots of parts. 'Not mine, not mine, not mine' is what Rachel is thinking. But there isn't a period at the end of it. Instead the sentence keeps going, almost as if it is a run-on sentence, and at the end of it Mrs. Price is ignoring Rachel, turning to page 32.

"I'm realizing that Cisneros sometimes uses long, run-on sentences, and in this instance, she does so in a way that shows that Rachel's voice gets lost in her teacher's actions."

You'll want to show children that you shift between very close reading of the text and consideration of your claim. "Now how might this connect to my thesis? Hmm . . . Maybe Cisneros's sentence structure reinforces the idea that Rachel feels voiceless? Rachel's thoughts get lost in this long sentence that ends up being all about the

---

MID-WORKSHOP TEACHING **Recognizing Symbols**

"Writers, can I stop you for just a minute? I want to add one more thing to our list of literary devices, and that is an author's use of symbols or images. Often in books, an object stands for more than what it seems. Like Fox. We could say that Margaret Wild decided to make him the bad guy just because she felt like it. But she could have just as easily made the character a moose or a donkey or a turtle. Why a fox? Does it stand for something more? Take a moment and talk to the person beside you. What might the fox stand for?"

Literary Devices

- Comparisons (metaphors and similes)
- Sound effects
- Dialect or words from another language
- Alliteration
- Repetition
- Descriptive words or sentences
- Symbols or images

(continues)

I gave children a moment to talk and then called for their attention. "I heard many thoughts. Sophie remembered fairy tales where the bad character is a fox. She thinks the fox stands for evil. Richard and John said that when they think of foxes, they think of characters that are sly and sneaky.

Brandon thought about symbols and made a connection to his story, *Number the Stars*. He is thinking that the Star of David necklace that is mentioned again and again might be something worth exploring.

"Continue on with your work, but remember that authors also send messages through repeated images or objects. If you notice something that stands out, chances are the author wants you to stop and ask, 'What does this stand for?'"

teacher's actions and decisions. Perhaps 'Eleven' is not just the story of Rachel but also of Sandra Cisneros and how she struggles to find and claim her own voice. Perhaps the story culminates in the fact that Cisneros gets the last word in. She—that's Cisneros but also Rachel—perhaps *does* find her voice because look, she's writing this essay! She's gotten the last word in, even if at the time Mrs. Price rolled right over her."

You'll need to demonstrate this in an efficient manner so that the conference is not a soliloquy. Shift soon to a second passage, and suggest that children assume there's a craft move in that paragraph that relates to each child's different thesis. (Of course, this may prove incorrect, but that is unlikely.) Then support children in identifying that move.

Considering Purpose in Crafting

Recruit writers to not only look at what the author *did* do in her text, but also what she did *not* do.

After calling students back to the meeting area, I said, "In today's session, you learned that it is important to notice not only *what* an author has written about, but also *how* that author has written, noting ways that the author's craft supports his or her message. This minilesson could launch another whole bend in the road of our unit! But time is short. Let's extend today's lesson at least for our share, anyhow. One way to do this is to reread the text under study and to notice what the author *did* do by noticing what he or she did *not* do!

"If you think back to when you were writing your own stories, you'll remember that you made choices about what to expand and what to skip past. You looked over your own writing and thought, 'What is the heart of the story?' and then you stretched out that part. The authors of these texts you are reading have made similar choices. They write with a lot of detail about some things and bypass others altogether. So one way to learn what matters to an author is to think, 'What has this author written about with extensive detail? What has the author skimmed past? And how might this support the meaning?'

"For example, today Raffi looked at Cynthia Rylant's story 'Spaghetti' and asked himself, 'What's missing here? What has the author seemed to pass right by?' And what he noticed was that she never mentions Gabriel's family. Not once! And since Raffi knows that authors make choices about what to include and what to leave out for a reason, he decided to push himself to try to figure out what that reason was.

"Here's what he ended up writing. It's really cool. Listen." (See Figure 13–1.)

> I think Cynthia Rylant left out Gabriels' family to show how alone he is. Some kids have their family around them all the time, but Gabriel isn't like that at all, and maybe that's why he's so lonely.

"Later, Raffi told me that maybe that's why Spaghetti meant so much to Gabriel, because Spaghetti could fill the space left by his missing family. Do you see how Raffi found something that's *missing from* the story and used that as evidence

FIG. 13–1   Raffi finds something missing from the story "Spaghetti."

for his thesis about Gabriel's loneliness, just the same way he could have used something that's *included in* the story, like a quote or a mini-story?

"Right now, will you reread the story you have been studying and notice what your author has developed and what your author has skimmed past? Notice the details that are missing. Does one character not have a name? Are there people, or events, left out of the story entirely? Once you have noticed what's missing in the story, ask yourself, 'How does the author's decision reflect the message of this story?' Write your thoughts down on a separate piece of paper, because they might be important enough to include in your draft."

SESSION 13 HOMEWORK

FROM THOUGHT TO REVISION

You're almost done revising your essay, so tonight, play with one last revision that will really wow readers. Sift through your list of ideas from the share about information that is missing from the story, and find one that would fit well with the big idea of your essay. You may need to add a couple more items to the list before you find the perfect one, and if so, that's okay! You're finding something that few readers will have noticed before, and that's worth taking some time and patience. When you've found an idea that fits, draft how you would write out your idea and incorporate it into a paragraph of your essay. You can decide to revise your draft to include that idea or save it for another writing project.

Editing

Dear Teachers,

As you come to the end of Bend II, you will likely want to provide some time for your students to edit their essays. You will probably collect your children's essay folders where they have been keeping their drafts and pore through them in preparation for this instruction. We recommend that you examine the work, noticing the demands this unit places on their writing conventions. Just as kindergartners and first-graders write with incomplete, approximate spellings when writing is new for them, your children will in a similar fashion write with an incomplete and approximate command of the conventions as they tackle the still unfamiliar genre of academic writing. That is, when your children talk and write about *contemporary* objects or events, they can rely on what some refer to as the register of social English. This is the sort of English they use during everyday interactions, and it will be more accessible to them. But when writing literary essays, children write about times, places, and texts that are distant and unfamiliar, and this means they are called to use what some refer to as *academic English*. The linguistic demands on children who attempt to write literary essays are high. This is especially true for English language learners.

In your students' work there will be a number of telltale signs that suggest to you they are having difficulties with the syntax of academic English. Sometimes they will write their thoughts in a brief, bare-bones fashion. Other times, the child will restate the same idea over and over. Yet other times, the child will write in garbled prose: "The influence shown by the character on his interactions with others shows the relationships and the tensions and the feelings that are important to all." In this instance, the tangled prose represents a child's efforts to sound impersonal, objective, and scholarly, relying on passive tense and strings of noun phrases. Be forgiving; it's impressive that the child is trying to take on a new role and a new way of using language. To some extent, what the child needs is time to become more at home with this register.

COMMON CORE STATE STANDARDS: W.4.1, W.4.5, RFS.4.4, SL.4.1, L.4.1, L.4.2, L.4.3

MINILESSON

You might begin the minilesson by sharing with the students what you have noticed in their writing, applauding their efforts as literary essay writers and laying out some of the common difficulties you see in their writing. As part of this, you might point out to students that there are different challenges when talking and writing about texts than when talking and writing about stuff: dogs, yo-yos, baked beans. In this unit, kids have been asked to use language to talk and think about language. There are some special tips that writers can learn to do this.

Your teaching point will be different based on the decisions you make about your content. We detail two options below.

For your teaching today, you can decide if you want to teach just one tip or several. If you want to address one major area for now, you might decide to take up the question of whether, when writing about a text, the writer writes in past tense or present tense. It makes sense that writers would be confused. After all, Dog already did welcome Fox. That happened on page 9 of the story. It is over. So for the reader who is retelling the story of *Fox*, it makes sense to use the past tense. Dog welcomed Fox. But, meanwhile, on the other hand, for readers who have yet to read the story, Dog *will* welcome Fox. That is still to come. For those readers, it will be an event that happens in a while. And finally, in the book, on that particular page, Dog welcomes Fox. It happens every day a reader reads that page. Therefore, present tense also makes sense.

How confusing! The good thing is that there is a rule for what people do when writing about the events in a text. And that is to write in present tense. It is happening now. Dog is still there, carrying Magpie in his mouth, welcoming Fox.

Stories are not usually written in present tense. They are more apt to be in past tense. "Once upon a time, long long ago . . ." For this reason and others, your children will quite frequently be confused, shifting between present and past tense. Don't be surprised about this, but don't refrain from teaching them the rules of the genre.

You might want to rally the class to join together to think about how to revise for tense in a selected piece of student writing. For example, Max uses both past and present tense in his summary. Max is an exceptional writer, so showing the class that he struggles over tense is actually a heartening message—and doesn't dim Max's rather abundant confidence. Of course, Max was given a chance to say he'd rather his work not be used as a problematic case in point. He, in fact, was glad for the help. This is one of the passages that reflects his confusion.

In the story, Rachel sits at her desk, staring at the red sweater Mrs. Price made her keep. She was disgusted with it, and wanted to cry like she is three . . . she then realizes that she was not just eleven . . .

You can demonstrate how to make the writing clearer and more powerful by shifting all the verbs to present tense. You will likely want to read the piece aloud with the class, noticing the verb tense and thinking aloud, "Hmm, is this in present tense? Does it sound like it's happening right now?" Then, model for the students how to put the entire summary in the present tense.

> Rachel sits at her desk, staring at the red sweater Mrs. Price made her keep. She is disgusted with it, and wants to cry like she is three . . . she then realizes that she is not just eleven . . .

During the active engagement, students can then try this work with another piece of writing you select, or you can ask them to open up their folders and choose an entry to work on, reading it to notice their tenses and to work toward writing consistently in present tense. You will want to coach them as they read, asking them to notice when the verbs make the writing sound as if it already happened or as if it is happening in this moment.

If you'd like to take up a second common confusion, we suggest you address the problems that accompany pronoun references. You've all seen children writing about a book like this: "He gives him the bread and he goes to the store with him and his father." How confusing! Who is he, who is him, and which he is whom? Remind your students that their readers always need to be able to discern the person to whom a pronoun refers.

There are a few concrete suggestions you can make to address this. First, children make dramatic progress toward this goal when they learn and use characters' names—instead of making vague references to "this guy" and "that other guy." It's best to use the specific names often, too.

Secondly, children need to be able to reread their own writing as if they are strangers to it, noticing places where the pronouns aren't clear. You can demonstrate this work by calling up a partner and exchanging pieces. You can ask your partner to read aloud your writing, asking your partner to stop at points of confusion, saying, "I'm confused! Could you rewrite this part using the characters' names?" Or "Wait! Who are you talking about here?"

To practice doing this, you might want to encourage children to exchange their essay folders and observe their partners' efforts to comprehend their entries. You may suggest that partners read each other's writing aloud quietly, adding (in oral parentheses) the proper name referenced by each pronoun. If the reader is unclear of the antecedent, the writer then needs to use the proper name or a more precise reference.

You can send your students off to continue their work. Some will want to devote time to editing; others will have other work to do. As you send them off, you might want to let them know that this is the last day they will have with this essay. This can be a way for you to create a drumroll around the importance of today's work. It is their last chance to do everything to make their strongest writing the strongest it can be.

CONFERRING AND SMALL-GROUP WORK

For your conferring and small-group work today, you will want to continue supporting students with editing. If you have taken some time to look through the students' entries, you likely noticed some common challenges the students face with this type of academic writing. Just as you used this data to plan the minilesson, you will want to use it to plan your small-group work and conferences.

You might notice that some students are working on making their writing sound more academic, and in this attempt, their writing becomes convoluted. It is crucial to let children know that getting an idea across to the reader is more important than a scholarly tone. If a child says or writes something you sense is important, but you can't discern the message because of the convoluted syntax, tell her! Don't think for a moment that you do the child a favor by neglecting to mention that the message is confusing to you. You might say, "I'm trying to follow what you are saying, but I don't understand." If the child tries to explain by making unwarranted assumptions, such as saying "you know" when in fact you don't know, then let the child know you are not exactly sure what she means. "I don't know what you are getting at," you could say, "but I want to understand. Can you try again to explain it and let me see if I can follow you?"

You might find that some students are confusing singular and plural verbs, which impacts the clarity of their writing. Pronoun-verb agreement becomes more complicated when the pronouns are indefinite. In this instance, you may want to teach students that words such as *anybody, anyone, nobody, no one,* and *neither* are all singular. It is correct to say, "Neither of his friends *is* going." When subjects are separated by *or* (as in Paul *or* Jerry) the verb must be singular (is going).

Gabriel *is* a lonely boy who *wants* company.

Gabriel and his cat *want* a home, but Gabriel *sits* on the stoop.

MID-WORKSHOP TEACHING

During the mid-workshop teaching, you might decide to interrupt the class to do a quick lesson on descriptive clauses. You can teach them that descriptive clauses enable the writer to tuck tiny bits of information about a character immediately after mentioning what the character has done or said. You might say, "The added information can allow readers to picture not only what is being done, but also how that action occurs." You can provide a few examples, instructing students, "Watch how the meanings become more specific as sentences become more complex":

Gabriel picked up the kitten.
Gabriel, the main character in this story, picked up the kitten.
Gabriel, bursting with pleasure, picked up the kitten.
Gabriel, bursting with pleasure, picked up the kitten, putting it close to his cheek.

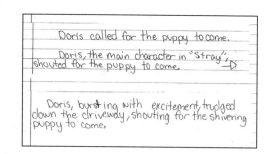

FIG. 14–1   Celia tries to write more complex sentences.

Or

Gabriel ate his sandwich.

Gabriel, ravenously hungry, ate his sandwich.

Gabriel, sitting alone on the stoop, ate his sandwich, savoring the thin layer of mayonnaise between two slices of Wonder bread."

You can then ask students to look at their writing to find places where adding more character information could help the reader picture the action and make their writing clearer and more powerful.

SHARE

As the students finish their second essay in this unit, you might want to take the time to celebrate the work they have done before moving onto Bend III. Now would be a good time to pull out the Opinion Writing Checklist for students to hold their writing against, noticing where they fall and what their next steps will be. (The Opinion Writing Checklist, Grades 4 and 5 can be found on the CD-ROM.) You can remind students that they can self-assess and set goals to become more powerful writers. You might say, "As we've seen in past units, charts and checklists can help you set goals for yourselves because they remind you of all the things you know to do that make your writing stronger. You can use our Opinion Writing Checklist to help you with this work today." You will want to have copies of the checklist for each student and possibly have an enlarged chart version to keep up in the classroom.

As the class reviews the checklist, remind students how to assess themselves using this tool. "As you know from other writing units across the year, and from the end of Bend I in this unit, you look at the checklist and ask 'What on this checklist have I already done in my essay? What am I

Opinion Writing Checklist

	Grade 4	NOT YET	STARTING TO	YES!	Grade 5	NOT YET	STARTING TO	YES!
	Structure				**Structure**			
Overall	I made a claim about a topic or a text and tried to support my reasons.	☐	☐	☐	I made a claim or thesis on a topic or text, supported it with reasons, and provided a variety of evidence for each reason.	☐	☐	☐
Lead	I wrote a few sentences to hook my readers, perhaps by asking a question, explaining why the topic mattered, telling a surprising fact, or giving background information. I stated my claim.	☐	☐	☐	I wrote an introduction that led to a claim or thesis and got my readers to care about my opinion. I got my readers to care by not only including a cool fact or jazzy question, but also figuring out was significant in or around the topic and giving readers information about what was significant about the topic.	☐	☐	☐
					I worked to find the precise words to state my claim; I let readers know the reasons I would develop later.	☐	☐	☐
Transitions	I used words and phrases to glue parts of my piece together. I used phrases such as *for example, another example, one time,* and *for instance* to show when I was shifting from saying reasons to giving evidence and *in addition to, also,* and *another* to show when I wanted to make a new point.	☐	☐	☐	I used transition words and phrases to connect evidence back to my reasons using phrases such as *this shows that . . . .*	☐	☐	☐
					I helped readers follow my thinking with phrases such as *another reason* and *the most important reason.* I used phrases such as *consequently* and *because of* to show what happened.	☐	☐	☐
					I used words such as *specifically* and *in particular* in order to be more precise.	☐	☐	☐

starting to do but might do more of? What have I forgotten?' I've also given each of you a blank checklist to assess yourself with. You can refer to this checklist later on to remind yourself of the goals you are still working toward as a writer."

Give students time to assess their writing and coach them through this work, reminding them of previous goals they have set in earlier units. "What are you noticing about your writing? Are there goals from our personal and persuasive essay unit, or earlier in this unit, that you still have?"

You will want to tell the children that today, the last day of Bend II, is an important time to celebrate their growth as essayists. You might do this by asking them to take out their drafts from Bend I and lay them beside their drafts from Bend II. You might say, "I'm guessing that most of you are noticing huge growth in your writing from Bend I to Bend II. We aren't even done with this unit, and already you've accomplished so much! Would you take a moment and share your growth, your successes, with your writing partner? Don't worry about trying not to boast. Brag away! And partners, will you try to *really see* what your partner is pointing out? It may be that they've done something that you can try in Bend III."

Giving students time to look across their writing in this unit to assess, set goals, and celebrate their accomplishments will give them the knowledge and motivation to continue to grow. It is important to allow time for your students, and you, to reflect on the writing that has occurred so far and use the goals they set and accomplishments they are proud of to propel the class into the next bend in this unit.

You might mention to students that instead of reading their pieces to others, today they will be celebrating their growth as essayists, and that at the end of the next bend, they will choose one essay to publish for a broader audience. This essay may be the one!

PRIORITIZING GOALS

Today you looked across the writing you have done so far in this unit and assessed yourself using the Opinion Writing Checklist. Then you set goals and celebrated what you have accomplished. Tonight I want you to look back over your checklists and the goals you set and prioritize them. As we start our last bend in this unit, think about what is the most pressing work you have to do to see even more growth in yourself as a writer. Then write a plan that includes not just what goals you are going to work toward but *how* you will work toward them. Come to school tomorrow ready to put those plans into action!

Also tonight to celebrate your writing and your growth as an essayist, read your piece to your parents, sister, brother, neighbor, or babysitter and tell them about all the ways that you have grown.

Building the Muscles to Compare and Contrast

IN THIS SESSION, you'll teach students that essayists notice the similarities and differences between texts and categorize their observations into patterns or ideas, in preparation to write a compare-and-contrast essay.

GETTING READY

✔ Concrete objects for students to compare (e.g., an apple and an orange) (see Connection)

✔ Chart paper and markers, to record the class's compare-and-contrast essays (see Teaching and Active Engagement)

✔ A collection of concrete objects for students to compare and contrast, set up at individual tables so students can move from one table to the next in centers (see Link)

✔ Students' writer's notebooks

✔ Sentence strips and markers, for students to record what they've learned about comparing and contrasting (see Share)

✔ "Tips for Comparing and Contrasting" chart (see Share)

O VER THE PAST SEVERAL DECADES, teachers who care about the teaching of writing have found it transformational to participate in their own adult writing workshops, experiencing from the inside what it is they are asking students to do. At one point, the Reading and Writing Project decided to offer similar opportunities to teachers of reading. We created a study group to support adult reading clubs, and soon teachers in more than 100 New York City schools were meeting together several times a month to talk about shared adult literature. Meanwhile, the Reading and Writing Project staff studied those reading clubs, trying to understand what made some of the conversations seem especially thoughtful and productive. We wanted to be able to teach youngsters by drawing on our own insider experiences as readers.

It soon became clear to us that one of the lasting, enduring features of a productive book club conversation was the fact that the conversation spanned more than one text. Somehow, the breakthroughs almost always came when one reader would say, "Isn't that sort of like the way _____ did that in _____?"

We puzzled over why intertextual references were so important to the caliber of a conversation. What we decided was that talking across texts required us to move up the ladder of abstraction, and required us to create links that did not exist in life. Cross-text conversations required participants in the conversation to form and shape ideas and to construct meaning.

The education world agrees that an ability to make connections across texts is an important part of academic literacy. The Common Core State Standards spotlight the importance of textual comparisons. The fourth-grade standard for textual analysis and comparison states, "Compare and contrast the treatment of similar themes and topics . . . and patterns of events" (CCSS RL.4.9).

This kind of thinking and writing demands that a writer synthesize and analyze, and requires a writer to pay attention not only to the subject of a text but also to an author's

COMMON CORE STATE STANDARDS: W.4.1.b, W.4.4, W.4.7, W.4.8, RL.4.9, SL.4.1, L.4.1, L.4.2, L.4.3

treatment of that subject. This leads a person to notice matters of point of view, emphasis, and interpretation, and it also leads that reader to be aware of the different craft moves that the authors of the different texts have used.

"The education world agrees that an ability to make connections across texts is an important part of academic literacy."

You will recall that when teaching writers to work within an essay structure, we created essay boot camp and channeled students to flash-draft an essay based on the thesis, "I love ice cream." Today we return to this sort of work, this time for the purpose of helping students grasp the gist of what it means to write a compare-and-contrast essay.

You'll see that the session suggests you begin by asking students to compare and contrast not texts, but something concrete—a football and a baseball, an apple and an orange, Brian's shoe and Melissa's. You choose the objects; the important thing will be to help students experience the form of compare-and-contrast essays.

You may be perplexed. Why, in a unit of study on writing literary essays, would students be writing about footballs and baseballs? You are right to ask. This session is a break from the usual tradition. It is meant to be a boot camp, a drill session—a time for students to develop their muscles so that tomorrow they'll be able to put those new muscles to important use.

Building the Muscles to Compare and Contrast

CONNECTION

Contextualize this lesson by telling students about places in life where you see compare-and-contrast essays and by talking up the importance of this kind of essay in future schooling.

"One of my favorite parts of the Sunday paper is a section called 'Book Review.' In it, there are lots and lots of literary essays—in many ways, they are like the essays you've been writing. But there is one big difference. Often, the essays that are published in *The New York Times* are not about one story—one text. Instead, these essays often discuss two texts. They might be two texts written on the same theme or by the same author or that use similar techniques. The essayists generally write about ways those texts are the same and ways they are different.

"These are sometimes called compare-and-contrast essays. Those terms—*compare* and *contrast*—mean noticing similarities and noticing differences. So a compare-and-contrast literary essay talks about the similarities and the differences between two texts and shows the significance of each.

"Trust me—this is a kind of essay that you want to be able to write and to write in a flash. It's a kind of essay that you'll be asked to write when you are in middle school, high school, and college and when you want to publish your literary essays in *The New York Times* or *Cricket* or on Amazon. But more than this, it is a kind of essay that can help you develop really keen ideas about texts. I'll show you that over the next few days.

"But first I want to tell you that writing a compare-and-contrast essay can also help you develop really keen ideas about apples and oranges."

❖ Name the teaching point.

"Today I want to teach you that writers can compare and contrast by putting two subjects side by side and asking, 'How are they similar? How are they different? What might the significance of that be?' Then, they write about their observations in a structured, seesaw, organized way.

◆ COACHING

It actually is a bit of a challenge to figure out how to explain to kids how this genre fits into the world of published texts because kids don't tend to read literary essays. In an ideal world, we should make sure that children do read about texts in ways that help them make choices about what to read and also help them bring more ideas to a text.

144

TEACHING

Recruit students to compare the two concrete objects you brought to the meeting area, asking them to notice the similarities and differences between them.

"Let's take apples and oranges and give this a go," I said, producing the two pieces of fruit.

I held up the apple first, and then the orange, in my hands, and solemnly inspected them. I looked up at the kids, as if to say, "Well, what are you thinking?" and said, "I don't know about you, but I could talk right away about some similarities and some differences, couldn't you?" The kids nodded, and I said, "So try that. Say what you see," and I gestured for them to turn and talk.

After a minute I stopped them. "What you just did—yammering on about a heap of ideas, all thrown together, about ways these are the same and different—that is what tons of kids do when asked to compare and contrast two texts! You had lots of good ideas, and lots of kids will have good ideas. But there was no order to your thinking, and that's how it usually is with kids who haven't studied this kind of writing. They talk about a difference," I flicked up one hand, "a similarity," I flicked up the other, "another similarity," I flicked that hand again, "some other random points." This is a good place to start, but it is not the end product that your readers need.

Scaffold students' observations by telling them that a compare-and-contrast essay has a specific structure.

"After they create a random collection of observations, the writer needs to proceed in a very methodical way. If you want to write an essay that says that apples and oranges are mostly the same, one way to do that is to take a trait—name it—and then say how that trait is the same for both items—item A and item B. Then you take a second trait—name it—and say how that trait is also the same for both items—item A and item B. Of course, the items that you compare and contrast can be as complex as different people or different nations or different theories.

"Let's try this work with apples and oranges. I'll start with one trait. Then you do the next. I'll say that apples and oranges are mostly alike. They are alike because they both have skins that cover the fruit. They are also alike because . . . Turn and talk."

After a minute, the children had spouted out some other possibilities, and I'd noted a few. "They are also alike because of their shape. They are both shaped like a baseball. And both are tougher on the outside than on the inside." So now our essay goes like this."

I've modeled making this mess-up because it is one of the most common things to avoid doing. Though the main focus of today's lesson is on structures for comparing and contrasting, you will want to take every opportunity to plant the seed that observations about similarities and differences (like any other kind of observations we make in essays) are grouped in logical ways.

Eventually, we'll talk with students about how the point of a compare-and-contrast essay is not only to say something is mostly similar or mostly different from something else. We'll talk with them about the real point of a compare-and-contrast essay: the reasons for and meaning behind and implications of the similarities and differences. For now, though, we are focusing on the need for orderly writing.

Apples and oranges are alike in many ways. They are both shaped in the same ways—round and small, like a baseball. Also, both apples and oranges have skins that are similar. The skins cover the entire surface of the fruit. The skins can be peeled off. The skins are tougher than the inside fruit, making both apples and oranges tougher on the outside than on the inside.

Debrief. Name what you've done in ways that make the work transferable.

"Do you see how we took the two items we are comparing and said, 'Are these mostly alike or mostly different?' We decided to argue they are mostly alike. So then we took one trait—named it—and said how item A and item B are similar for that trait. Then we took a second trait—we named it—and we said how that trait is also the same for both items—item A and item B. Next we could go to differences, starting with the sentence, 'But they are also partly different.' And then we'd talk about reasons why those similarities and differences exist, or maybe what the implications might be for how the fruit fits into the world because of those features."

ACTIVE ENGAGEMENT

Channel children to try the same work using different objects. Invite two children to put their shoes in the front of the classroom for all to see.

"Let's try this again. I need a shoe. Please, could I have a shoe?" Sam produced his shoe, then he hopped back to his seat. I laid the shoe on an upside-down crate covered with a lovely tablecloth.

"Class, we could study this shoe—ta da!—and write about it. Think what you'd write if you were to observe Sam's shoe, and I'll do that too." I was quiet, thinking of what I would say. Then I said, "Here's the thing. To *really* understand the unique features and character of Sam's shoe, it's helpful to contrast it to an another shoe." I'd already chosen Melissa's shoe as a contrast, and now I laid the small pink slipper alongside the sprawling high-top sneaker.

"To compare and contrast Sam and Melissa's shoes, decide if they are mostly alike, or mostly different. Which would you say?" The consensus was that they were mostly alike—after all, they both were shoes. "Okay, think of a general trait on which they are similar—something like their shape, their component parts, their appearance, their purpose. Then be specific. Try writing an essay in the air about the two shoes that is like our essay in the air about the two fruits," and I produced the latter as a model, with key phrases underlined.

<u>Apples and oranges are alike in many ways.</u> <u>They are both shaped</u> in the same ways—round and small, like a baseball. <u>Also, both apples and oranges have skins</u> that are similar. The skins cover the entire surface of the fruit. The skins can be peeled off. The skins are tougher than the inside fruit, making both apples and oranges tougher on the outside than on the inside.

Teachers, in this lesson, we could have gone past the superficial comparison such as stating that the fruits are similar because both have tough skins. I could have led the student to consider why this might be. I didn't do that because the next sessions dig deeper into significance. Often when planning teaching it's helpful to save some content to teach as a next step.

Soon I called on the class to jointly construct a compare-and-contrast essay on Sam and Melissa's shoes. This is what they pieced together.

> Sam and Melissa's shoes are alike in many ways. They both have the same basic shape. Both are like tubes that go around the foot, and both have a space in the middle for the foot. They also have the same purpose. Both cover the person's foot to keep it safe and clean.

"You also need to write about the differences between their shoes. How are Sam and Melissa's shoes different? Turn and talk." As the children talked, I wrote the essay they'd constructed thus far onto chart paper, and soon we'd added a second paragraph.

> But Sam and Melissa's shoes are also different in some ways. Their sizes are very different. Sam's shoe is about as big as a loaf of bread, and Melissa's is more the size of a piece of bread. They are different in color, too. Sam's shoe is black and white, with dirt. Melissa's is pink, with sparkles.

Ask children to debrief. Recall the teaching point and put today's work in a bigger context.

"Have any of you ever written a haiku? That is a kind of poem that has all these rules—like the first line has five syllables, and the next line has seven syllables. Writing one of those, I have always felt like I'm partly writing a poem and partly doing a math equation. As you can see, compare-and-contrast essays have all these rules as well. Will you talk with your partner about what the steps might be for writing compare-and-contrast essays?"

Children talked, and after a bit I intervened. "I think you've got the important points. One way to write a compare-and-contrast essay is to discuss both similarities and differences—one at a time. The writer chooses a trait and looks at it across the two items, then chooses another and looks at it across the two items."

LINK

Set students up to go off and work in centers.

"Today will be a different kind of writing workshop. Normally, I remind you of the strategy I've just taught and then send you off to work on your own important writing projects. Today I'm sending you off to move through a series of centers where you'll have a chance to flex your compare-and-contrast muscles.

"You won't be writing about literature just yet. Instead, I've set up different objects for you to compare and contrast in your writer's notebook, just as we practiced here in the meeting area. One of you will find photographs at your table, another will find vegetables; I've made a table of objects from our writing center, and even a table with the names of people who work at our school. I've made two ways to compare and contrast essay samples. One way we used today.

Be creative when setting up today's centers. You'll want to create several tables, each with a different theme, and usher children through each center during the writing workshop. So, for instance, you might choose to have a center where children study and then compare and contrast photographs of famous landmarks. Another might have the names of school staff— teachers, office staff, custodial staff, administrators. You might choose to put objects like fruits, vegetables, or tools that children can compare and contrast at other tables. Depending on the number of centers you have, plan on giving students approximately seven to ten minutes at each table, ensuring that they have the opportunity to visit each of the stations.

I also added a new way. So you can refer to them as you work at your center. Start at your own table, and then I'll call for you to switch to another in seven minutes or so. Off you go to get writing!"

Example of Way #1

Apples and oranges are alike in many ways. They are both shaped in the same ways—round and small, like a baseball. Also, both apples and oranges have skins that are similar. The skins cover the entire surface of the fruit. The skins can be peeled off. The skins are tougher than the inside fruit, making both apples and oranges tougher on the outside than on the inside.

Example of Way #2

Apples and oranges are alike in many ways. An apple is round. For example, it's shaped like a baseball. It also has a tough skin that goes all the way around the fruit. You can peel the outside layer and get to the softer inside. An orange also is round. An orange also has tough skin that goes all the way around the fruit. Its skin is thicker, but can also be peeled to get to the softer inside.

Deepening Students' Initial Observations

I T IS LIKELY THAT WHEN YOUR CHILDREN FIRST START DOING THIS WORK, they will compare and contrast on a somewhat superficial level—noticing the way one teeny detail in a picture is different from another or how one vegetable is a different sort of green than another. There is nothing wrong with this. In fact, you modeled doing some of this work yourself a moment ago. You will, however, want to immediately intervene and teach children to search for larger traits under which they can situate their minute observations.

I pulled up next to John, who was at the school staff center and working to compare and contrast Mr. Meyer, the school custodian, and Mrs. Bryant, the art teacher. I immediately noticed that he was creating what amounted to a list of superficial comparisons (Mr. Meyer has short, brown hair; Mrs. Bryant has long, brown hair; they are both young; they both use tools to do their work, but Mrs. Bryant uses art supplies and Mr. Meyer using cleaning supplies, and so on).

"John," I began, "as you look across the similarities and differences you've identified for Mrs. Bryant and Mr. Meyer, are you noticing any patterns or big categories?" John thought for a minute. "Well, I saw that they both need supplies to do their jobs but that the supplies are different," he said.

"Yes, that is exactly what I mean. Here's the thing, John. What you have done beautifully is to dedicate yourself fully to uncovering all the similarities, big and small, between these two people. But let's go back to apples and oranges. It helps to compare apples and oranges by thinking of categories. For instance, I might compare and contrast their taste, their appearance, and their health benefits. If I could push myself to say a lot about each of those categories, then each could have its own paragraph.

(continues)

MID-WORKSHOP TEACHING
Finding Patterns and Ideas in Our Observations

"Can I stop you for a moment? I've met with many of you today, and you've worked hard to notice even the tiniest differences and similarities between the objects at your centers. I wanted to share a bit of work John and I just did together, because I think it will be important for us all.

"When we are writing about similarities and differences, we want to be on the lookout for big patterns or ideas that start to emerge. What I mean by this is that you don't just want to be the kind of writer who lists ten things that oranges and apples have in common and ten ways that oranges and apples are different. Instead, you want to sort your observations into groups. As I taught John, there are two ways to do this. You can group your observations into categories, or you can group your observations into ideas.

"John started off by grouping what he noticed into categories. For instance, he realized he could write a whole paragraph alone on the similarities and differences between the supplies Mrs. Bryant and Mr. Meyer use. He could also write about the similarities and differences in the way they look and dress.

"But instead, John decided to formulate an idea—that Mrs. Bryant and Mr. Meyer are important to our school—and write a paragraph all about how they are important because of how they treat people. Let's take a look at his entry and notice what he did that we might try also."

"Another possibility is that I develop a few *ideas* about apples and oranges and then write about the way the idea is true for oranges and the way the idea is true for apples. So, for example, I might write that fruit is essential to a healthy diet. Apples and oranges are both good for you and provide vital nutrients. They both give you potassium and vitamin A. But they are different because they provide different amounts of nutrients. Oranges have more potassium and vitamin A than apples, but apples have more fiber than oranges.

"So let's take a look at your writing and see if we can do something similar. What ideas are you having about Mrs. Bryant and Mr. Meyer?"

Before long, John developed the following idea: "Both Mr. Meyer and Mrs. Bryant are important to our school." (See Figure 15–1.)

If your students, like John, are making superficial comparisons or when John compared the hair color on Mr. Meyer and Mrs. Bryant, you'll want to move them towards noticing patterns that are more significant. It can also help if you push them to ask, "So what?" and to reflect on the significance of those patterns. What does this show? Doing this work in centers will help students eventually do it also when they think about characters and themes in their books.

> Mr. Meyer and Mrs. Bryant are both important to our school because of how they treat people. They are similiar because they both treat kids really well. They also both make school feel like a nice place, kind of like a second home. They are also different, though. Mr. Meyer is a fun kind of custodian. When someone throws up in the classroom he always comes in with his mop and makes a big joke. 'Boy, it stinks in here!' he says, and we all start laughing. Mrs. Bryant is different. She is more like a mom kind of teacher. She talks really calm and never yells. She gives kids hugs when they are sad and when you are having a bad day she let's you come into the art roon and play around with paints and oil pastels.

FIG. 15–1   John's compare-and-contrast entry

Strategies for Comparing and Contrasting

Orchestrate an inquiry into what makes for good comparing and contrasting.

"Some of you might be thinking, 'I thought we were studying literary essays in this unit! What's up with the apples and oranges?!' And you'd be right to wonder. The work we did today will play an important role in the literary essay work you do across the next couple of days, when you compare and contrast two texts. On most days I'd say, 'So class, here's the really important stuff I hope you got from today' and then I'd show a chart that sums up all of the learning you did. But today is going to be different.

"Right now, I'm going to ask *you* to figure out what you learned about comparing and contrasting today. What is the really important stuff you discovered that we need to chart and remember over the next week? With your table groups, will you go off and figure this out? I've left some sentence strips and markers on your tables. You'll want to look back over all you've done today and, as a group, decide on one or two or three important things you've learned about comparing and contrasting. Then we'll come back together and make a chart of our sentence strips."

I sent the children off to work, coaching into each group as they studied their writing and attempted to name the work they'd done that was worth replicating. When each group had written on one or two sentence strips, I called them back together, asking the children to form a circle.

Help children decide which sentence strips are most important and form a class chart.

"You are the leaders of this chart we are making, and the choices about what goes on the final chart will be up to you. Sophie, will you be in charge of collecting sentence strips the class decides should go on the chart and pasting them up onto this blank piece of chart paper? We'll need a title for the chart, of course. How about 'Tips for Comparing and Contrasting'?"

Harrison began, sharing his sentence strip on behalf of his group. "We thought it was really important to have John's strategy on here. So we wrote 'We need to group our similarities and differences into categories or ideas.'" He looked around the carpet at the other children, and many shook their heads in agreement or indicated that they, too, had charted something similar. Sophie taped the sentence strip onto the chart.

Jill spoke next. "Our group looked at all our notebook entries, and we saw that we were using lots of transition words we know. They made our ideas more connected. We wrote, 'Use transition words to connect your ideas.'"

"That is very important," I said. "Maybe we can leave a little space under your sentence strip so we can fill in some specific transition words kids might use."

At the end of the share we had a chart that looked like this.

Tips for Comparing and Contrasting

- Group our similarities and differences into categories or ideas.
- Use transition words to connect your ideas.
  - They are similar because . . .
  - They are different because . . .
  - Also . . .
  - For example . . . Another example . . .
  - In addition . . .
- Write all about the similarities and then all about the differences OR you can be like a seesaw and write something about one thing and then something about the other thing, then something about the one thing and something about the other thing.

TIPS FOR COMPARING and CONTRASTING

★ GROUP OUR similarities and differences into Categories or IDeas

★ Use tRANSition WORDS to connect your IDeas
  • They are similar because...
  • They are also different because...
  • Also
  • For example... Another example...
  • In addition
★ write all about the similarities and then all about the Differences OR you can be like a seesaw and write something about one thing and then something about the other thing, then something about the one thing and something about the other thing.

SESSION 15 HOMEWORK

REVISING ENTRIES

Today you wrote a bunch of different compare-and-contrast entries as you moved from center to center. I think you'll agree you know a lot more compare-and-contrast strategies now than you did before today's workshop. Tonight return to your entries and revise them using what you've learned. Then, find things you would like to compare and contrast in your own life—the items on your kitchen table, clothes or books in your room, your movie or CD collection. The more time you spend building your compare-and-contrast muscles, the better off you will be, because you'll use these skills when you are comparing and contrasting two texts. You may want to copy the chart we made earlier into your notebook so you can use it tonight as you revise your entries.

Comparing and Contrasting Familiar Texts

THINK ABOUT HOW A YOUNGSTER learns to ride a bike, and you'll grasp the logic of this session and the last. The child first aspires to ride a bike. Then the child gets out on a little two-wheeler, with training wheels firmly in place. Voilà! He can do it! Now the training wheels come off, and Mom is there, running behind, a hand firmly on the bike seat. Yes! You are doing it! No training wheels (but yes, a hand on the seat). And then Mom lets go, and the youngster is peddling on his own, momentum building, with Mom, just fifty feet back, racing to catch up to be there to dust him off when he falls, get him back onto the bike, and run behind, hand on the seat, for a time.

In the previous session, you began the complicated work of teaching kids to compare and contrast. First, you simply put the apple and orange in front of them, explained the ground rules of discussing similarities and differences, and nudged them to have a go. Hey—that wasn't so bad. They all had something to say. But like any kids who haven't been taught otherwise, their work was disjointed. You said to them, "There's just one tip that will make a world of difference," and followed that up with, "Let me get you started." By the end of the session, when following a model closely, your students could compare two pieces of fruit, two shoes, and an array of other objects.

This session, then, lifts the level of student work, providing lots of support as expectations escalate. Think of all the supports you will provide. You will have chosen two texts that are ripe for comparison. One has already been mined, explored. You now do similar work with the other text, laying out themes that can be compared to the first text. For example, in both *Cinderella* and *Fox* good wins out over evil.

After students work together with tons of support to compare and contrast these two familiar texts, they are invited to do similar work comparing and contrasting any texts of their choice—including the two that you have already helped them to get a start on. This final challenge sets them up for the work on their final essay of the unit.

IN THIS SESSION, you'll teach students that essayists write compare-and-contrast essays by looking at similar themes across texts, or similar characters, and naming how the texts approach the themes differently or how the characters are similar and different.

GETTING READY

✔ "Finding Texts to Compare in Deep Ways" chart (see Teaching and Conferring)

✔ "Possible Leads for Compare-and-Contrast Essays" chart (see Mid-Workshop Teaching and CD-ROM)

✔ List of literary terms, written on chart paper for students to reference (see Share)

COMMON CORE STATE STANDARDS: W.4.1.a, W.4.4, RL.4.1, RL.4.2, RL.4.9, SL.4.1, L.4.1, L.4.2, L.4.3, L.4.6

Comparing and Contrasting Familiar Texts

CONNECTION

Tell students that after school yesterday you saw all of life through a compare-and-contrast lens. Suggest that the more interesting insights came when you went from surface to deeper-level comparisons.

"Writers, after yesterday's lesson I found myself continuing to compare and contrast things all day and all night. As I was waiting at the bus stop, I found myself comparing and contrasting the signs in storefront windows, the way different drivers park their cars. I even found myself comparing and contrasting how people walk down a block. I realized something that I never noticed before: some people are swingers when they walk, while others are not. The nonswingers keep their arms alongside their bodies even if they are dashing to catch a bus. But those who do swing their arms do it in different ways. Some swing just one arm because they are carrying something or clutching a bag," I demonstrated, "and some swing in sync with their legs." I demonstrated again.

"When I got home yesterday, I noticed that some of the people in my family are swingers, and some are not. I started to theorize that swingers are different sorts of people in other ways—personality ways. I'm still doing that research (and anyhow I don't want to offend anyone who is or is not a swinger by stereotyping you), but anyhow, from doing all this thinking, I came to an idea I want to share with you today."

✿ Name the teaching point.

"What I've learned is that the most interesting compare-and-contrast ideas are ones that go beneath surface traits to deeper relationships. One can say, 'These two texts are alike because they both contain the word *the*' but—*boring*. On the other hand, one of the greatest ways to have a good book talk is to wrestle with how two literary texts address the same theme or include similar characters, but do so differently."

◆ COACHING

This may sound frivolous to you, but actually comparing and contrasting are habits of mind, and you want your kids to be living the same way. You want them to be looking at the knapsack their brother carries and their own, thinking, "How are these the same? How are they different? What is the significance of those differences?"

TEACHING

Suggest that the class practice making theme-based comparisons by doing so with a familiar fairy tale, then unpack some themes associated with that tale as preparatory work for the upcoming comparisons.

"Writers, I was trying to imagine how we could begin this work of comparing and contrasting texts, and I thought it might be helpful to start off by comparing simple childhood tales such as *Cinderella* to some other texts.

"The first step needs to be to interpret—to think about themes—in one of the texts. Let's do that with *Cinderella*. You remember the story, don't you, of the beautiful, good Cinderella, who works all day, without complaining, while her evil stepsisters mistreat her? Let me recall the story for you, and will you think, 'What's this story really about? What lessons does it teach?'

"After mistreating Cinderella, the evil, rich stepsisters go off to a ball, intent on snaring the prince. Cinderella is left home to clean the ashes in the fireplace. A fairy godmother arrives on the scene, produces a pumpkin coach and a gown, and in the end, Cinderella marries the prince.

"So what life lessons might that story be teaching? What themes might it address?" I left a millisecond of silence, then continued. "Could you say it is about how good wins out in the end? Or about how the person, with goodness, can win over the more evil person?" The children agreed, adding another thought or two.

"Now we need to think, 'What other stories or books carry that same theme?'" I again left some silence. "Remember that the big ideas in one text will always relate to lots of other texts. That is why they are called *big ideas*. They are universal. Think of a few other stories where the younger, less powerful ends up triumphing over the powerful, richer, fancier (and less good). Turn and talk."

The children came back with suggestions. Soon we'd likened *Cinderella* to *David and Goliath*, *Charlotte's Web*, *The Lion, the Witch and the Wardrobe*, *Peter Pan*, *Skinny Bones*, *Pinky and Rex and the Bully*, and the list continued. "So you could easily write a compare-and-contrast essay showing how *Cinderella* is like and unlike any one of those texts—and, I would add, you could do so with *Fox*."

Debrief in ways that pop out the replicable, transferable work you have just done.

"So, writers, as I told you yesterday, *The New York Times Book Review* often publishes essays that compare and contrast two texts. Usually the essayist gets at something deep and important that is the same across the two books and then discusses ways those books do that same thing differently. So far this minilesson has helped you know how to find texts that can be compared by theme. And just finding those texts and setting them alongside each other is half the challenge." I unveiled the following chart.

The work you're asking students to do here—-to think about themes and how they relate across texts—is work the Common Core Reading Standards for Literature expect your students to be able to do as fourth-graders. The standards expect students to "determine a theme of a story, drama, or poem" (CCSS.RL.4.2) and to "compare and contrast the treatment of similar themes and topics (e.g., opposition of good and evil) and patterns of events (e.g., the quest) in stories, myths, and traditional literature from different cultures" (CCSS.RL.4.9).

> **Finding Texts to Compare in Deep Ways**
>
> - Think about the larger theme of one text, list other texts that address the same theme, and choose a second text that seems to especially "go."
> - Think about how the two texts both address the same theme. How are they similar? Why is this significant? How do they address the theme differently?

Remind students that when comparing and contrasting, they can use the template they learned the previous day.

"So, writers, once you have your shared theme, remember that you will write how the books develop that theme similarly and differently. So let's say I am comparing *Cinderella* and *Charlotte's Web*. Watch how I start my essay, and get ready to list across your fingers three tips that you learn by watching me do this."

> Both <u>Cinderella</u> and <u>Charlotte's Web</u> teach the lesson that sometimes in life, characters who are pushed to the side and thought of as nothing end up being heroes. In many ways, the stories are the same. They are the same because in both, the protagonist is at first pushed to the side. In <u>Charlotte's Web</u>, Fern's father wants to kill Wilbur despite Fern's protestations. In <u>Cinderella</u>, Cinderella wants to go to the ball, but her stepmother and stepsisters forbid her from going.
>
> They are also the same because in both stories, the protagonists don't succeed on their own. In <u>Charlotte's Web</u>, it is really the spider Charlotte who helps save Wilbur. In <u>Cinderella</u>, it is the fairy godmother who helps Cinderella get to the ball and meet the prince.

I gave the children a few seconds to list the tips with their partner.

ACTIVE ENGAGEMENT

Channel students to compare and contrast two stories.

"To practice comparing texts by theme, I'm going to suggest you and your partner think between *Cinderella* and *Fox*, and do so by thinking of how they address the same theme, similarly and differently, or how Cinderella is like and unlike a character in *Fox*. Turn and talk."

I moved among children, coaching them.

If you want to provide extra scaffolding, you could spell this out more. You could say, "You could compare, for example, how both stories address the theme we mentioned earlier of the good person triumphing over someone who is evil."

"Don't just run through a list of how they are the same and different, but spend time explaining the first similarity you notice before you switch to a second, and before you shift from similarities to differences. It might sound like this: 'These characters are the same in many ways. The first way . . . To add on . . . Also . . . For example . . . The second way . . . '

"Remember the power of *because*. Say it once and follow with another and another.

"Add on to your partner's thinking by saying, 'But . . . Also . . . In addition . . . '

"Use your thought prompts, like 'This shows . . . ' and 'This is important because . . . '

"Don't just stop talking. If you aren't sure, remember you are just exploring, so use 'Maybe . . . ' 'Perhaps . . . ' 'It could be . . . '

"Make sure your evidence matches your claim. You are not talking about all the ways they are the same. You are talking about ways the two texts develop the same theme."

LINK

Send youngsters off to start writing their own compare-and-contrast essays, on texts of their own choice. Let them know that this project will culminate the unit.

"For two days now, you have worked on developing your muscles for comparing and contrasting. All of that has prepared you for this moment. Now is the time for you to do the work that is the very hardest work you'll do in this whole unit. Your job over the next four or five days is to write one last essay. It will be a compare-and-contrast essay. I suggest you use at least one of the texts you have already written about in this unit—*Fox* or the short text you wrote about initially: 'Eleven,' 'The Marble Champ,' or 'Spaghetti'—or you could write about your favorite book of all time. You'll want to start and think, 'What is that text really about?' and once you have a sense for a possible theme, you'll want to think about some other texts that address the same theme. I often find it helps to come up with a short list, and then to ask myself, 'Of all the possibilities, which would work best?'

"You have about fifteen minutes to choose your texts and to think about what the similarities are that matter to you. You don't even need to think about differences just yet. For now, you may not even be writing. You might instead be jotting, mapping, planning. This is gigantic work, so don't waste a minute. Get started."

Teachers, if there are two steps that children are expected to do during one workshop, it is helpful that you give them a sense of how much time part 1 will take, or children could spend the whole time making a plan and never executing it. We have found this to be especially true of children new to a workshop.

Bringing All You Know to This Important Work

IT IS HELPFUL IF YOU TAKE A BIT OF TIME to anticipate the predictable problems your students are apt to encounter today, because this will make you able to be more responsive more quickly. First of all, don't be surprised if your students make incredibly simplistic comparisons between the two texts. The child might be arguing that in both *Because of Winn-Dixie* and *Charlotte's Web*, the theme is that friendship matters, and

in both, there is a girl with a name that contains only four letters: Fern, Opal. You'll have a hard time maintaining a straight face over some of their blunders.

When this happens, you might as well get a kick out of the kids. Their mess-ups reflect the fact that this is utterly new work. The good news is that if they are showing

---

MID-WORKSHOP TEACHING **Using Templates to Craft Comparative Essays**

"Writers, remember earlier, you learned about templates that you could use to make a thesis." I pointed at the "Possible Templates" chart from Session 10 (see CD-ROM). 💿

"I thought it might help to add templates to this chart for the sorts of leads that comparative essayists often use when they are writing. You and your partner can try these on for size and see if any of them work for you." I unveiled the following templates.

> Possible Leads for Compare-and-Contrast Essays:
>
> • Both (first title) and (second title) are stories about...
>
> Ex: Both "Those Shoes" and "Stray" are stories about longing and learning to accept.
>
> • Both (first title) and (second title) teach readers that... In (the first text) and in (the second text)... Although both stories teach readers... they do so very differently because in one... whereas in the other...
>
> or
>
> • Both stories, (first title) and (second title) deal with the theme of ... but while (first text)

> suggests that... (second text) suggests that...
>
> Ex: Both "Charlotte's Web" and "Because of Winn Dixie" teach readers that it's not always the big and important people who make the biggest difference. In "Charlotte's Web," a little spider turns the barnyard into a community, and in "Because of Winn Dixie," a stray dog does the same for a town. Although both stories show the amazing influence that one character can have, in one book, the character gives her life to this cause, and in the other, the character lives happily ever after because of this.
>
> • The characters in (first title) and (second title) are both... and both learn to...
>
> Ex: The characters Opal from "Because of Winn Dixie" and Doris from "Stray" are both lonely and both learn to open their hearts to a new friend.

After a few minutes I said, "So writers, you might find it helpful to use these templates when you are writing. Remember, you can try things out not just once, not just twice, but three or four times to help you get the most powerful essay. Let's get back to work."

---

themselves to be total novices at this, then just think of how easy it will be for them to improve in giant steps.

The challenge, of course, will be, first, to not get discouraged yourself and to not let them get discouraged, and second, to figure out ways to not just say, "Wrong," but to instead let them know more productive ways of proceeding. If a child has said Fern and Opal are similar because both have four letters in their name, we imagine two tactics that might be especially helpful. First, you'll want to remind children that they are now looking not just for any ol' similarities, but for similarities that show how the two texts develop the theme, which in this instance, is the theme that friendship matters. It usually helps to start with one book and to think about concrete ways that theme is shown. Are there patterns in the actions that support the idea that friendship matters? Soon the writer will be saying something like "Wilbur relies on Charlotte to help him with his problems." Now she will be situated to make a much more substantial comparison with her next text.

The second way to steer children toward making more substantial comparisons is to remind them of the aspects of books that they already know matter. So, for example, they already know that when writing about a story, it pays off to notice the characters—their traits, motivations, struggles, changes, and relationships. So a child wanting to compare *Charlotte's Web* and *Because of Winn-Dixie* would find it productive to compare any one of those important aspects of the texts.

Depending on your reading instruction, you may also find that some students are unsure of their thinking about themes. You might want to pull these students together and teach them a way to do so. We usually begin a small group by telling the students why we have gathered them together. This helps students focus. You might say something like "I've gathered you all together because I noticed that you are having a hard time coming up with a theme that ties two books together." Then you could name the teaching point of the small group and the work you'll do together. You might say, "I thought it might help you to know that when it is hard to compare themes across books, often it helps to start by comparing the main characters in two books. Again, it helps to start by settling on one thing. You might decide, for example, that you definitely want to write about *Cinderella*. Then you could say to yourself, 'Okay, what

character do I know whose life and circumstances are a lot like Cinderella's?' It could be that Harry Potter pops into your mind, and it is true that there are similarities. Then you could list those similarities. Both Harry and Cinderella are adopted by reluctant family members. Both are then abused by a family member. But both rise above their situation with the help of a powerful, magical character—the fairy godmother for Cinderella and Dumbledore for Harry. Both characters go, literally, from rags to riches."

I might then ask children to think about the process I'd just gone through. What did they notice me doing? I'd want them to realize that if it is hard to think about a theme that relates to two books, usually one can think about characters who are similar, and by thinking about that, one can get to comparisons of theme.

After this small-group lesson, we added a new bullet to our chart.

Finding Texts to Compare in Deep Ways

* Think about the larger theme of one text, list other texts that address the same theme, and choose a second text that seems to especially "go."

* Think about how the two texts both address the same theme. How are they similar? "How do they address the theme differently? Why is this significant?"

* Look at two similar characters from different books and think about how they are similar. Do they both learn similar lessons?

Being Literary Scholars

Share with the class one student's draft that demonstrates especially powerful literary work, such as using the language of the discipline.

"Writers, I want to talk to you about something I noticed Parker doing that I think all of you could benefit from. Parker was sitting at his desk with his several quick drafts of an introduction to the side and another piece of paper in front of him. On this page, he was trying to write his ending in three different ways. I was curious to see what he was on about, so I sidled over to check, and what I saw blew me away! So, Parker, come up here and explain your work."

Parker displayed his work to the class and began, "I decided to revise this one part over and over, trying to use better words."

"Explain what you mean by 'better words.'"

"I was trying to use words like *author, protagonist, theme*, and, um, I think that's it."

"So you were trying to write with words of your discipline? Like we talked about a few days ago during one of our mid-workshops? Read us a little of the before draft and then the after draft."

Parker said, "My 'before ending' goes like this."

> Both Gloria from the story "Gloria Who Might Be My Best Friend" and Dog from the story "Fox" are characters who are willing to put themselves out there and take risks to make friends.

"And my new ending goes like this."

But before he could finish his sentence, I interrupted to say, speaking in my most erudite voice, "Parker, read as if you are a literary scholar or a college professor of lit-er-a-ture and this is your masterpiece." Parker did.

> The character Gloria, the protagonist in the fiction story "Gloria Who Might Be My Best Friend" by the author Ann Cameron and Dog, the protagonist in the fiction story, "Fox" by the author

FIG. 16–1 Parker uses literary language in his introduction.

Margaret Wild, are stories that deal with the same theme that in order to make friends sometimes you have to take risks in life.

"Writers, doesn't this version of Parker's ending make him sound so professorial!"

The kids nodded and Parker went to sit down. "I'm pretty sure that some of the rest of you will want to be sure you are using academic language. And I also want to teach you one more thing that Parker could do, and that all of you could do, to make your essays scholarly. You can mention archetypes."

Introduce students to the literary term *archetype* and encourage them to think about the term and use it in their own essays.

"Let me explain what an archetype is. Let's start with Fox. If I say that a character was foxlike, tell your partner what that character is like. Turn and talk." The children talked for a minute, and then I called them back. "The fact that you have a lot of knowledge of what constitutes a foxlike character shows that you have a deep understanding of archetypes. You just haven't been taught the term—which is no wonder because it really is a concept most people are taught in college.

"An archetype is a kind of character that one meets often in stories. The gallant knight is an archetype, and the wicked stepmother is an archetype. Turn and talk about the archetype of the stepmother in *Cinderella*. The children did, and of course, they said she is an evil person who makes Cinderella's life miserable.

"So my question, writers, is whether one of the characters in your story is an archetype. If so, you probably get the feeling you have seen this character often. This is the younger brother who is—what?" I left a pool of silence.

The kids called out that he is lazy and foolish, but he turns out to not be so bad after all.

"And what about the man who lives alone in a shack by the sea? If he is an archetype, what's he like?

"What about the librarian. What does she look like if she is an archetype?

"What about the wolf?

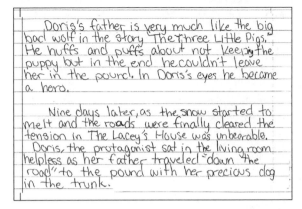

> Doris's father is very much like the big bad wolf in the story "The Three Little Pigs." He huffs and puffs about not keeping the puppy but in the end he couldn't leave her in the pound. In Doris's eyes he became a hero.
>
> Nine days later, as the snow started to melt and the roads were finally cleared the tension in The Lacey's House was unbearable. Doris, the protagonist sat in the living room helpless as her father traveled "down the road" to the pound with her precious dog in the trunk.

FIG. 16–2   Celia rewrites two parts of her draft using literary terms.

> Both "Spaghetti" by Cynthia Rylant & "Journey" by Patricia MacLachlan are fiction stories that deal with the theme of loneliness. Gabriel, the protagonist from "Spaghetti" & Journey, the protagonist from "Journey" both find the cure when they befriend an animal.
>
> Loneliness is the theme that runs through both "Spaghetti" by Cynthia Rylant and "Journey" by Patricia MacLachlan. Although these stories are set in different places each character solves their loneliness by befriending an animal.

FIG. 16–3   Jessica revises her introduction by using literary devices.

"Turn and talk to each other about whether one of your characters could be regarded as an archetype. If not, you'll still want to make sure you are using literary language in your essay, so help each other insert words like those on this list into your essay where they are needed."

point of view	theme
protagonist	lead
character	tension
setting	symbol
plot	tone

OPENING UP POSSIBILITIES

For homework tonight you'll want to continue thinking, "What are my texts really about?" If you started to write about one theme, you will probably not want to zero in on this one theme, but you'll want to come up with different possibilities. You can do this by rereading your texts and thinking about other themes you can uncover. If you are struggling to come up with different themes, you may want to think about your characters and their traits, motivations, struggles, changes, and relationships. All of these will lead you to compare your stories in deep ways. Try to get a lot of writing down tonight, not only by exploring different ideas, but also by exploring different templates. Remember, you can try things out not just once, not just twice, but three or four times to help you get the most powerful ideas for your essay.

Using Yesterday's Learning, Today and Always

THE HALLMARK OF TRUE UNDERSTANDING is the ability to take a strategy, a skill, or a lesson and apply it to new situations independently. And, of course, this philosophy is at the core of the writing workshop. As children ventured from personal narrative to personal and persuasive essay, we reminded them to use what they know about narrative craft to angle their anecdotes and evidence. As children moved from personal and persuasive essay to literary essay, we emphasized the fact that what they know about essay structure and craft still applies.

Today, you will remind children that all they have learned across the past units is still important as they draft this new form of literary essay. "Weighing one thing and another thing and thinking deeply about their similarities and differences is important thinking work that students will need to apply across their schooling."

We have hinted all along that the skills of comparing and contrasting are important because of the Common Core State Standards' expectations for your children. And indeed, it is clear that analyzing themes across texts is one of the messages to be gleaned from the CCSS. But we also believe that weighing one thing and another thing and thinking deeply about their similarities and differences is important thinking work that students will need to apply across their schooling—to the content areas of math, science, and history—and in their college essays, scholarship essays, and so forth. Comparing and contrasting requires students to synthesize what they know about a subject or a text, think critically about that subject or text, and categorize their thinking so that it applies to something larger. This type of intellectual work gets students to think more deeply about the texts they are reading and to move more effortlessly up and down the ladder of abstraction. It is these skills you have been teaching children over the past several sessions, and today's session builds on that work, reminding children that as writers, they must carry forward all they know and use it in service of writing to compare and contrast.

IN THIS SESSION, you'll teach students that essayists draw on all they know about essay writing as they tackle new projects. You'll remind students that compare-and-contrast essays are a kind of literary essay, so they can use prior learning as they continue to draft and revise their essays.

GETTING READY

✔ Charts from across the unit, hanging around the classroom for children to see (e.g., "How to Write a Literary Essay" from Session 11; "A Few Ways to Transition to Quotes from a Text" from Session 6; "How to Angle a Story to Make a Point" from Session 5; "Ways to Push Our Thinking" from Session 11; and any others your children use often)

✔ Students' notebooks and drafts, their writing to learn, and their personal goal sheets from Session 14, to be brought to the meeting area

✔ Sample student's compare-and-contrast essay, to use as a model for making a revision plan based on all she knows to do but hasn't yet done in her writing (see Connection)

✔ Conferring tools, such as copies of student drafts and essays, class essays, your essay in various stages of development, conferring sheets, the Opinion Writing Learning Progression, and mentor text, such as *Fox*

✔ "Literary Devices" chart from Session 13 (see Conferring and Small-Group Work)

COMMON CORE STATE STANDARDS: W.4.1, W.4.5, W.4.10, RL.4.1, RL.4.9, RL.5.1, SL.4.1, L.4.1, L.4.2, L.4.3, L.4.6

Using Yesterday's Learning, Today and Always

CONNECTION

Remind students that as they move to new kinds of essay writing, they are still writing essays and need to draw on all they know.

"Writers," I began, "you might notice that our classroom looks a bit like a laundry room, with all our charts hanging from strings and wooden clothes hangers around the room. I've done this on purpose, because I want to make sure that all the learning you've done across this unit is front and center. You see, even though you have begun a new endeavor (compare-and-contrast essays), it is important, imperative really, for you to use *all* you've learned about writing literary essays in particular as you tackle this new project. After all, even though this is a new project, you are still writing in general and writing literary essays.

"I flew to Florida once and needed to rent a car. I hopped in, ready to put the key in the ignition and drive off, only to find that there was no key and there was no keyhole. I sat there for ten minutes, trying to figure out how to turn the car on, until I finally realized that this particular kind of car started when you pushed a button. I turned the car on and sat there. I was scared to drive off! What if there are other things I don't understand about how this car works? What if I can't figure it out? My mind was racing.

"I could have sat there for ages, scared to drive off. But instead, I reminded myself of all I *do* know about driving. I knew enough to drive this car, even if it was a bit different than those I had driven before."

❖ **Name the teaching point.**

"I am telling you this today, because like me in that new car, you are in the process of drafting a new kind of essay. You may think, 'Wait, I don't know how to do this! I've only learned about compare-and-contrast essays for two days!' But really, you know enough about writing essays to do it well. Essayists ask, 'What do I already know that will help me do this well?' and then they hold themselves accountable to drawing on all they've learned before.

"Yesterday, Emily and I were talking. She showed me the compare-and-contrast essay she has been working on, comparing 'Thank You, Mr. Falker' and 'The Marble Champ.' She is trying to show that both of these stories are about the importance of support and determination in hard situations. Whenever I reread drafts of compare-and-contrast essays that I'm working on, I always check to see if I've remembered to do all that I know. For me, the important thing is that

◆ COACHING

Throughout these units of study, we make anchor charts with children, and we intend for those charts to be resources again and again until the steps and strategies on them are internalized. There are also charts that are less crucial, less central to the learning of each unit, but nevertheless helpful. You will have to find the balance between a bounty of helpful charts and an upsetting, overwhelming overload of charts. Keep present only the additional charts you know your children can use, above and beyond the anchor charts for each unit. You may want to type up smaller versions of these less central charts and have them at the writing center for children to use when they need them. You can also add these to your conferring toolkit.

I can draw on what I know about stories and essays of all sorts, to help me with structure and elaborating. I don't just think about whether I'm using what I have learned from literary essays.

"I want to show you what we saw when Emily and I looked at her body paragraphs. Look with us, thinking about whether Emily has used everything she has already learned." (See Figure 17–1.)

"When Emily and I looked at her writing, we noticed a lot of things she is doing well. We noticed right away that she writes with generalizations—at the top of that ladder of abstraction—and with the concrete specifics. Also, she not only *tells about* a part of the text that matches her claim, but she *cites* that part. She also writes a bunch of sentences, and not just one sentence, to prove her point.

"But we also thought about things that Emily has learned to do that she hasn't yet done in this essay. It is, after all, a rough draft. Emily realized that there is just one example to support each of her points. She realized that she's forgotten to push her thinking and that she can work on that by using some of the prompts we've learned, like 'Another example is . . . ,' and then provide a second example, so she will be working on that today. Then too, she realized that she cites the text but doesn't 'unpack' the citation, discussing how it matches her thesis, and she knows how to do that.

"Emily made a plan for how to get started today by looking back at all our class charts and thinking about all she's learned about essay writing. The important thing is to check that you do all the things you know how to do as you revise your draft today."

FIG. 17–1 Emily's body paragraph shows what she's doing well and where she can add things she's learned.

ACTIVE ENGAGEMENT

Rally your students to review their own work in progress, thinking about whether they, too, have forgotten to do some of the things they know how to do.

"Right now, will you take out the drafts you are working on and place them in front of you? I want you to pore over the writing you've done so far and ask, 'What is on these charts? What prior learning have I forgotten to apply to my writing?' You'll also want to look at your personal goal sheet. Have you remembered to hold yourself accountable to the goals you've set for yourself? Turn and talk with your partner."

As the children talked, I moved among them, coaching into their work.

LINK

Remind writers to draw on all they know, and send them off to work.

"Writers, will each of you think about the goal—or goals—that today's investigation has revealed for you, and add those goals to your personal goal sheets? After you have done that, you can get started on your writing. And always remember that all that you learned last week and last month is always still precious today."

Essayists Think about *How*, Not Just *What*

IN YOUR CONFERRING TODAY, you'll want to make sure to watch not just for *what* kids are writing, but *how* they are writing it. You might consider pulling a small group of children whose ideas seem tentative. When you looked over their drafts, you were struck by the number of phrases these children used like *possibly*, *it could be*, or *maybe*. These words were so overused it detracted from the idea the writer was trying to make and made the writer seem uncertain and unsure of the validity of her thesis. There is, of course, a beauty to mulling things over in an essay, and you'll want to give children the freedom and space to meander their way to an idea. In fact, some people think it is a good thing for an essayist to journey through thinking in a more questioning, wondering way. Others, however, say it is better to have an authoritative voice and believe that the use of "hedge words" like *probably*, *possibly*, *maybe*, and *perhaps* weaken a writer's ability to be persuasive.

In light of this, you might explain that it is important to think about *how* writers convey their ideas. After all, they want others to agree with them! Essayists have to decide on the tone of their essay. They ask themselves, "What will my essay sound like? Will it be more assertive? Will it be more tentative? Will there be some places where I assert my views and then some places where I'm journeying through my thoughts?" To explain this to your students, you might liken this to talking to adults versus to kids their own age. You might ask, "Have you ever noticed that you talk differently to different people? For example, if you talk to our principal at recess you sound different than when you talk to your friends." If your children need this explained further, you might say, "Do you remember when I called you together for our writing boot camp? That day I was pretty strict with you. You'll probably remember I said things like 'Do this now' and 'No, not like that. Like this.' You might even say I was being a bit of a bossy-pants. But from my language it was clear that I knew what I wanted you to do. We call this being authoritative."

MID-WORKSHOP TEACHING
Pushing Initial Ideas and Thoughts about Texts Further

"Writers, can I stop you for a second? I want to caution you against seeing drafting as a robotic capturing of ideas you've already had about books. Instead, drafting can be a time to push your own thinking further. One way to do this is by asking, 'What does this similarity or difference teach me about the world?'

"Drafting is not just about jotting down what you already know, what you already think. Instead, use drafting time to develop new thinking and journey yourself through your thinking.

"Here's how to do it: when you notice a similarity or difference between two books, you can stop and ask yourself, 'What does this similarity or difference teach me about the world?'

"For example, Raffi has noticed that *Snow White* and *Fox* both have the theme that it's hard to be all alone, but Snow White deals with this by making friends with everyone around her, and Fox deals with this by trying to hurt everyone around him. When I talked to him about what this difference teaches us about the world, do you know what he said? He said, 'The bad stuff that happens to you matters, but what you decide to do about it matters even more.' What a cool thought! That could really change the lives of people who read his essay. And the way he got there was by looking at what he'd written and asking himself, 'What does this similarity or difference teach me about the world?' Please take a moment and in your essays try the same work Raffi did. Essayists push themselves to not just record ideas, but develop new ones."

You might then say, "You have a choice when you write about a text. You teach others the smart theory that you've settled upon. If you decide to play this role, you'd probably talk a bit like an announcer, using a strong, declarative voice like I did in boot camp." You'll then want to illustrate the tone by altering your own voice to match what you are describing. "For example, if I were writing about 'Spaghetti' I might talk like this."

> In the story "Spaghetti," by Cynthia Rylant, we meet Gabriel, a lonely, serious boy who learns to love when he finds a cat. This is evident from how he handles the cat. He holds the cat in his hands. He holds him to his cheek. He holds him "under his chin." He holds him so close that he notices the cat smells like "pasta noodles." It is important to notice that Cynthia Rylant spends so much time talking about how Gabriel holds the cat for a reason. All these details clearly show that Gabriel bonds with the cat and opens his heart to him.

You might also choose to model for children what the other option would sound like (the one that many of them have adopted), in which they take on a meandering, tentative tone. "On the other hand, you could decide to talk and write about the text as if you are an explorer, a wanderer. In that case, your voice would be tentative and exploratory. For example, in this voice I might write":

> "Spaghetti" is a story about a boy who learns to love. He learns this from a cat. Some people might say it's not really love he felt. He just held the cat and his heart opened. Or was it already open? Would he have picked up the cat and put it by his cheek if he was so hardened? I don't think so. He maybe learns love from his own life, not just from the cat, but I'm not sure.

To bring the small group to an end you might sum up by saying, "Both the authoritative and meandering tones can lead to beautifully written essays, and so writers must choose which tone they will use or if they will use both. But remember that essayists make that choice deliberately, based on what they want the reader to get out of their essay. Some essayists want to take their readers along with them on the writing journey, and it's almost as if the reader is discovering the big ideas at the same time as the writer. But other times, essayists want to get their readers to be persuaded by their ideas, and so even if they wrote a lot of tentative ideas at first to get to their big idea, they then go back and revise some of that tentativeness out of their writing so that their reader knows exactly the claim the writer is putting forth." Then you will send them off to revise parts of their drafts by taking on the different tones. Tell them both have value, and so they will need to be able to do both.

Another way to watch for *how* they are writing it is to study craft with children. So as you set out to confer today, remember to tuck *Fox* in among your conferring tools, such as copies of student drafts and essays, class essays, your essay in various stages of development, conferring sheets, the Opinion Writing Learning Progression, and so on. You will never know what you might need to help you make concrete to children what you are teaching them. You might remind the students that an author deliberately crafts a story—or any text—in ways that highlight the deeper meaning. If you are saying that you might choose to go back to parts that you studied earlier in *Fox* more specifically, have on hand a small version of the "Literary Devices that Highlight Meaning" chart to give to each child. This might be a time you teach into a device you haven't studied with the rest of the class yet.

Being Critical Friends

Recruit children to read their partner's draft critically, looking for ways to revise it by drawing on past learning.

"Writers, did you know that writing partners wear different hats? There are times when your job as a writing partner is to cheer each other along or pat each other on the backs after a long day's work. But writing partners also have to be critical friends. What I mean by this is that, as a partner, it is also your responsibility to help your partner see what he or she may not notice on their own. Sometimes this means saying, 'Hey, I'm noticing you have a problem here,' or 'This part is confusing. Can I help you make it clearer?'

"Today, you will meet with your partner and help each other with the work we began in the minilesson—holding yourself accountable to past learning. This will work best if you take one person's piece and study it carefully. Remember to use the charts and together name the goals you both think the writer still needs to work on. After all, part of being a good friend is being an honest friend."

> My Goals
>
> · I need to use more transitions so that readers can follow what I'm saying. I could write things like "this shows that..." or "another place" where this is true is..."
>
> · Spice up my introduction and conclusion a little bit, maybe by telling the reader why this book or topic is so important
>
> · Make sure I don't have any run-on sentences.
>
> Still need to work on:
> - transitions to quotes from a text
> - use more literary devices
> - explain the significance

FIG. 17–2 Parker updated his personal goals after meeting with his partners.

SESSION 17 HOMEWORK

REVISING DRAFTS BASED ON PARTNER SUGGESTIONS

Today you met with your partner for a bit of time and both of you really pushed yourselves to be critical friends. You took seriously your responsibility to help each other see what you each may not have noticed on your own. You now have a list of suggestions and notes in the margins of your draft of the work that needs to get done. Make sure you set aside enough time to work on these suggestions. You might want to spend time tonight collecting the tools you'll need to do your work. Think about the charts you may need, mentor essay texts, and also your old drafts. You only have a few more days to finish your essay, so use your writing time as productively as possible.

Developing Distinct Lines of Thought

T EACHERS OF READING collect careful evidence of children's miscues and then study them to understand the logic that informs their efforts. The child who reads a sentence, "I got on my horse and galloped away," as if it says "I got on my *house* and galloped away" is relying on phonics and not meaning. The miscue functions like a window, letting us understand this. In the same way, the chaos and ambiguity and confusion that we often see when children try to write literary essays can also give us a window into the logic that informs children's writing. Study your students' work with great care, and then expect to invent teaching—conferring, small-group work, and minilessons—in response to what you see.

This is one such minilesson. We're quite sure that you'll find that your kids, like so many students the world over, often write in what the great researcher, Mina Shaughnessy, once called "sentences of thought" instead of passages of thought. This minilesson is an attempt to talk to kids about what we see.

You can expect that the problems will not go away as a result of today's minilesson. You are teaching extremely complicated things: elaboration, logic, following a line of thought, discerning ambiguity. The good news about today's session is that it may give you a language with which to talk about your students' tendencies to tangle up their thinking.

The session relies on a method of teaching that by now you will know well. Because we aim to teach something complicated, the minilesson relies on something concrete and tangible. For the session to work, however, it also needs for you to be intent on communicating, on reaching your kids. Lean forward. Watch their faces. Sense their response. And be prepared to go to great lengths to be sure you are reaching them.

IN THIS SESSION, you'll teach students that writers elaborate on each of their distinct, individual supporting ideas, ensuring they have developed their essay with enough evidence for their claim.

GETTING READY

✔ Tangled knots of string, for students to help you untangle (see Connection)

✔ Sample student draft that demonstrates a tangle of thoughts and ideas, to model to children how to untangle ideas in their writing (see Teaching)

✔ Smaller versions of the anchor charts from the unit, such as the "How to Write a Literary Essay" chart (see Conferring and Small-Group Work)

✔ "Ways to Push Our Thinking" chart (see Share and Homework)

COMMON CORE STATE STANDARDS: W.4.1.b,c; W.4.5, RL.4.1, RFS.4.4, SL.4.1, L.4.1, L.4.2, L.4.3, L.4.6

Developing Distinct Lines of Thought

CONNECTION

Recruit children's help to untangle knots of string. In a way that will connect to their writing, say back what they did to untangle the knots.

"Writers, can I get some help? I wanted to hang some charts up in our room, but all of my string seems to be in tangles. If I give you some of these tangles, would you see if you can straighten them out?" I distributed tangled knots of string to triads of children. "I've been tugging and pulling and haven't been able to get rid of the knots. I probably just need to go buy more string."

After a minute or two, clusters of children started completing their untangling job. I looked totally floored that they were done so quickly. "How did you do it?" I asked. "I have pulled so hard and they didn't come undone for me."

The children hastened to tell me that the answer hadn't been to pull harder—which only tightened the wad of string. Instead, the job required them to *loosen* the tangle, to separate the strings, to give each strand of string some space.

When they said this, I took in their words, repeating them. "So you found the strings all smushed together," and I clasped my hands, "and what you needed to do was to loosen the string a bit, to let there be more space in there?" I unclasped my hands. The children confirmed this.

I know. This one takes the cake. It will seem odd, but I think it actually makes an important point.

❖ **Name the teaching point.**

"That is amazing, writers, because today I was going to talk to you about how sometimes your writing is like a tangled knot of thoughts, twisted together. The way that you loosen the tangle of strings might also be the way you loosen your writing. Perhaps you need to separate lines of thinking, to give each line of thinking a bit more air, a bit more space."

TEACHING

Show children one writer's tangled thoughts, and suggest that to untangle the ideas, she needs to focus on one thought at a time, saying more about each one.

"Writers, yesterday when Jessica and I looked at her draft, the first thing I realized was that she had a ton of brilliant moves in her essay. But because she twisted all her good thinking tightly together so that her writing was like a knot of ideas, it was hard to see and to follow all the brilliant stuff she'd written. Everything was so tangled into her passage, so tightly combined, that it was easy to miss her brilliant thinking.

"Listen to the start of her essay. You'll see that it begins with her thesis and then goes on to elaborate—fast, in her smushed-together way. Listen, because I think you'll find that many of you do a lot of what Jessica does as well." (See Figure 18–1.)

> Jessica
>
> Both Spaghetti by Cynthia Rylant and Journey by Patricia MacLachlan are stories about lonely characters who find the cure when they befriend an animal. In Spaghetti, Gabriel, being lonely reminds me of Journey being lonely. When Journey was lonely, "and then the cat came," Patricia MacLachlan said. Bloom, the cat, helped cure Journey's loneliness. Bloom also helped connect Journey to the rest of his family. ...

FIG. 18–1 Jessica's introduction twists her good thinking into a knot of ideas.

> Both "Spaghetti" by Cynthia Rylant and "Journey" by Patricia MacLachlan are stories about lonely characters who find the cure when they befriend an animal. In "Spaghetti," Gabriel being lonely reminds me of Journey being lonely. When Journey was lonely, 'and then the cat came,' Patricia MacLachlan said. Bloom, the cat, helped cure Journey's loneliness. Bloom also helped connect Journey to the rest of his family. There are italics that show how important it was.

"Writers, I'm sure you noticed that Jessica has a ton of brilliant moves in her essay. She has said that Gabriel, from one story, and Journey, from another story, are both lonely. She has said that in both, an animal comes to help. She has suggested that animals can cure loneliness.

"That is all great thinking. But this is her problem. She tangles all her good thinking tightly together into a knot of ideas, and it is hard to see all the brilliant stuff she's got tangled so closely together. The funny thing is that Jessica actually thought the problem was she didn't have *enough to say!* She was going to try to get more stuff to twist into her knot. That is exactly the opposite of what she needs to do. She needs to piece apart her knot of thinking like this is a ball of string, pulled really tightly. If she starts to loosen and separate the different ideas, then she can say more about each one. Let's help her together."

ACTIVE ENGAGEMENT

Set students up to help untangle the student's draft, stretching out each thought before moving to the next one. Scaffold their work by naming the first idea.

"Let's help her together. Take this line."

> In "Spaghetti," Gabriel being lonely reminds me of Journey being lonely.

"How can Jessica say more about that, stretching it out so she writes a whole paragraph about that? Turn and talk."

After a minute, I said, "Writers, eyes back here. You are right. She can tell evidence she has for Gabriel being lonely and evidence for Journey being lonely. Perhaps she could get a quote from each or tell a micro-story. Writers, would you read on in Jessica's draft and see if there is another place where she has written, in one sentence, what really should go in a whole paragraph?"

Soon the children had found other examples. The supporting idea, "Bloom, the cat, helped cure Journey's loneliness," for example, is undeveloped. The children thought Jessica could explain *how* the cat helped cure Journey's loneliness, and provide specific details about what the cat did.

We concluded by saying that Jessica has some good thinking, but that rather than jumping quickly from one supporting idea to another, she should instead work on developing each idea by providing evidence and examples in support of her reason and claim.

LINK

Tell students that untangling their thoughts and providing more evidence for their different supporting ideas might be work they want to do today.

"I'm telling you this because we have a lot of people who smush their brilliant ideas so close together that they almost don't make sense: Remember that each of your supporting ideas needs to be developed with evidence and examples.

"Today some of you will work to loosen the tight knot of ideas on your paper, perhaps copying over a sentence on a fresh piece of paper, then elaborating on it, then copying another. Others of you have other work to do on your essay."

In Spaghetti, Gabriel being lonely reminds me of Journey being lonely. One way, Cynthia Rylant shows Gabriel's loneliness is that she had Gabriel looking longingly at people in his neighborhood "talking quietly among themselves." He is not sitting with them but is alone on a stoop. He is not part of a group but seems to want to be because "he wished for some company." It is like Gabriel is on the outside looking in at his neighbors and hoping that one of them or someone will invite him in. Journey is a lot like Gabriel in this way. Journey feels on the outside of his family and he longs to find a connection with them, especially with his absent mother. Another way, the author shows Gabriel's loneliness is through the description of the building. In the text is said that Gabriel sat in

front of a "tall building of crumbling bricks and rotting wood." This image of a run down building is used to show how like the building Gabriel has no one to take care of him and the building represents that Gabriel is depressed because he is lonely. Patricia MacLachlan like Cynthia Rylant also shows Journey's loneliness through an object. The pictures of his mother tell the story of a mother who wasn't really there. The grandmother tells Journey, "Your mama always wished to be somewhere else." Journey like Gabriel are trying to fill their holes of loneliness.

FIG. 18–2 Jessica develops each idea by providing evidence and examples in support of her reason and claim.

Simplicity Versus Complexity

OVER THE LAST FEW SESSIONS, your teaching has asked students to ratchet up the level of sophistication of their essays. You have taught them to reach for themes that tie two texts together and to elaborate by thinking about what the similarities or differences between the two texts are and what they teach them about the world. These are all good things to teach, but they are challenging.

You should be aware, then, that some of your students will struggle—and for good reason. Often children who struggle accept confusion and chaos. If things don't make sense, they assume that is the way things are meant to be. You'll want to let children know that actually, clarity matters a lot, and there is real value to aiming for the straight and simple ideas. It may help to tell a story about the genius Albert Einstein. He insisted always on using hand soap for shaving, despite the discomfort. When asked why, Einstein replied, "Two soaps? That is too complicated!" This, from the man who created theories of relativity! Many people believe that Einstein's genius came from being dissatisfied with anything that wasn't simple, elegant, and clear.

If you shared that story with some of your students, you could then suggest that they reread their writing, looking for parts where they tried to write in fancy ways and may have ended up writing in confusing ways. Teach writers that one of the most important habits a writer develops is the habit of stepping back to see what works and what doesn't work.

If some of your children seem to be struggling, remember that during Bends I and II, you provided very strong scaffolding to support your students' efforts to gather information around each of their topic sentences. You suggested they collect micro-stories, quotes, and lists in booklets, and then you helped them piece those together to make essays.

By now, however, you have removed those scaffolds and suggested that children plan using outlines, or templates. This is more challenging work, and the time frame around it is more abbreviated, allowing you fewer opportunities to see what youngsters are

MID-WORKSHOP TEACHING
Using Your Partner to Make Sure Your Writing Is Clear

"Writers, can I stop you for a minute?" I waited for all the children to turn and look at me.

"Earlier, I asked that you begin the day by rereading your draft to make sure you hadn't tangled your ideas together. So, as you continue to reread your writing to make sure your thoughts aren't smushed together and that you're writing with clarity, you'll also want to look for places where the reader might be confused or where some of the writing does not make sense, obscuring all the brilliant things you have to say. Personally, I find it hard to catch all of those places, so it is helpful to have my partner read my piece to make sure it is clear. That is what an editor does. Editors read over drafts and leave little questions and notes on the places where they are confused, and then they also leave suggestions. For a few minutes, will you and your partner swap your drafts and be each other's editors? I will signal you when it is time to go back to working on your own piece. When you get your piece back, you should read over the feedback and spend some time revising your piece to make it clearer."

doing and intervene. Then, too, your students are now writing compare-and-contrast essays, so that adds to the level of challenge. So again, don't be surprised if children have some difficulties.

You might take a step backwards toward the booklets you used earlier in the year, rather than channeling all students to write directly into drafts. You needn't literally have students return to the system of collecting components of essays in separate booklets, but you may want to suggest that each new part of the essay be developed on a new sheet of paper, and you may want to encourage children to note along the margin the sort of material that will go in that part of the essay. That is, a child can label the first quarter of his page "introduction" (with "thesis" as part of it) and then the next part, "topic sentence" or "reason" and "one example" or "one piece of evidence" and so forth.

You might also find that there are a few children in your classroom who are like Teflon. You've laid out all of this rich work for them to try, and they have not incorporated much of it into their piece at all. It would be helpful to bring smaller versions of the anchor charts from the unit (such as the "How to Write a Literary Essay" chart) as well as a list of the latest work in this bend when you confer with them. When you meet with them you might begin by reviewing these. Next, ask them to show you where in their drafts they tried some of this work. After it is revealed that little was tried except the bare minimum, you might explain that you understand that some of this work is hard, such as using academic vocabulary and micro-stories, but you expect them to try it. You might want to share with them the quote "Not to have tried is the true failure." Then get them to look back at the list and check off what they are going to try. You will want to check back in with them to make sure they are holding themselves accountable to the work they agreed to do."

Freewriting for New Ideas

Celebrate the work students have done today and set them up to do some freewriting to generate new ideas.

"Writers, today during workshop I walked around for a bit and noticed all the wonderful things you were doing as essayists. I saw many of you searching both of your texts trying to find the perfect evidence to support your thesis. I saw a few of you writing and rewriting micro-stories. Some of you were working on introductions and conclusions. I could brag on and on about all the great work I saw in here.

"But I want to give you all a suggestion. I don't think many of you have been spending enough time developing your thinking.

"So what I thought you could do right now is to read over one of your body paragraphs and then turn your paper over and freewrite. Remember, you can use the 'Ways to Push Our Thinking' chart to help you develop your thinking. Also remember that this kind of writing is fast and furious. I should see your hand moving quickly down the page. Ready? Freewrite!"

After a few minutes I asked the students to read over their freewriting and underline new thoughts that they would like to add into their drafts. I reminded them that they don't want the structure of the essay to stop them from having new ideas and that they can always choose to put their draft aside and get a new piece of paper and freewrite. Freewriting, I restated, can get new ideas flowing and enrich their drafts.

Ways to Push Our Thinking

In other words...
That is...
The important thing about this is...
As I say this, I'm realizing...
This is giving me the idea that...
An example of this is...
This connects to...
I see...
The thought I have about this is...
To add on...
The reason for this is... Another reason is...
This is important because...
On the other hand...
This is similar to... this is different from...
This makes me think...
This proves...

REVISING TO LIFT THE LEVEL OF YOUR ESSAY

Today you got new ideas flowing by freewriting off of one of your body paragraphs. Tonight do the same thing with your remaining paragraphs. You might want to bring home a copy of the "Ways to Push Our Thinking" chart to help you develop your thinking.

Remember to be your own boot camp instructor and push yourself to write fast and furiously. This is particularly important because you have a deadline looming and other work you know you have to do. So look back over your checklists, the goals you set, and your partner suggestions, and prioritize them so you spend time on the revision work that will lift the level of your essay the most.

Exploring Commas

ear Teachers,

Today is the day when you'll help children finish up their revision work and polish up their pieces so they are ready for publication. You could specifically focus your teaching and their learning on the conventions of language; specifically, exploring commas. In this letter, we will help you imagine the teaching you might do today.

MINILESSON

We suggest that you begin your connection by reminding your children to make sure their literary essays are clear for their readers. You could have a prewritten editing checklist (on the CD-ROM), or together as a class make a list of the editing work they have previously learned, to use as an editing checklist. Some of the things on the list could be rereading their piece for missing words, editing for punctuation, and correcting run-on sentences as well as accidental sentence fragments. They will also need to have on hand the Opinion Writing Checklist, and they will need to focus on the Language and Conventions category in particular.

You could frame today's lesson by saying that in addition to the general editing they'll do, they'll need to focus, from time to time, on particular ares of editing. For example,

Opinion Writing Checklist

	Grade 4	NOT YET	STARTING TO	YES!	Grade 5	NOT YET	STARTING TO	YES!
	Structure				**Structure**			
Overall	I made a claim about a topic or a text and tried to support my reasons.	☐	☐	☐	I made a claim or thesis on a topic or text, supported it with reasons, and provided a variety of evidence for each reason.	☐	☐	☐
Lead	I wrote a few sentences to hook my readers, perhaps by asking a question, explaining why the topic mattered, telling a surprising fact, or giving background information. I stated my claim.	☐	☐	☐	I wrote an introduction that led to a claim or thesis and got my readers to care about my opinion. I got my readers to care by not only including a cool fact or jazzy question, but also figuring out was significant in or around the topic and giving readers information about what was significant about the topic.	☐	☐	☐
					I worked to find the precise words to state my claim; I let readers know the reasons I would develop later.	☐	☐	☐
Transitions	I used words and phrases to glue parts of my piece together. I used phrases such as *for example, another example, one time,* and *for instance* to show when I was shifting from saying reasons to giving evidence and *in addition to, also,* and *another* to show when I wanted to make a new point.	☐	☐	☐	I used transition words and phrases to connect evidence back to my reasons using phrases such as *this shows that . . . .*	☐	☐	☐
					I helped readers follow my thinking with phrases such as *another reason* and *the most important reason.* I used phrases such as *consequently* and *because of* to show what happened.	☐	☐	☐
					I used words such as *specifically* and *in particular* in order to be more precise.	☐	☐	☐

COMMON CORE STATE STANDARDS: W.4.4, W.4.5, RFS.4.4, SL.4.1, L.4.1, L.4.2.b,c; L.4.3

writers sometimes edit their pieces by paying particular attention to their use of commas. You might talk to your students about how comma usage seems to be mysterious to many of them and that if they don't understand when to use commas, they may use commas incorrectly and confuse their reader.

Then you'll want to name the teaching point. We suggest saying something like "Today I want to teach you that whenever you want to unlock one of the mysteries of writing, you study and analyze the mystery—such as comma usage—in mentor texts. Then you can extrapolate from the mentor text how the author did that thing—in this case, how the author used commas."

Then for the teaching and active engagement, you might decide to send the students on an inquiry. If so, you can tell the children that instead of a regular minilesson, today they will do an inquiry. Remind them that they did this earlier in the unit when they inquired about what, exactly, a writer does to be a powerful essayist. You might want to tell your children, "When people think of grammar and punctuation, they usually think of *rules*. They worry about doing things 'right,' versus doing things 'wrong.' It is true that there are some important rules to learn about commas—because following these rules will help make your writing more readable to others. But the important thing is that you think about the sound of your writing and what makes sense." Tell them that the use of commas lets the reader know how to read your writing. Commas empower the writer to slow bits down or speed them up, as well as tucking in a quick reference or bit of information to have an effect on the reader and help bring out the meaning of your piece.

For a mentor text, you'll want to either write a literary essay yourself or find one to use as an exemplar that highlights the particular thing—in this case, commas—you want your students to learn. The essay you choose should be written about a text your students are familiar with so that they can focus on the mechanics of the piece rather than wondering about the story or characters the essay highlights. You will want to make copies or project the piece for the whole class to see and read the text aloud to the class as they follow along. Or you may choose for them to chorally read it with you so they are reading it using the commas as the author intended. Then reread it, asking them to pay close attention to the writer's place-ment of commas. We use an essay we wrote about "The Marble Champ," by Gary Soto, but of course you can choose to use another.

> Lupe, the main character in "The Marble Champ," by Gary Soto, works hard to become better at sports. In the beginning, Lupe wants to be good at sports just like her friends. She is a good student, but she can't run, skip, or hop too well. Lupe shows determination by practicing right after school instead of doing homework. The text says, "she tried again and again," and didn't give up even when her thumb was sore and aching. Finally, she learns how to play marbles and is the marble champion! This shows that if you have determination you can do anything.

As you reread each sentence, and highlight the commas, ask the children to talk with their partner about why they think the writer put the commas where he did. What effect does the comma or commas have on the reader? What does the comma do? No doubt, your children are familiar with the use of com-mas in lists. What they may not be sure of—and what much of the world disagrees on—is whether or not a comma should be used before the last object being listed. For instance, some might write, "The dog is small, brown, and soft." Others might write: "The dog is small, brown and soft." The British tend to rely on the former, the Oxford Comma, whereas Americans may forgo the last comma, although there are exceptions to this because some publishers follow the Oxford Comma rule. Either way is correct, and I suggest illuminating this disagreement for children.

As children are talking, listen in to what they are saying, coaching them to say more. You might say, "If you aren't sure, remember that you are just exploring, so use 'Maybe . . . ' 'Perhaps . . . ' 'It could be . . . '" What your students think will give you ample data about what they truly understand about the use of commas.

Then gather your students to share their thoughts. You might want to make a chart that looks something like the following so that the inquiry produces a concrete tool the children can reference not just today but in the future.

When you do this with your class, encourage your children to put what they are noticing into their own words. You'll need to crystallize their words in order to record something in the chart.

Example	What do you notice?	What does this let you know about the use of commas?
• Lupe, the main character in "The Marble Champ," by Gary Soto, works hard to become better at sports.	• The author put a comma after a character's name and then told us who she is. • A comma is used after the title and again after the author.	• The comma is followed by a description of the character. • Two commas can be used to set off more information for the reader, like the author's name.
• In the beginning, Lupe wants to be good at sports just like her friends.	• The author put a comma after telling the reader where in the story the information about a character was seen. • The comma makes you pause and pay attention to the information that is coming.	• A comma is used when information is added to the front of the sentence. This can give the reader more information about "where" or "when" or "how" something is done. • If you read the sentence carefully, you'll notice a natural pause where the comma is situated.
• She is a good student, but she can't run, skip, or hop too well.	• There is a comma after a sentence that describes a character and before the word *but*. • After the word *but* there are two commas that separate a list of actions of the character.	• Commas are used to glue two sentences together with a conjunction (such as *and* or *but*). • The comma is used when listing three or more items in a sentence.

At the end of the minilesson, before you send the children off to continue to do this work, you'll want to add "Reread your writing for commas usage" to the class's editing checklist and have them add it to the copies they have in their writing folders.

CONFERRING AND SMALL-GROUP WORK

During the workshop today you will want to move around, quickly addressing children's editing needs. First and foremost, you want to make sure that children are rereading their essays to catch the most basic of errors and using the checklists as needed. So many times our children aren't catching in their own writing something they will spot in someone else's writing or on a chart you've made. You might want to suggest to these students that they read their own writing as if they were a stranger to the piece. You might further suggest they read it not from the beginning to the end following the flow of the text, but out of order, looking closely at sentences. Explain to the writers that often when we read our own piece we don't catch the most obvious of errors. For example, we don't catch that we left off periods, capitals, or quotation marks. This happens because when we read over our own writing, we read it not as it's written but as we meant to write it.

You may want to observe children editing their pieces and watch for what they are catching and what they aren't. Compliment the child for what you see is a talent of theirs and tell the whole table that sits around them what that talent is. Ask those writers to comb through the rest of their piece with those expert eyes and share their expertise by reading their partner's and table-mates' pieces too. Write these observations down. You will use these observations in your teaching share today.

If you see children reading over their work and not catching many errors, you might want to suggest to these writers that they read their text aloud to themselves and listen. Tell them that being able to listen closely is a tremendously important part of being a writer. The way our writing sounds on the page helps us to convey meaning. As they are reading their writing aloud, ask them to think about how their writing sounds. Ask them to think, "Does my word choice (and sentence structure and punctuation) convey what I'm trying to say?" Then have them underline places where their writing has a strong sound—lonely or confused or elated. Then have them ask, "Is this the feeling that I want my reader to have?"

You might be on the lookout for writers in your classroom who seem to be writing with an inconsistent use of mechanics. One thing you might do with them is to find places in their drafts where they have written beautiful, well-crafted sentences and teach them to use these as mentor sentences for the rest of their writing. Remind them that today in the minilesson, students noticed the technique of other writers and are now trying to emulate those techniques to improve the quality of their writing. Tell them that they can use their own well-crafted sentences as mentors as well. First, have them specifically name what they did well, and then ask them to search through their writing and find other places where they might do that same work.

If you have students who continue to struggle with spelling words conventionally, they may need to spend extra time not just today but at the end of each workshop, and each time they write, rereading their writing to check their spelling. It is helpful to teach them to live their lives as students of spelling. You've taught them that writers live wide-awake lives and pay attention to the sights and sounds in their environments. Well, good spellers live a similar life. They listen to words and study their spellings, develop curiosities and theories, and in the process develop the experiences needed to accurately spell words in their writing. Remind them that today they should be checking their list of commonly misspelled words, circling the words they think they spelled incorrectly, and looking them up in the dictionary as well as checking the word wall.

180

MID-WORKSHOP TEACHING

For your mid-workshop teaching, you might remind writers that peers can be helpful editors, and then have writers exchange pieces with a neighbor to help each other catch final errors. Encourage them to use the editing and Opinion Writing checklists. Then stop the class and share with them an example of how one partner helped another.

SHARE

You may want to set aside a longer period of time today for the share so that your writers will be given the opportunity to meet with more than one other writer for a peer editing conference. To do this, you'll set children up to work with other writers who are editing experts in some way. One way you can do this is to reveal a chart with students' names and their editing talents listed. Writers will identify who they think can help them the most and sign up for quick editing conferences. It is kind of like speed dating in that you'll set a timer, and each time the buzzer goes off, kids will move onto their next conference.

If you want, the chart of editing experts you create today can later be turned into a guide sheet that taps into each writer's expertise. Children can use this guide as a way to get help and support throughout the following units. Tapping into all your writers' talents will help move your whole class in huge ways.

Best of luck!

Lucy, Ali, and Kathleen

SESSION 19 HOMEWORK

BEING WIDE-AWAKE READERS OF OUR OWN WRITING

At the beginning of this unit I told you that to write literary essays you needed to be a wide-awake reader, paying attention to little details that others might pass by, and then you wrote to grow ideas about those details. Well tonight, for your final work time on your essay, I want to give you one more tip. For you to write beautiful, compelling essays, you have to be a wide-awake reader of your own writing, looking closely at the little details that you may have passed by that distract from your essay. So tonight, reread your essay over and over looking for those distracting details, whether it be a misplaced comma, confusing pronouns, or run-on sentences. I know you have writing work in mind for tonight based on the last few days, but before you begin on your list, step back and reread your essay as a wide-awake reader. Find those places that need fixing. You will need some tools, so make sure you gather those up and put them in your folder. In particular, you'll need your editing checklist and perhaps the chart we made earlier today on comma usage, which I typed up and have copies of for you to take with you. Remember, I told you earlier in the year that deadlines can be "lifelines" because they have a way of making a person spring to life. Good luck!

A Celebration

Dear Teachers,

Today marks the end of the unit. In this unit you and your students took on big and important work. You and they have witnessed growth in their abilities to write about texts across the last few weeks—no easy task. Today, the culmination of that hard work, is cause for a momentous occasion.

Today is the day when you will want your students to understand that they are joining a long list of people who write about texts. In the real world, there is a group of people who spend their lives thinking about the message behind a beloved story, noticing the ways an author's craftsmanship supports the author's message. The people who do this are literary scholars, and they write essays about texts. For examples, hundreds of literary scholars have written about the deeper meanings in Mark Twain's *Huckleberry Finn*. These literary essays are then circulated among the people who are interested in this text or in literary scholarship. It is fitting, then, that your children celebrate their literary essays by circulating them among other literary scholars.

THE CELEBRATION

In the real world, literary scholars often publish their writing about texts in books with other essays about these same texts. Take out a text of literary criticism on *Hamlet*, for example, and you will be greeted by twenty different essays, exploring the meanings of various themes and symbols in the play. On the other hand, sometimes a volume of literary criticism will not be about one text, but instead will feature essays all grouped around a type of text—Romantic poetry, for example. Literary scholars organize their work in ways that are designed to influence others' thinking about texts, and your students might do the same.

Here, then, is our idea: you and your students might create different anthologies featuring student essays. One type of anthology that your students might create could be around a text—"Spaghetti," for example, or "Gloria Who Might Be My Best Friend." The same way that a volume of literary criticism for adults might be organized about different interpretations of *Hamlet*, so can all the students who have written essays on "Spaghetti" now compile their work in one anthology of literary essays for and by children.

Yet, students can create different types of anthologies as well. Perhaps, many of your students have written literary essays of their favorite texts. Now imagine creating an anthology of essays titled something along the lines of "On Our Favorites" and compiling all the literary works of the students who spent time interpreting their favorite story. (You might even help students extend this work by letting them meet with students from another class on the grade who have also compiled an anthology of writing about their favorite texts. Children can read each other's essays and take notes on the connections they see between their favorites. Each child might also prepare for a two-minute pitch to convince others to read her own particular beloved text.)

Another choice for an anthology might be around the type of essays students wrote. You might create an anthology called "Compare and Contrast" and include all of the essays focused on comparing and contrasting literary works. (This anthology might also feature a chart that students have constructed about what is most essential to writing a strong compare-and-contrast essay, and students might have even annotated their own essays to show key features.)

Or, the essays might be sorted into anthologies based on similar ideas or themes on which the children wrote. So, there might be an anthology based on characters who were lonely and alone in the world and then found a friend. Or another anthology on essays that address good triumphing over evil and so forth.

We suggest talking to your class about the different choices and letting each child decide in what sort of anthology his or her essays belong. You might even have a few essays which end up in multiple places. Perhaps the child who wrote about his favorite story, "Spaghetti," might place that essay in both the "On Our Favorites" anthology and the "Thoughts about 'Spaghetti'" anthology. Our suggestion is to involve the students in the work as much as possible, letting them make decisions; their investment in the project will be sky-high. Imagine the final products—volumes of literary criticism just for children! The school library will no doubt be thrilled to shelve these insightful works.

Yet, there is another way that your children's literary essays can have influence over others' ideas about texts. Just as professors assign students in colleges and universities to read literary essays about great works of literature and then charge students with using these essays in their discussions, so can your students bring their essays to other classrooms and let other students use them in book talks. You might send a few of them off to a classroom where you know "Spaghetti" has been read. Let them listen to some of the book talk going on in the room and then offer their essays that connect to and extend the story.

"Read this," your student might say to a group of students in the classroom, handing over her essay on "Spaghetti." "Mark it up. Get ready to cite it in your book talk." When the children in the book talk resume their conversation, they'll be asked to bring the thoughts of the author of the literary essay into their discussion, actually reading bits of the essays aloud to support their thinking. All the members of the book club will be expected to talk back to the ideas of (eavesdropping) essayists.

What would be ideal is to have students go to other classrooms on the grade where the children have also been writing literary essays. Then, when these students take on the literary essays in their conversations, they can also study and discuss these pieces as writers as well as readers of the texts.

Today's celebration, then, could have children dispersed across a few classrooms where colleagues are doing this unit. Children will celebrate their anthologies in different ways and might even give copies of them to the class in which they celebrated.

AFTER THE CELEBRATION

Finally, to wrap up the unit you may want to have the children take out their goal sheets and reflect on the work they did not just this month but across the two essay units. These reflections will help you see what they learned and what each student feels he or she still has to learn.

Congratulations, literary scholars!

Lucy, Ali, and Kathleen

Literary Essay to "Eleven"
By Maxwell

Some people think that growing up is fun, or exciting, having birthday parties and blowing out candles. But smart kids know that growing up is not all fun. Your old clothes don't fit anymore, and you can't play the same games, and you need to worry about new things, like money or work. In the story, "Eleven," by Sandra Cisneros, Rachel comes to an understanding of what being eleven really feels like.

Rachel comes to understand that when you are eleven, you are also ten, nine, eight, seven, six, five, four, three, two, and one. In the story, Rachel sits at her desk, staring at the nasty red sweater Mrs. Price made her keep. She was disgusted with it, and wanted to cry like she was three. She tried not to let her three come out though. Why did she want to cry over a sweater? She thought she was eleven,

old enough not to cry over something silly like a sweater. She then realizes that she was not just eleven, but ten, nine, eight, seven, six, five, four, three, two, and one. There are other sections of the story where Rachel understands that when you are eleven, you're also all the ages inside. For example, she says "when you are scared and need to sit on your Mama's lap, that is the part of you that is still five." And "When you say something stupid, that is the part of you that is still ten." Another section of the story where Rachel sees that she has all the ages is "When you are sad and need to cry, that is the part of you that is still three." And one more place is when she blabbed and stuttered to Mrs. Price when she wanted to say something. That was the part of her that was still four. Her understanding that when you are eleven you are also all the ages inside is important because the way Sandra Cisneros stretches out "10, 9, 8, 7, 6, 5, 4, 3, 2, and 1" instead of just saying

"all the other ages"—she really wants to show that that is the most important part.

Something else that Rachel comes to understand is that turning eleven can be a let down I see this in the text here: Rachel expected to feel eleven on her birthday as soon as she woke up. But she did not. She opened her eyes and everything was just like yesterday but it was today. She went to school and expected to feel like a big eleven year old, but instead has a terrible day. Mrs. Price forces her to wear a nasty, disgusting sweater. She cries in front of the whole class like she was three. At the end of the day, she just wanted it to be gone and forgotten. Other parts in the text where I see that Rachel understands being eleven can be a letdown are "You don't feel eleven. Not right away. It takes a few days, weeks even, sometimes even months until you say eleven when they ask you." And "You are not smart eleven. Not until you are almost twelve." And when she realizes that

she does not know what to do when Mrs. Prices forces her to wear the sweater. She does not have enough ages yet. I can really tell that Rachel does not feel eleven because Rachel says "I'm eleven" or a variation on that a lot, and that shows that she really has to remind herself, because that is not the way she feels. Also, Sandra Cisneros made a list of examples at the end of the story of things that are far away like "I wish I was 102 or anything but eleven" and "far away like a runaway balloon" or like "a teeny tiny little o in the sky." This really shows how much Rachel wants the day to be over with. Because she did not have a happy birthday. She had a letdown birthday.

Literature can help you understand things better. For example, I have come, through Rachel's thoughts and experiences, to a conclusion that growing up is not all birthday parties and blowing out candles. And I have learned that I should appreciate being young, while I am.

FIG. 20–1   Max's final draft

"Eleven" by Adam

In literature, authors write a lot about one character being upset and taking it out on another person. Sandra Cisneros' essay, "Eleven," is about a girl named Rachel who is mistreated by her teacher and in return mistreats her classmates.

Rachel is mistreated by her teacher. Mrs. Price finds an ugly, old sweater in the coat room and forces Rachel to put it on. Rachel says "That's not . . . mine." But Mrs. Prices moves on to the next math problem without understanding Rachel, saying "of course it's yours." Mrs. Price says, "I remember you wearing it once." This is mistreatment because Mrs. Price isn't respecting Rachel. Mrs. Price doesn't care about what Rachel has to say. Later, right before the bell rings, Mrs. Price pretends as if everything's ok, ignoring the real pain Rachel is feeling.

In return for Mrs. Price mistreating Rachel, Rachel then goes on to mistreat her classmates. Rachel thinks of her classmates in a derogatory way. An example of this is when Rachel commented, "Maybe because I am skinny, maybe because she doesn't like me, that stupid Sylvia Saldivar says" . . . I think it belongs to Rachel!" Then later on, Rachel comments " . . . But the worst part about it is right before the bell that stupid Phyllis Lopez who is even dumber than Sylvia Saldivar says she remembers the sweater is hers." In both these examples, Rachel is calling her classmates dumb and stupid. She's doing this in her mind, but her feelings probably affect her actions too. Sandra Cisneros also shows Rachel mistreating her classmates when Rachel describes the sweater as smelling like "cottage cheese" and " . . . all itchy and full of germs that aren't even mine." This shows that Rachel is disgusted with wearing her class-mate's clothes. The sweater, it turns out, belongs to Phyllis and she must feel awful, seeing Rachel cry over the fact that Rachel needs to wear her sweater.

This story teaches me that when someone mistreats a person, that person needs to protest so that they don't pass on their fury to other people. When someone gets mad at me, I sometimes don't protest and instead pass it on to someone else. Sandra Cisneros in "Eleven" teaches me to speak up.

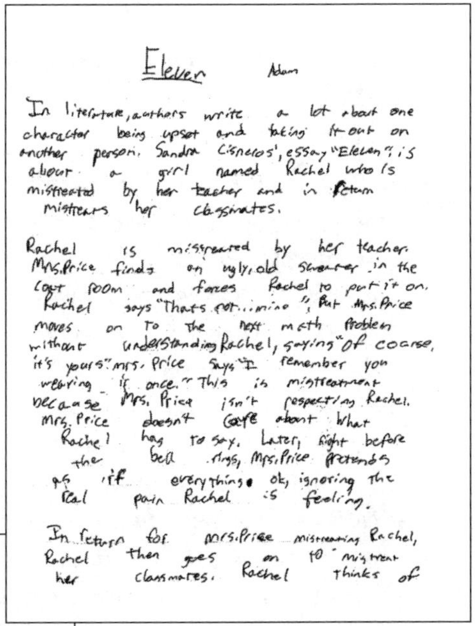

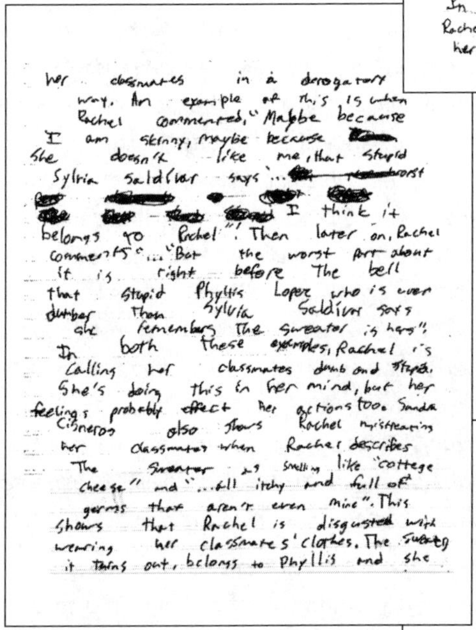

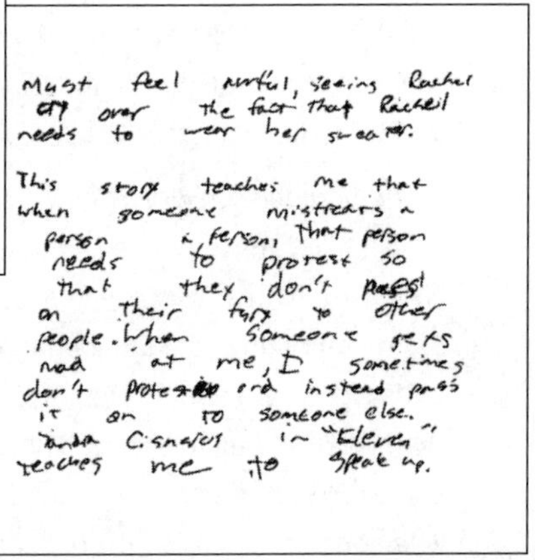

FIG. 20–2 Adam's final draft

"The Marble Champ" by Judah

In literature, characters face challenges and learn to survive. In the short story "The Marble Champ" by Gary Soto, Lupe learns to overcome her difficulties by working hard and believing in herself.

Lupe overcomes her difficulties through hard work. Soon after Lupe decided to become skilled at marbles, she came home from school and decided to waste no time before playing marbles. But this wasn't just play. This was serious work. Lupe had never been good at sports. So this time she was determined to become good at marbles. She picked five marbles that she thought were her best. Lupe didn't practice on any old table; she smoothed her bedspread to make it into a good surface for her marbles. She really thought about what to do to get good at this sport. She shot softly at first to get her aim accurate. The marbles rolled and clicked against one another. Lupe was disappointed, but didn't give up. She decided her thumb was weak and decided to strengthen it. Lupe worked to get her thumb strong by spending three hours flicking at marbles. She worked to get her wrists strong by doing twenty pushups on her fingertips, and she worked to get her thumb even stronger by squeezing an eraser one hundred times. Gary Soto uses a lot of repetition to emphasize that Lupe worked hard to become good. For example, he wrote, "she tried again and again," and "Practice, practice, practice. Squeeze, squeeze, squeeze." Lupe overcame her difficulties, not only by hard work, but also because she believed in herself. She practiced and practiced and practiced. She squeezed and squeezed and squeezed. She believed that this would work. Lupe became pretty good. Marbles became her goal—not anything academic. She beat her brother, who played marbles. And, she beat a neighbor friend who, not only played marbles, was a champ. She believed in herself to play against them and she might win. The friend said, "She can beat the other girls for sure, I think." This didn't stop Lupe. It didn't even make her nervous! She kept going and still believed in herself. Lupe believed in herself to try and win the academic awards. Lupe believed in herself to work and try to become good. Lupe believed in herself to go to the games and try to win.

In the beginning, Gary Soto writes, "Lupe Medrano, a shy girl who spoke in whispers . . . " It is important to notice that Gary Soto is writing about a character who is complicated. He writes that she is shy. But she sits and looks at all of her awards. Then, as the story goes on, Lupe changes to a girl who believes in herself. In the beginning, Lupe was shy. Then, in the end, she shook hands with people who watched her, even a dog! At first, her thumb was "weaker than the neck of a newborn chicken." Then, after she exercised it, it was swollen because of the muscle. Her thumb was so strong, that when she shot, she shattered a marble. Gary Soto writes to make us think that Lupe is determined to become good at marbles.

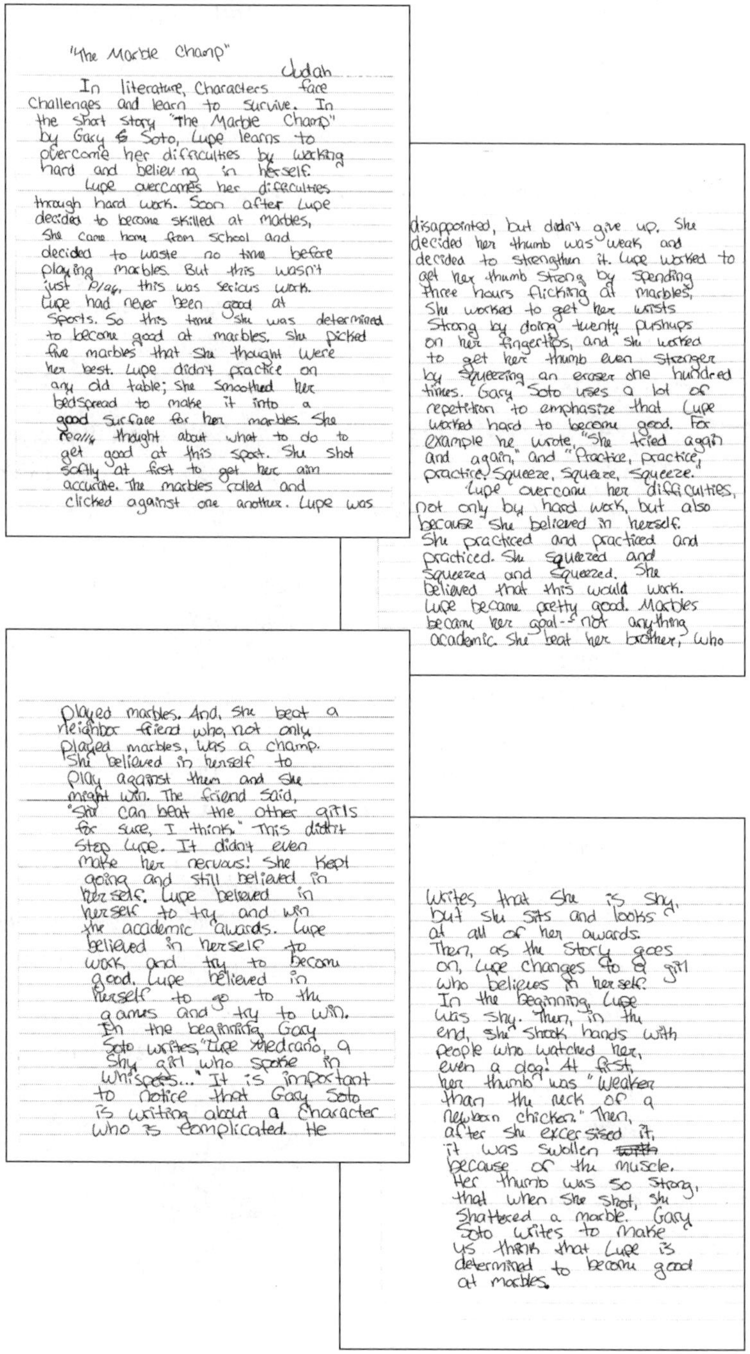

FIG. 20–3 Judah's final draft

A Literary Essay on "The Marble Champ" by Ali

When I read I am often drawn to stories that are about people my own age who have problems that I might have, because than I can really feel how the character is feeling. In the short story "The Marble Champ" by Gary Soto a girl named Lupe has never been good at sports, but through determined effort she will do something she has never done before–win a sport.

At the start of the story Lupe had never been good at sports. She could not catch a high pop, kick a soccer ball, or shoot a basketball. One afternoon, Lupe lay on her bed staring up at the shelves that held her awards. Her awards were for spelling, reading, science, piano, chess and for never missing a day of school. Not one of her awards was for a sport. "I wish I could win something, anything, even marbles."

Gary Soto uses lists in the beginning of the story to convey the point that Lupe has been a winner. For example " . . . the school's spelling bee champion, winner of the reading contest three summers in a row, blue ribbon awardee in the science fair, the top student at her piano recital, and the playground grand champion in chess." Soto wants readers to notice that although Lupe has excelled in many areas in her life she has not been good in sports.

Through determined effort Lupe will win in a sport. One night after dinner, Lupe and her dad went outside. It was dark, but with a couple of twists the porch light went on. The light shone down on the circle Lupe had drawn earlier in the dirt. Lupe set the marbles inside the circle and she dropped down to her knee, she released her thumb. Even though she completely missed the marble she did not stop. She was determined to perfect her shot. She practiced again and again and again. It started to become a regular movement in her thumb. It was getting late and she continued to work her way around the circle. Dropping, aiming, releasing. Lupe prepared for the championship by squeezing an eraser 100 times, by shooting marbles for three hours, and by pushing up and down on her fingertips 20 times.

Gary Soto uses repetition to illustrate determined effort as an important part of Lupe's character. For example "Squeeze, squeeze, squeeze . . . practice, practice, practice." Repeating these words show how Lupe's determination to work hard in order to succeed.

From this story I have learned that determined effort can have surprising results. Lupe had motivation to succeed, but I don't think she was expecting to win her first game. I think she had prepared herself as best she could and she was going to try her hardest. What I realize is that having determined effort to always do your best is important, because it can help make your wishes come true.

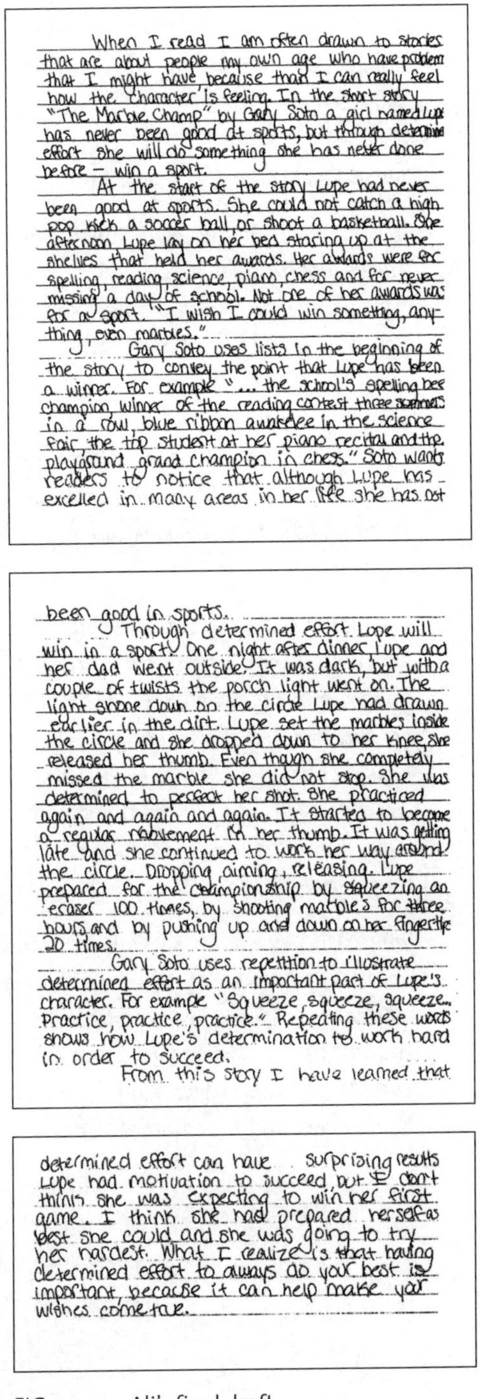

When I read I am often drawn to stories that are about people my own age who have problem that I might have because than I can really feel how the character is feeling. In the short story "The Marble Champ" by Gary Soto a girl named Lupe has never been good at sports, but through determined effort she will do something she has never done before – win a sport.

At the start of the story Lupe had never been good at sports. She could not catch a high pop, kick a soccer ball, or shoot a basketball. One afternoon, Lupe lay on her bed staring up at the shelves that held her awards. Her awards were for spelling, reading, science, piano, chess and for never missing a day of school. Not one of her awards was for a sport. "I wish I could win something, anything, even marbles."

Gary Soto uses lists in the beginning of the story to convey the point that Lupe has been a winner. For example "... the school's spelling bee champion, winner of the reading contest three summers in a row, blue ribbon awardee in the science fair, the top student at her piano recital and the playground grand champion in chess." Soto wants readers to notice that although Lupe has excelled in many areas in her life she has not been good in sports.

Through determined effort Lupe will win in a sport. One night after dinner Lupe and her dad went outside. It was dark, but with a couple of twists the porch light went on. The light shone down on the circle Lupe had drawn earlier in the dirt. Lupe set the marbles inside the circle and she dropped down to her knee, she released her thumb. Even though she completely missed the marble she did not stop. She was determined to perfect her shot. She practiced again and again and again. It started to become a regular movement in her thumb. It was getting late and she continued to work her way around the circle. Dropping, aiming, releasing. Lupe prepared for the championship by squeezing an eraser 100 times, by shooting marble's for three hours and by pushing up and down on her fingertips 20 times.

Gary Soto uses repetition to illustrate determined effort as an important part of Lupe's character. For example "Squeeze, squeeze, squeeze... Practice, practice, practice." Repeating these words shows how Lupe's determination to work hard in order to succeed.

From this story I have learned that determined effort can have surprising results Lupe had motivation to succeed, but I don't think she was expecting to win her first game. I think she had prepared herself as best she could and she was going to try her hardest. What I realize is that having determined effort to always do your best is important, because it can help make your wishes come true.

FIG. 20–4 Ali's final draft

A Literary Essay on "Spaghetti" and <u>Journey</u> by Jessica

Loneliness is something that everyone experiences in life. It can make people feel isolated, depressed and even angry. It is with us throughout our lives and we all have to figure out how to deal with it. Both "Spaghetti" by Cynthia Rylant and <u>Journey</u> by Patricia MacLachlan are stories about lonely characters who find the cure when they befriend an animal.

In Spaghetti, Gabriel being lonely reminds me of Journey being lonely. One way, Cynthia Rylant shows Gabriel's loneliness is that she had Gabriel looking longingly at people in his neighborhood "talking quietly among themselves." He is not sitting with them but is alone on a stoop. He is not part of a group but seems to want to be because he "wished for some company." It is like Gabriel is on the outside looking in at his neighbors and hoping that one of them or someone will invite him in. Journey is a lot like Gabriel in this way. Journey feels on the outside of his family and he longs to find a connection with them, especially with his absent mother and father. Journey's loneliness makes him angry. When his grandfather takes a family picture, instead of the picture looking like a family who is together, it looks like Journey is separate from the rest and reveals his anger.

Another way, Rylant shows Gabriel's loneliness is through the description of the building. In the text it said that Gabriel sat if front of a "tall building of crumbling bricks and rotting wood." This image of a run down building is used to show how like the building Gabriel has no one to take care of him and the building represents that Gabriel is depressed because he is lonely. Patricia MacLachlan like Cynthia Rylant also shows Journey's loneliness through the use of objects. The pictures of his mother tell the story of a mother who wasn't really there even when she was physically there she wasn't emotionally. The grandmother tells Journey, "Your mama always wished to be somewhere else." Journey like Gabriel are trying to fill their holes of loneliness.

When Journey was lonely, "and then the cat came," Patricia MacLachlan said. Bloom, the cat, showed up one day at Journey's window and walked right into his life. Bloom being there made Journey less lonely, because he loved Bloom and she loved him. Gabriel also found a cat for his friend. His cat was named Spaghetti. When he found Spaghetti, he stopped wanting to live alone outside and started wanting to "live together" with Spaghetti in his room. Both boys started off being apart and then had someone to be "together" with once they found Spaghetti and Bloom.

So both stories show that the protagonists got less lonely when they found an animal to befriend. Maybe sometimes when you feel very alone, it's easier to make friends with an animal who loves and needs you. Then when you have done that, you can start to make friends with people, too.

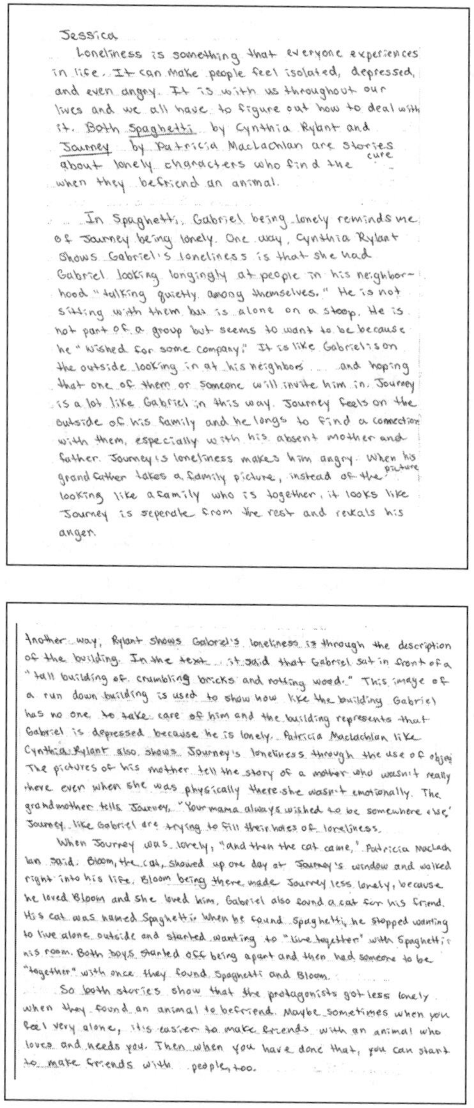

FIG. 20–5   Jessica's final draft

A Literary Essay on <u>Gloria Who Might Be My Best Friend</u> and <u>Fox</u>

In life things don't always turn out well like in the movies or even books. People do try and try but they don't always succeed because nothing in life is a guarantee. In both stories, Gloria Who Might Be My Best Friend by Ann Cameron and Fox by Margaret Wild, deal with the theme that in order to make friends you have to take a risk. But Gloria Who Might Be My Best Friend suggests that if you take a risk it will turn out in the end while Fox suggests it is important to take a risk, but you might not be happy in the end but perhaps wiser.

Gloria Who Might Be My Best Friend taught me that to make friends you have to take risks. In Gloria Who Might Be My Best Friend, Gloria wants to be friends with her new neighbor Julian. She could have just been safe and waited to see if he would come talk to her first, but that probably wouldn't have worked because he thought, "If you have a girl for a friend, people find out and tease you." So he probably would have just ignored her. But instead, she took risks. She started talking to him first, and then she showed him cartwheels. And then she was the first one to say, "I wish you live here a long time." She took a risk by being the first one to talk to him when he could have ignored her. And then she took a risk by trusting him with her feelings when he might have been mean about them. But her risks worked, and they became best friends.

Fox taught me the same lesson, even though the story was very different. In Fox, Dog has to risk his life by running hot ash to rescue Magpie before they become friends. Then to make friends with Fox, he risks letting Fox stay with him even though Magpie says, "He belongs nowhere" and "He loves no one." Like Gloria, Dog took a risk with Fox by trusting him, but the difference is that his risk didn't work. But he also had to take a risk with his body in order to become friends with Magpie, and that did work and got him his best friend. So even though some risks didn't work, it was still important that he took risks to make friends.

The character Gloria, the protagonist in the fiction story Gloria Who Might Be My Best Friend by the author Ann Cameron and Dog, the protagonist in the fiction story Fox by the author Margaret Wild, are stories that deal with the same theme that in order to make friends sometimes you have to take risks in life.

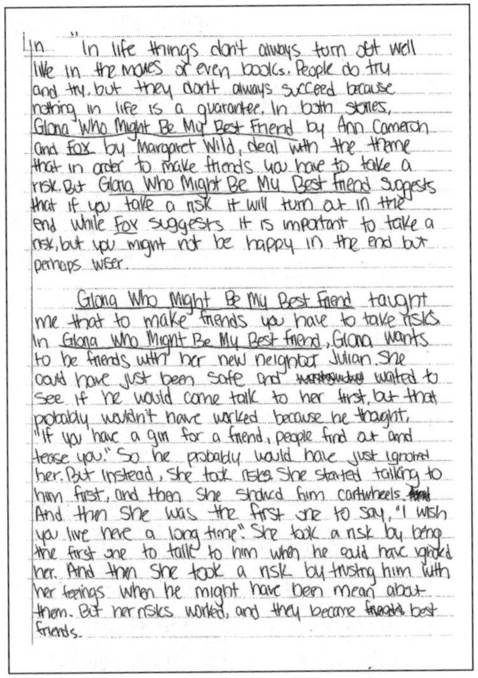
In "In life things don't always turn out well like in the movies or even books. People do try and try but they don't always succeed because nothing in life is a guarantee. In both stories, Gloria Who Might Be My Best Friend by Ann Cameron and Fox by Margaret Wild, deal with the theme that in order to make friends you have to take a risk. But Gloria Who Might Be My Best Friend suggests that if you take a risk it will turn out in the end while Fox suggests it is important to take a risk, but you might not be happy in the end but perhaps wiser.

Gloria Who Might Be My Best Friend taught me that to make friends you have to take risks In Gloria Who Might Be My Best Friend, Gloria wants to be friends with her new neighbor Julian. She could have just been safe and waited to see if he would come talk to her first, but that probably wouldn't have worked because he thought, "If you have a girl for a friend, people find out and tease you." So he probably would have just ignored her. But instead, she took risks. She started talking to him first, and then she showed him cartwheels. And then she was the first one to say, "I wish you live here a long time." She took a risk by being the first one to talk to him when he could have ignored her. And then she took a risk by trusting him with her feelings when he might have been mean about them. But her risks worked, and they became best friends.

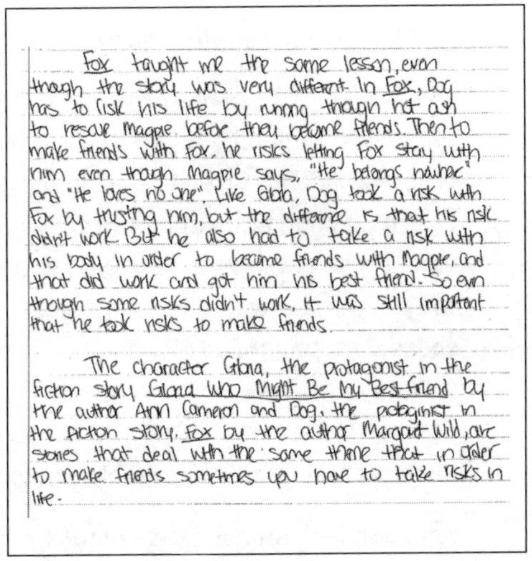
Fox taught me the same lesson, even though the story was very different. In Fox, Dog has to risk his life by running through hot ash to rescue Magpie before they became friends. Then to make friends with Fox, he risks letting Fox stay with him even though Magpie says, "He belongs nowhere" and "He loves no one". Like Gloria, Dog took a risk with Fox by trusting him, but the difference is that his risk didn't work. But he also had to take a risk with his body in order to become friends with Magpie, and that did work and got him his best friend. So even though some risks didn't work, it was still important that he took risks to make friends.

The character Gloria, the protagonist in the fiction story Gloria Who Might Be My Best Friend by the author Ann Cameron and Dog, the protagonist in the fiction story, Fox by the author Margaret Wild, are stories that deal with the same theme that in order to make friends sometimes you have to take risks in life.

FIG. 20–6 Parker's final draft

A Compare-and-Contrast Literary Essay on "Freedom Summer" and "The Marble Champ" by Kenneth

Both "Freedom Summer" and "The Marble Champ" are stories many readers will enjoy and connect to because in both stories, the main characters want to do something. In "Freedom Summer," John Henry wants to be able to do everything his friend Joe does, but because of segregation laws, John Henry cannot. In "The Marble Champ," Lupe wants to win at marbles. However, "Freedom Summer" unlike "The Marble Champ," teaches sometimes you don't get what you want.

In "The Marble Champ," Lupe, a girl who was never good in sports, is determined to excel at a sport. Lupe won many awards from the academic standpoint, but not a single one in sports. Lupe is not satisfied with that so she sets out to become a champion marble player. Playing marbles wasn't easy for her so Lupe "tried again and again," and "Practice, practice, practice, squeeze, squeeze, squeeze." Eventually, hard work and determination pays off as Lupe wins her first marbles trophy. Many kids have Lupe's determination when they work toward their goals.

In "Freedom Summer," John Henry, an African-American boy, wants to be able to do everything his best friend Joe gets to do. Unfortunately, John Henry can't do that because of segregation. He cannot use the same water fountains, get ice pops from the same store, and especially swim in the town pool, which is for whites only. John Henry, like Lupe wants something he hasn't had. Lupe wanted a trophy and John Henry wanted to swim in the town pool. Both characters wanted so badly to get what they want.

One way the stories are different is in "Freedom Summer," unlike "The Marble Champ" the character John Henry didn't get what he most wanted. When he got a chance to swim in the town pool, the pool was closed down. In the story "Freedom Summer," Joe tells John Henry that the laws have changed and now he can swim in the town pool. John Henry hollered: "I'm going to swim in the town pool!" He was so excited to finally get to do what Joe gets to do. But later in the story, the pool is filled with "steaming asphalt." John Henry responds with "angry tears." He faces disappointment. However, in "The Marble Champ," because Lupe was determined and she worked hard, she finally reaches her goal of winning a trophy in sports. In a nutshell, "Freedom Summer" has an ending where the main character doesn't get what he wants, which is a bit more realistic than "The Marble Champ" which has a "perfect" ending.

Although both stories have characters that wanted to accomplish something, "Freedom Summer" teaches sometimes you don't get what you want. Sometimes, there are things like laws or other people that get in the way of your goals, not your lack of hard work or determination.

The two outcomes don't just apply to stories, they apply to real life situations. Sometimes, your plans work out perfectly, like in "The Marble Champ," sometimes your plans don't work out the way you want them to, as in "Freedom Summer." It's just a fact of life that everything isn't perfect.

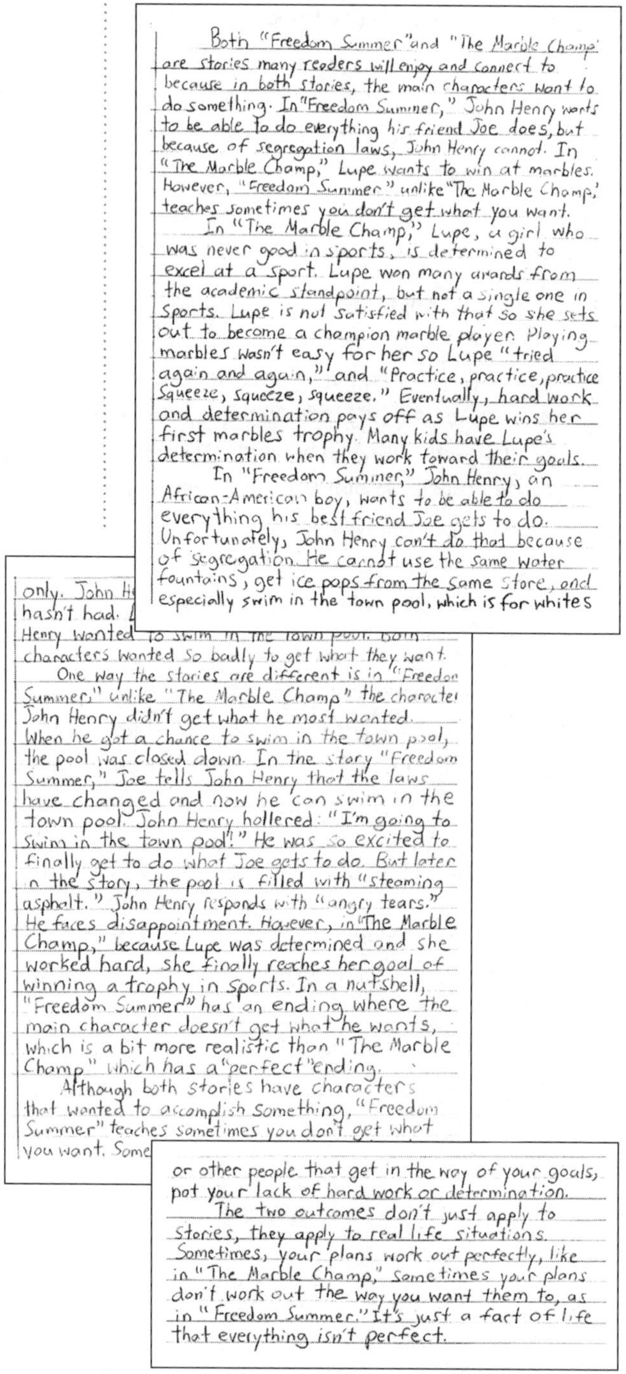
Both "Freedom Summer" and "The Marble Champ" are stories many readers will enjoy and connect to because in both stories, the main characters want to do something. In "Freedom Summer," John Henry wants to be able to do everything his friend Joe does, but because of segregation laws, John Henry cannot. In "The Marble Champ," Lupe wants to win at marbles. However, "Freedom Summer" unlike "The Marble Champ," teaches sometimes you don't get what you want.

In "The Marble Champ," Lupe, a girl who was never good in sports, is determined to excel at a sport. Lupe won many awards from the academic standpoint, but not a single one in Sports. Lupe is not satisfied with that so she sets out to become a champion marble player. Playing marbles wasn't easy for her so Lupe "tried again and again," and "Practice, practice, practice Squeeze, squeeze, squeeze." Eventually, hard work and determination pays off as Lupe wins her first marbles trophy. Many kids have Lupe's determination when they work toward their goals.

In "Freedom Summer," John Henry, an African-American boy, wants to be able to do everything his best friend Joe gets to do. Unfortunately, John Henry can't do that because of segregation. He cannot use the same water fountains, get ice pops from the same store, and especially swim in the town pool, which is for whites

only. John H

hasn't had.

Henry wanted to swim in the town pool. Both characters wanted so badly to get what they want.

One way the stories are different is in "Freedom Summer," unlike "The Marble Champ" the character John Henry didn't get what he most wanted. When he got a chance to swim in the town pool, the pool was closed down. In the story "Freedom Summer," Joe tells John Henry that the laws have changed and now he can swim in the town pool. John Henry hollered: "I'm going to Swim in the town pool!" He was so excited to finally get to do what Joe gets to do. But later in the story, the pool is filled with "steaming asphalt." John Henry responds with "angry tears." He faces disappointment. However, in "The Marble Champ," because Lupe was determined and she worked hard, she finally reaches her goal of winning a trophy in Sports. In a nutshell, "Freedom Summer" has an ending where the main character doesn't get what he wants, which is a bit more realistic than "The Marble Champ" which has a "perfect" ending.

Although both stories have characters that wanted to accomplish something, "Freedom Summer" teaches sometimes you don't get what you want. Some

or other people that get in the way of your goals, not your lack of hard work or determination.

The two outcomes don't just apply to Stories, they apply to real life situations. Sometimes, your plans work out perfectly, like in "The Marble Champ," sometimes your plans don't work out the way you want them to, as in "Freedom Summer." It's just a fact of life that everything isn't perfect.

FIG. 20–7 Kenneth's final draft